Psychoanalysis, COVID and Mass Trauma

'*Psychoanalysis, COVID and Mass Trauma*, by Katalin Zana and Tihamér Bakó, is a brilliant and extremely thought-provoking book on the effects of massive trauma.

In light of the recent COVID pandemic, which has produced a worldwide experimental field, among others, the authors re-discuss classic themes of psychoanalysis such as trauma, the relationship between material reality and psychic reality, and the role of intersubjectivity in psychoanalytic theory.

On the one hand, they devote particular attention to the intergenerational transmission of psychic suffering; on the other hand, to the ways in which in the here-and-now of the therapeutic relationship it is possible to activate transformative processes starting from the quality of the therapeutic relationship, and this leads them to integrate in their toolbox new tools of contemporary psychoanalysis, such as those elaborated by the post-Bionian theory of the analytic field.

However, the book is also enriched with original concepts, such as that of the "transgenerational atmosphere". One can safely say that it represents an extraordinarily significant contribution to a debate that no analyst can now afford to ignore. Suffice to say that everyone has been touched by the trauma of the pandemic both personally and in professional practice, having found themselves perhaps for the first time reflecting on what the extreme social isolation required by preventive hygiene measures means, as well as disrupting the usual parameters of the analytic setting and learning to work remotely.

We are only at the beginning of radical new changes in the way we think about psychoanalytic treatment. Filled with compelling clinical material and an uncommon ability to delve into complex theoretical concepts, *Psychoanalysis, COVID and Mass Trauma* is essential reading for all psychoanalysts and psychotherapists, as well as for those more generally interested in the subject of psychic trauma.'

Giuseppe Civitarese, *SPI, APsaA, IPA member, is author of*
Sublime Subjects: Aesthetic Experience and Intersubjectivity
in Psychoanalysis *(Routledge, 2017)*

'This book is a psychoanalytic page turner, impossible to put down. One feels more human and able to be with patients' traumas and one's own trauma reactions. Bakó and Zana offer containment and symbolising with their concept of the "Atmosphere", a psychological space and intersubjective sphere where shock and trauma transform. They use the form of diaries and snapshots to bring forth the emotional encounters with patients during the chaotic upheavals of COVID. Evocative writing about their own deep experience of the pandemic enlightens felt hauntings of annihilation fears and the possibiities of creativity and human contact made available when witnessing is active. The reader is enriched as a therapist working in the trauma atmosphere of now and as a human being desiring connection with others.'

Nancy R. Goodman, *Ph.D., training and supervising analyst with the Contemporary Freudian Society, IPA member, editor of,* The Power of Witnessing: Reflections, Reverberations, and Traces of the Holocaust—Trauma, Psychoanalysis, and the Living Mind *(Routledge 2012)*

"Constructed as a psychoanalytic diary, the authors of this book reflect on clinical observations from their work with patients during the COVID-19 pandemic, tracking these singular experiences to arrive at broader understanding of the psychological characteristics of collective trauma.

Based on the theoretical framework of their previous book, which focuses on the transgenerational, psychological effects of large-scale social-historical traumas and introduced new concepts such as the "Transgenerational Atmosphere," the authors here explore the trauma itself, especially those deep traumas which affect a large group of people or even the whole of humanity, including pandemics, natural disasters, terrorism, and war. In this volume, the authors progress toward the potential immediate and long-term psychological effects of such trauma, including the possibility of the activation of unprocessed transgenerational traumatic experiences, but also the potential for growth.

Rich in clinical material and methodological suggestions, this book will appeal to mental health professionals, including psychiatrists, psychologists, psychoanalysts, and social workers, in addition to professors in other academic disciplines such as sociology, history, philosophy, and anthropology.

Tihamér Bakó is a psychologist, psychotherapist, training psychoanalyst of the Hungarian Psychoanalytical Society, and training therapist for the Hungarian Psychodrama Association. He works in private practice in Budapest. He is the author of many textbooks and articles dealing with trauma, transgenerational trauma, crisis, and suicide.

Katalin Zana is a doctor, psychotherapist, psychoanalyst, and a member of the Hungarian Psychoanalytical Society. She is the author of many books and articles on trauma, transgenerational trauma, and creativity. She has a private practice in Budapest."

Psychoanalysis, COVID and Mass Trauma

The Trauma of Reality

Tihamér Bakó and Katalin Zana
Translated by Richard Robinson

Routledge
Taylor & Francis Group

LONDON AND NEW YORK

Designed cover image: "the *me* in the *we*" by Tihamér Bakó

First published 2023
by Routledge
4 Park Square, Milton Park, Abingdon, Oxon OX14 4RN

and by Routledge
605 Third Avenue, New York, NY 10158

Routledge is an imprint of the Taylor & Francis Group, an informa business

© 2023 Tihamér Bakó and Katalin Zana

British Library Cataloguing-in-Publication Data
A catalogue record for this book is available from the British Library

ISBN: 978-1-032-04646-4 (hbk)
ISBN: 978-1-032-04644-0 (pbk)
ISBN: 978-1-003-19406-4 (ebk)

DOI: 10.4324/9781003194064

Typeset in Garamond
by Apex CoVantage, LLC

Contents

Acknowledgments

We are deeply indebted to all the colleagues who participated in the genesis of this book.

Our thanks go to Andrea Sinkovics and Ágnes Kléger-Sipos for their close reading and expert reviewing of the Hungarian version of the book, for their useful advice, and their valuable comments that shaped both our approach and ultimately the final form of the book.

We thank Giuseppina Antinucci for her careful reading of the English text.

We are grateful to our translator Richard Robinson for his work.

Special thanks are due to Vamık D. Volkan, who wrote the foreword for the book. His sensitive, perceptive words inspired us to think more deeply and further enriched the ideas in the book.

Foreword

In their thought-provoking book *Transgenerational Trauma and Therapy*, Tihamér Bakó and Katalin Zana (2020) explored the psychological impacts of collective traumas. The COVID pandemic motivated them to write another book, *Psychoanalysis, COVID and Mass Trauma*. Reading this second book brought some personal memories related to a collective trauma to my mind.

I was born to Turkish parents on the Mediterranean island Cyprus in 1932 when it was a British colony. I came to the United States in 1957 as a newly graduated physician and went through my personal analysis in the 1960s. During that time, a deadly ethnic conflict was taking place as the island became an independent state (Volkan, 1979). My former Cypriot Turk roommate, who was like a younger brother to me when we were attending medical school together in Turkey, was shot and killed near his family home due to his ethnicity. While I was safe in the United States, my parents, sisters, and friends on the island were exposed to such personal and collective traumas on a regular basis.

As I recall now, while I was on my analyst's couch, there was no focus on my anxiety linked to these traumas thousands of miles away, or on my feelings of guilt for being safe while my loved ones were suffering, or my inability to mourn my former roommate's death in my new environment. Much later, after I became a psychoanalyst, I realized that my history related to events on Cyprus was the key motivation for my decades-long studies of collective traumas, especially traumas at the hand of "others" (Volkan, 1997, 2013; Volkan et al., 2002). Reading Bakó and Zana's book once more reminded me of the importance of psychoanalysts' paying attention to the impact of collective traumas in the clinical setting.

There are various types of shared catastrophes. Some result from natural causes, such as tropical storms, floods, earthquakes, forest fires, or volcanic eruptions. Some are accidental man-made disasters, like the 1986 Chernobyl accident that spewed tons of radioactive dust into the atmosphere. Sometimes, the death of a leader, or of a person who functions as a "transference figure" for many members of the society, creates individualized as well as societal responses – for example, the assassinations of John F. Kennedy in the United States (Wolfenstein & Kliman, 1965) and Yitzhak Rabin in Israel (Erlich, 1998; Raviv et al., 2000). Other collective traumas are due to the deliberate actions of an enemy group in an ethnic, national, or religious conflict. Such catastrophes themselves range from terrorist attacks to wars and genocides.

Even though they may cause societal grief, anxiety, and change as well as massive environmental destruction, natural or accidental disasters should generally be differentiated from those in which the catastrophe is due to ethnic or other large-group conflicts. When nature shows its fury and people suffer, victims tend ultimately to accept the event as fate or as the will of God (Lifton & Olson, 1976). Even after a man-made accidental disaster, survivors might blame a small number of individuals or governmental organizations for their carelessness, but there are generally no "others" who have intentionally sought to hurt the victims. When a trauma results from war or other types of ethnic, national, or religious conflicts, however, there is an identifiable enemy group who has deliberately inflicted pain, suffering, and helplessness on its victims. Such trauma affects large-group (i.e., ethnic, national, or religious) identity issues in ways entirely different from the effects of natural or accidental disasters.

Yet, as this book demonstrates, discriminating between only two major types of collective traumas doesn't fully account for a phenomenon like COVID-19, which perhaps deserves its own unique category. The trauma has a natural cause, but unlike many natural disasters, it has not been specific to one locale or region and it has not been short-lived. It is a trauma that has affected the entire globe – and it has caused damage and death not just for a day but for months and now years. Further, many of the governmental and societal responses to the pandemic have themselves triggered their own traumas with far-reaching political, economic, developmental, and psychological effects. Indeed, as a non-visible enemy, COVID-19 threatened and still threatens all human beings: old people, young people, rich people, poor people, famous people, and refugees in different countries.

As the title of this book suggests, Bakó and Zana draw from their own professional practice in Hungary to discuss the various ways their patients have responded to the COVID-19 epidemic. Reading about these cases caused me to recall my own past experience with large-group trauma for good reason: I was responding to many of the cases reported in the book, which vividly demonstrates how facing a new collective trauma brings about memories not only of personal childhood difficulties but also of previous collective traumas. For example, some of the authors' patients whose ancestors were survivors of the Holocaust faced the shadow of the past and "experienced" the losses for themselves. Many of the experiences they report also mirror the ones I have previously described (Volkan, 2021).

Although I no longer have a clinical practice, I continue to be a supervising analyst to analysts practicing in various countries, including Turkey, the United States, and Germany. Through my supervisory role, it became clear to me that initial responses to the pandemic increased some analysands' investments in their large-group identities. For example, at the start of the pandemic, a Jewish man who lives in Turkey filled his first telecommunication session with his Turkish analyst with references to his identification with Anne Frank. By not being able to go to his analyst's office, he felt as though he was being forced into hiding, like her. He had linked the natural threat of the coronavirus to the devastating large-group threat faced by Anne Frank and all European Jews in the Holocaust.

While the first part of the "diary" focuses on the clinical, the second part focuses on the theoretical, as the authors consider the mutual interaction of the *me* (the individual or subject) and the *we* (the group or intersubjective community). They introduce a novel concept that they call "the Atmosphere." It refers to "a constant presence, a psychological milieu simultaneously embracing and penetrating the *me* within." They examine how group-level trauma can lead to a dysfunctional operation of the Atmosphere and show how mass trauma changes perceptions of reality within both individuals and groups.

This latter discussion points to a highly salient idea that we – as psychoanalysts, psychiatrists, psychologists, and other mental health workers – should keep in mind. While our clinical work is often directed at helping the individual heal from trauma, we should also look for ways to administer "medicine" to societies following collective trauma so that they might heal in healthy ways. Tihamér Bakó's and Katalin Zana's book is an important contribution for finding avenues to practice this type of large-group "medicine" and to change the Atmosphere for the better.

Vamık Volkan
Emeritus Professor of Psychiatry, University of
Virginia, and the founder and the first president of
the International Dialogue Initiative

References

Bakó, T. & Zana K. (2020). *Transgenerational Trauma and Therapy. The Transgenerational Atmosphere*. Routledge, London and New York.

Erlich, H. S. (1998). Adolescents' Reactions to Rabin's Assassination: A Case of Patricide? *Adolescent Psychiatry: Developmental and Clinical Studies*, 22, 189–205.

Lifton, R. J. & Olson, E. (1976). The Human Meaning of Total Disaster: The Buffalo Creek Experience. *Psychiatry*, 39, 1–18.

Raviv, A., Sadeh, A., Raviv, A., Silberstein, O. & Diver, O. (2000). Young Israelis' Reactions to National Trauma: The Rabin Assassination and Terror Attacks. *Political Psychology*, 21, 299–322.

Volkan, V. D. (1979). *Cyprus – War and Adaptation: A Psychoanalytic History of Two Ethnic Groups in Conflict.* Charlottesville, VA: University Press of Virginia.

Volkan, V. D. (1997). *Bloodlines: From Ethnic Pride to Ethnic Terrorism.* New York: Farrar, Straus and Giroux.

Volkan, V. D. (2013). *Enemies on the Couch: A Psychopolitical Journey through War and Peace.* Durham, NC: Pitchstone Publishing.

Volkan, V. D. (2021). Sixteen Analysis' and Large Groups' Reactions to the COVID-19 Pandemic. *International Journal of Applied Psychoanalytic Studies*, 18, 159–168.

Volkan, V. D., Ast, G. & Greer, W. F. (2002). *Third Reich in the Unconscious: Transgenerational Transmission and Its Consequences.* Brunner-Routledge, New York.

Wolfenstein, M. & Kliman, G. (eds.) (1965). *Children and the Death of a President: Multi-Disciplinary Studies.* Doubleday, Garden City, NY.

Introduction

This book consists of two parts. Part I is a kind of psychoanalytic diary: our aim while writing this was to record our professional experiences and personal impressions during the COVID pandemic. How we (patient and therapist, individual and society) react to the continuously changing external reality. How personal experiences, the inner realities, are continuously influenced by an environment in constant flux, and how we can – or how we fail to – contain overwhelming experiences.

We are experiencing an intensive event that is bound to affect each one of us, and we therapists are experiencing it too (Goodman & Meyers, 2012; Székács, 2020). The COVID pandemic reinforced the impact of the group, the Intersubjective in the broad sense (the intersubjective community) on the individual. The effect of the group is always present, but in "peacetime" the group's influence is less striking, less obvious. We have all experienced how the sometimes rapid changes in "collective mood" have affected us too. Rather than observers, we became (or are) participants in a process that is underway in our environment (González, 2020b, 424; Bakó & Zana, 2021b).

We have reflected on this period through our own subjective filter, with the tool of analytical listening, taking subjective "snapshots" to document the various pieces of the reality accumulating within ourselves and our patients. In the diaries that we have been keeping since March 2020, we tried to capture changes in the collective mood, daily events, things that happened in sessions, and our own experiences. To keep a diary was a great aid at such a time: when the reality of the external world became "too much" for us, the very recording of experiences, putting them into words, as a kind of witnessing, gave us strength and kept us going (Goodman & Meyers, 2012).

We are both psychoanalysts who live in Hungary and work in private practice, offering psychoanalytic therapy and psychoanalytically oriented therapy. The therapy snapshots will be familiar to many: they reflect the effects of the pandemic on society, and may have been sensed by others in many parts of the world. In addition to the similarities, there are bound to be differences: local peculiarities (the Hungarian collective mood and the way it changed) are also apparent in the brief case vignettes.

DOI: 10.4324/9781003194064-1

The second, theoretical, part of the book focuses on the psychological effects of collective (or mass) trauma on individuals. Assuming that psychological processes underway at the individual level cannot be understood without taking into account the current external reality (the social and historical context) and the unconscious processes underway in the intersubjective community in the broad sense (the *we*), when recording these snapshots we tried to give special attention to the *we-in-me*, to listen to the voice of the *collective aspect* of the subject, which was reinforced by the crisis (Peltz, 2005; Bakó & Zana, 2018, 2020a; González, 2020a, 393–393, 397; Peltz, 2020, 420–422; González, 2020b, 424; Civitarese, 2021a, 134).

In previous publications, we dealt with the psychological effects of mass social trauma caused by humans (Bakó & Zana, 2018, 2020a, 2020b). Taking as a starting point the immediate deep psychological effects of individual trauma, moving toward the effect of group-level trauma down the generations, we have given special attention to the role of the social environment in both processing the trauma and in passing it on as a legacy.

The model we developed, the transgenerational atmosphere, describes the non-verbal sharing of experiences between the generations in mass societal traumas. In the victims of collective societal trauma and their descendants, the boundary between the *me* (subject) and the *other* – the internal worlds of the subject and of the other members of the community undergoing the experience – may become blurred. A shared psychological field comes into being, which we have termed the transgenerational atmosphere. The transgenerational atmosphere is a traumatized psychological space where boundaries disappear or become unclear: boundaries between the past–present and future planes of time, between external and internal (psychic) reality, between me and others, and between generations (Bakó & Zana, 2018, 2020a, 2020b, 2021a).

In a development of our earlier approach, in this book we introduce a new concept, which we have termed the Atmosphere. Similar to the transgenerational atmosphere, we conceive of this Atmosphere as an intersubjective field generated by the interaction of the *me* (subject) and the *we* (group, intersubjective community) in the *here-and-now*, which makes it possible to share feelings and experiences rapidly, in a non-verbal manner. Moving on from healthy functioning, we examine how a group-level traumatic event changes the complex, delicate relationship between the *me* and the *we*. We consider how a trauma experienced at the group level may lead to a dysfunctional function (a traumatization) of the shared intersubjective field, the Atmosphere, and how this manifests itself.

While experiencing the events of the COVID period, we rethought the concept of reality – while we were also trying to understand and process an increasing number of sometimes overwhelming feelings and experiences. In this book, by reality we mean a psychic construction which is the result of a process of symbolization (Bion, 1962a, 85). In this interpretative framework, reality is the end product of a process of dreaming: using its dreaming, transformative capacity, the mind changes the raw, objective reality of the external world (the real) into an integrated interior psychic reality (Ferro & Civitarese, 2013, 647).

In Chapter 3, we focus on how the concrete reality of the *here-and-now* becomes an internal, subjective reality. In addition to the outer reality and the individual's internal, psychic reality, we distinguish a third reality: *we* (or collective) reality, the reality of the group, the Intersubjective in the broad sense. In this chapter, we examine the mutual interplay of the *we* reality and the *me* reality. We consider how the individual's and the group's perceptions of reality are changed and distorted by the effect of mass trauma; how the reality of the *we* produced in the constantly changing *here-and-now* can color and shape the *me* reality. We discuss how changes in the *me* reality rebound on the *we* reality, and how past (emotional) reality is woven through the present individual and group realities.

Many thinkers, artists, and scholars have made and still are making continuous attempts to understand how destructive ideologies, such as fascism, extreme nationalism, or racism, manage to become so successful, influencing the emotions of masses and mobilizing them so rapidly. During the pandemic, we saw for ourselves how extremist views and feelings overwhelmed whole groups of people: collective fantasies related to the Virus and the Vaccine proliferate, and extreme feelings mobilize masses, giving rise to uncontrollable fears and aggression. Like many other psychoanalysts and authors, we too are concerned with this issue. The model we have created also incorporates the ideas of earlier writers, in an attempt to look at these age-old questions from a slightly different perspective. In this book, we take the concepts of Atmosphere and perverted Atmosphere as a theoretical framework to reinterpret the phenomenon.

Structure of the book

Part I is the Psychoanalytic Diary of the COVID Crisis. Our main aim with the case excerpts described in the Diary was not to present therapy cases in the classic sense, but to record this period with a series of subjective snapshots. The snapshots revealed a process: while we were writing, the reality of the external world was constantly in flux, the collective mood shifted, our patients changed, and our own internal realities, even our therapy attitudes, transformed. We tried to record these snapshots in the knowledge (or rather lack thereof) that these mosaic tiles would only much later (when the book was finished, or rather, when it was read) form a full picture, a subjective hologram of this period. Each reader can then continue shaping this with his or her own experiences and interpretations.

The second, theoretical part (The Reality of Trauma, the Trauma of Reality) deals with how a powerful unexpected experience at the group level, a shocking event, affects the individual, and at what point the shocking experience becomes traumatic. In Chapter 3, we revisit ideas that we advanced in our previous book on trauma and group-level trauma. We have integrated some of those insights, but in line with the topic of this book we have shifted the focus somewhat. Perhaps the more striking change is that unlike our earlier book, we purposely consider not traumatic experiences, but put the emphasis on the process itself: how an unusual, intense experience, by virtue of its power or nature, affects the individual, and at what point it becomes traumatic. Taking normal functioning as a starting point, we discuss the factors that influence the short- and long-term effects of an event, which factors help or hinder the processability of the event, and its integration into the life history. Moving on from the effects of the shocking event on the individual, we consider how different it is if the experience is group level, and what role the environment has on the short- and long-term effects. In Chapter 2, we advance our new theoretical ideas, which we illustrate with excerpts from cases drawn from Part I: Psychoanalytic Diary of the COVID Crisis. In this part, we consider the mutual interaction of the *me* (the individual or subject) and the *we* (the group, the intersubjective community). Setting out from our previous model, the Transgenerational Atmosphere, we develop it further to introduce the concept of the Atmosphere. The main difference to the previous model is that by the Atmosphere, we mean not a damaged psychological field, but a constant presence, a psychological milieu simultaneously embracing and penetrating the *me* within. Moving on from the healthy functioning of the Atmosphere, we examine how a group-level trauma changes the complex, delicate relationship between the *me* and the *we*. We consider how a trauma experienced at the group level may lead to a dysfunctional working (a traumatization) of the Atmosphere, and how this manifests itself. In Chapter 3, we examine the mutual interplay of the *we* (Intersubjective, group) reality and the *me* (individual, subjective) reality. We consider how the individual's and the group's perceptions of reality are changed and distorted by the effect of mass trauma, and how the reality of the *we* produced in the constantly changing *here-and-now* can color and shape the *me* reality. We discuss how changes in the *me* reality rebound on the *we* reality, and how past (emotional) reality is woven through the present individual and group realities.

This book provides a framework for understanding, in the full awareness, that many other interpretations of these phenomena are also possible. We encourage each reader to use the book in their own way, to enjoy it, and to form their own reading from the assemblage of small slices of (predominantly subjective) reality we have recorded. In this way each reader can continue to "write" the book, enriching it with their own interpretations. Our hope is that the book will start to live its true life after it is "born," or published. The excerpts from cases in the book are fictive cases, based on genuine cases from our own practice. All personal data (such as name, age, occupation, sex, nationality) have been changed in order to protect our patients' privacy.

References

Bakó, T. & Zana, K. (2018). The Vehicle of Transgenerational Trauma: The Transgenerational Atmosphere. *American Imago*, 75(2), 273–287.

Bakó, T. & Zana, K. (2020a). *Transgenerational Trauma and Therapy. The Transgenerational Atmosphere.* Routledge, London and New York.

Bakó, T. & Zana, K. (2020b). A Transzgenerációs Atmoszféra: Az Emlékezés Folyamata Kollektív Társadalmi Traumákban. *Lélekelemzés*, 2, 63–80.

Bakó, T. & Zana, K. (2021a). *A transzgenerációs trauma és terápiája. A transzgenerációs atmoszféra.* Medicina kiadó, Budapest.

Bakó, T. & Zana, K. (2021b). COVID and Mass Trauma: The Atmosphere as a Vehicle for Group Experience. *American Imago*, 78(3), 515–538. www.muse.jhu.edu/article/837107.

Bion, W. R. (1962a). *Learning from Experience* (pp. 1–116). London, Tavistock.

Civitarese, G. (2021a). Heart of Darkness in the Courtyard, or Dreaming the COVID-19 Pandemic. *Psychoanalytic Psychology*, 38(2), 133–135.

Ferro, A. & Civitarese, G. (2013). Analysts in Search of an Author: Voltaire or Artemisia Gentileschi? Commentary on "Field Theory in Psychoanalysis, Part 2: Bionian Field Theory and Contemporary Interpersonal/Relational Psychoanalysis" by Donnel B. Stern. *Psychoanalytic Dialogues*, 23(6), 646–653.

González, F. J. (2020a). Trump Cards and Klein Bottles: On the Collective of the Individual. *Psychoanalytic Dialogues*, 30(4), 383–398.

González, F. J. (2020b). With Fellow Travelers to Nodal Places: Reply to Dajani, Doñas, and Peltz. *Psychoanalytic Dialogues*, 30, 424–431.

Goodman, N. R. & Meyers, M. B. (2012). *The Power of Witnessing: Reflections, Reverberations, and Traces of the Holocaust – Trauma, Psychoanalysis, and the Living Mind* (Chapter 24, pp. 301–318). London, Routledge Press.

Peltz, R. (2005). The Manic Society. *Psychoanalytic Dialogues*, 15(3), 347–366.

Peltz, R. (2020). Living Entities that Join and Separate us: A Discussion of "Trump Cards and Klein Bottles: On the Collective of the Individual". *Psychoanalytic Dialogues*, 30, 417–423.

Székács, J. (2020). COVID Napló, külső és pszichés realitás karantén idején. *Kézirat.* [COVID Diary: External and Internal Psychic Reality during the Quarantine. Manuscript.]

Part I

Psychoanalytic Diary of the COVID Crisis

In our diary we have recorded our experience of working as psychotherapists through the pandemic. Writing a diary was a great help to us in this period, which is still ongoing: when events in the external world overwhelmed and overburdened us, the very act of recording events, of putting them into words, which can be seen as a kind of witnessing, gave us strength (Goodman & Meyers, 2012). During the pandemic, we – even we therapists – became participants in an intensive event which could not but effect each one of us. This event was shocking, and suddenly overturned the lives (both outer and inner lives) of all of us, had the effect of jolting us out of our customary modus operandi, that of the analyst, for shorter or longer periods (Goodman & Meyers, 2012; Levine, 2014, 221–222, Ellmann in Ellman et al., 2017, 23; Civitarese, 2021a, 133; Volkan, 2021; Nicolò, 2021). This is natural. A therapist cannot and should not pretend that nothing has happened. Not only are they forced to acknowledge and react to the threatening reality of the external world: that is their task, while they also try to reflect from a distance on external and internal events (Goodman & Meyers, 2012; Leuzinger-Bohleber & Blass, 2021).

What can we do as psychoanalysts, if an even is too overwhelming? Civitarese writes: "If . . . the theater is on fire, you have to close it down. But if you do keep it open, then you have to carry on with your job, in other words, you have to listen like an analyst" (2021a, 133). We experienced similar things in March 2020: the theater was indeed closed in the physical sense (from March 2020 we switched to online sessions). But in a psychological sense the play continued, in a space that was more safe and secure, at least physically. While in one respect the stage had become safer, the sudden switch to the online mode of working posed many new exciting questions. Reality became malleable: not only outer reality, but the inner one too.

Experiences like these have led me to conclude that cyberspace has provoked a dramatic change in our cultural understanding of reality. Ready

DOI: 10.4324/9781003194064-2

or not, excited about it or not, cyberspace, as Eigen (2007) observed, "is a part of our way of life." Reality is in flux.

(Hartman, 2011, 468)

The first large chapter in this book, the Diary, is a series of snapshots. As we progressed through the seasons and the stages of the pandemic, we followed through our own subjective filters how the emotional situation, or the "weather" of the external and internal world, was changing (Civitarese, 2021b, 10–11). We tried to grasp and record the changes in the collective mood, everyday events, things that happened in therapy, and our own experiences: emotional states, moods, and dreams.

Our diary is subjective in the sense that we did not attempt to make an accurate record of either events in the outer world or our own and our patients' internal "events." Excerpts from the cases and our own impressions found their way randomly into the diary, depending on what caught our attention when, or sometimes, what we had the mental capacity for.

When recording these snapshots we did not strive to understand and interpret them immediately. We recommend this mode of working to the reader too: allow yourself to be carried by the images, on the waves of these small slices of reality. Put together your own pictures as you experienced things in this period, maintaining a sense of curiosity as to what picture emerges at the end from this mosaic of realities. The picture that develops will naturally be unique, and slightly different for each reader. We followed events on the stages of therapy and of life outside with the method of analytical listening, and considered the resulting play as a joint dream (Faimberg, 2005, 19–30; Ferro, 1992, 58; Ferro & Foresti, 2008, 72; Civitarese, 2021b, 6). But the question arose in us: whose dream is it actually? This came up in one of the sessions: "But when the noise of concrete reality is deafening, who is the author of the dream and what is the dream about?" (Civitarese, 2021a, 134).

We worked on the assumption that in individual therapy we are in contact not with an isolated person (an individual, a subject), but with an individual who is a part of a group (the Intersubjective). González (2020a) writes:

> Individual unconscious life can be seen as having a double provenance: the intrapsychic world of conventional psychoanalysis, infantile sexuality, bodily drives, attachments, and individual object relations; and the radically intersubjective world organized by the group as the elemental structure of the social, with its implicit pacts, alliances, and inherent multiplicity. . . . A description of individual psychic life must include its collective aspect, the one-to-many object relation. This collective thread within the individual has a dual nature: both promoting a sense of coherence, perdurability, or consistency within the subject (who I tend "to be" when I am in any group) as well as a sense of multiplicity, instability, and inconsistency (how I am a "different person" in different groups).
>
> (González, 2020a, 393)

The pandemic particularly provides an opportunity to examine a new aspect of a question that has long concerned us: the interaction of the individual and the group (Civitarese, 2021a, 134). Although the majority of snapshots capture the experiences of individuals, our aim was also for these mosaic tiles to merge to depict another picture, that of the relationship, the dynamic interaction between the individual and the group. Thus, we listened to events in therapy, and even outside of therapy, not only as a dream of the dyad, but as dreamed by the intersubjective community, the *we*, assuming that where two people meet, the group (*we*), the whole of humanity is also always present. In our method, we have departed from the customary mode of analytic listening only in that beyond the individual layers, or rather *within* the subject, we listened very carefully for the overtones of the voice of the group, the *we* – the collective aspect of the subject, the "*we-in-me*" (Faimberg, 2005, 19–30; Ferro, 1992, 58, Bakó & Zana, 2018, 2020a; González, 2020a, 390–393, 397; Peltz, 2020, 420–422; González, 2020b).

Bion used experience from group therapy to aid understanding of individual therapy processes. "He tried to do as the Greeks did when they gave the Trojans a wooden horse. He hid a group soul inside his theory of individual psychoanalysis" (Civitarese, 2021b, 3). In the second half of the book, we attempt a similar experiment ourselves: in individual processes, we try to discern the ever-present spirit of the group, be it an accompanying familiar, or a haunting ghost. We also provide an interpretative framework, the Atmosphere (see Introduction and The Atmosphere), in the knowledge that the material is open to many other interpretations. We encourage each reader to use this material freely, and to supplement it with their own interpretations. Our book will thus continue to live, change, and transform, even after it has been written.

The Context

We have all experienced the current crisis:

> The COVID-19 pandemic is a health and economic crisis unprecedented in human history. It never happened that analyst and patient were immersed in the same potentially traumatic reality, nor that they had to use a different setting from the usual one. The author recounts his own experience in the period of time from the beginning to the closing of the first national lockdown in Italy from 9 March to 18 May 2020.
>
> (Civitarese, 2021a, 133)

The collective mood conveyed by the outside world affected/affects us therapists just as it did our patients. Although our capacity for self-reflection helped, we too were often perplexed and at a loss, asking ourselves: "What is right? What should we do?" Part of the therapy process is that the therapist represents the reality of the external world to the patient. But what happens when the therapist is uncertain too? When it is difficult to navigate through the external world, which changes by the minute, and which is colored by our own internal reality? During the pandemic, the tension in the external world was also felt in the professional community. Sometimes we were able to contain it easily; sometimes it was more difficult, and took more time. In the very early stages, the question arose as to what extent we therapists raise the issue of the threat, or if we only speak of it if the patient raises it. Psychoanalytic societies discussed whether the society should standardize practice (online versus face-to-face sessions, how groups could function) or allow members to make their own decisions.

We, the authors of the book, are both psychoanalysts who live in Hungary and work in private practice, offering psychoanalytic therapy and psychoanalytically oriented therapy. During the first phase of COVID-19, we both switched to working online. Later came periods of face-to-face and online therapy in which we did not switch from to one mode of working to the other at the same time. This reflected our own environment in Hungary, and within this, more particularly, the reality of our professional community: at the beginning of the pandemic, the "stay at home" mentality was dominant, and was reinforced by much stricter rules than later. Subsequently, from fall 2020, as well as various measures which were less clear than before, increasing space was given to individual decisions, which put more responsibility on the individual. The characteristics of the therapy snapshots and our own experience will be familiar to many: they reflect the effects of the pandemic on society, and may have been sensed by others in many parts of the world. In addition to the similarities, there are bound to be differences: local peculiarities, with the Hungarian collective mood and the way it changed, are also apparent in the brief case vignettes.

To help the reader understand the context better, while writing the diaries, as the stages of the pandemic progressed, we gave space to the subjective experience of our patients, or "others," or even ourselves, embedding them in social events and the collective mood, and reflecting on them. Thus, the Diary is a sequence of social and therapy snapshots alternating with our own experiences.

The story of some patients occurs several times in the Diary. They can be identified on the basis of their name, age, and occupation.

February 2020

That day Bergamo basked in happiness. The lads scored four goals against Valencia and only let in one. On the stands people hugged one another in delight, kissing. Previously nobody had thought that such a victory was possible. Everyone was dissecting the miracle on crowded public transport, in bars, in front of the TVs. It was in this overwhelming joy that one of the largest hotspots of the global pandemic came into being. Soon Italy had almost twice as many infections and fatalities as China, and in March

Spain too had more victims than the origin country of the SARS-CoV-2 virus, where hermetic lockdown was imposed with draconian force on infected towns and districts.

(Barát & Kemenesi, 2021, 33–34)

March/April 2020

Scapegoating

At the beginning of March, Hungarian prime minister Viktor Orbán announced that two people infected with the SARS-CoV-2 had been found in Hungary: two Iranian students.

> At a press conference given by the Operative Group, György Bakondi, the prime minister's chief advisor for interior security, spoke of the pandemic in an anti-migrant context. He opined that the reason for the spread of the corona virus pandemic was illegal migration.
>
> (Barát & Kemenesi, 2021, 50)

Over the next few days, news of the corona virus pandemic spreads in the Hungarian media, and it appears in the collective mood as a genuine threat that affects us. There is great uncertainty over the scale of the danger, and whether this pandemic is different from a large influenza epidemic. Meanwhile, the news from Italy gets more and more disturbing. "On March 11, the government announced a state of emergency, introduced restrictions on entering the country, and banned sports events and large-scale gatherings" (Barát & Kemenesi, 2021, 52).

Maskers and Antimaskers

The collective changes almost from day to day. As yet there are no large lockdowns or restrictions (schools are still open). Most people are still not wearing masks, but a few people have started to wear them. Sessions are still being held face-to-face, without masks, but without the customary handshake, and disinfectant appears in the consultation room.

Aliz (35 years old, a doctor), told of an experience she had:

> As a doctor I was a bit more cautious, so I put on a mask to go into the shop. Standing in line at the checkout I could feel people looking at me suspiciously. I felt increasingly awkward, so I unexpectedly said to myself: I'm not sick, I'm just careful.

Wearing a mask was not yet compulsory then, and in fact many people had an aversion to it. At the time, wearing a mask sent not the message that someone was careful, but that they might be ill, and be a risk for others. A couple of days later the schools closed, and wearing a mask became compulsory. At the same time, almost from one day to the next, the collective mood changed: now people were expected to wear masks, they symbolized care for the other, and someone might feel awkward for not wearing one. Shortly afterward, the mask acquired a new meaning, and for many became a symbol of a curtailing of their freedom (Bakó & Zana, 2021b, 515).

Eszter (38 years old, a financial specialist) has been going to analysis for four years. Indecisiveness in various situations was a recurrent theme in the sessions. She is a third-generation Holocaust survivor. The family's Jewish roots are shrouded in mystery: the grandparents destroyed all their documents so that no trace remain. This particular week she starts the session by saying that she can't decide whether or not to put on a mask in the shop. She cannot express what she is actually afraid of. As to what feelings arose in her when she approached the shop, she said:

> I don't really know whether we should be wary of the virus. I think that actually it wasn't the virus I was afraid of, or of being infected. I was looking at whether most people in the shop were wearing masks, whether the masks or the no-masks were in the majority. I decided that if it was the masks, I'd quickly put on my mask; if it was the no-maskers, I'd stuff it in my pocket.

The Enabling Act

The Hungarian Parliament passed the only Enabling Act in Europe. "Members of Parliament voted that the cabinet govern by decree, and that during the time of the health crisis private members' bills not be submitted" (Barát & Kemenesi, 2021, 54).[1]

The external world changed most rapidly: schools and offices closed, and a mode of working took root that was new for many: remote working. Most psychotherapists also shifted to an online space, although one or two colleagues continued to work face-to-face. In this period, we (the authors of the book) were also working completely online. When new restrictive regulations were declared, the collective mood was pervaded by uncertainty, growing fear, and anxiety. Meanwhile, solidarity also grew: people tried to care for one another and help others. For instance, people offered to go shopping for old people.

Mask and Shame

Károly (35 years old, an economist) started coming to therapy about once a week. He finds it very difficult to accept the regulations, and to wear a mask. He felt deep shame, humiliation, when he was warned in a drugstore to put on a mask and to keep his distance. He believes his freedom was being curtailed, and felt this was unbearable. Day by day, the anger within him grows, and he feels it overwhelms him completely. He experiences many atrocities, which fill him with a sense of injustice. He is angry with his friends too. They don't want to meet him in person, because they are afraid of the virus. It's more important for them to stay in contact with their families, with their elderly parents. He is a member of an online group where he constantly experiences tense anger when he reads that some of them are scared or cautious, and are staying at home. But he dares not write down his opinion, because he is scared they will judge him, or exclude him. He is angry at the day nursery: he can't take his son there because he has a cold. He's angry at the doctor who will not see him in person (he misses a routine annual screening) even though "that's his job." His experience is that the health service has deserted him, "as far as they are concerned I can drop dead." He cautiously tests me as a therapist, to see how wary I am of the virus. His assumption is that if we think differently on this topic, then I won't be able to understand him, that I'll reject him, and he will be excluded and alone. The shame he experiences in the *here-and-now* conjure up in Károly the memory of a previous shame, when he moved into a college hostel, and in the kitchen someone asked him who the dirty saucepan belonged to. He had brought the saucepan from his grandparents, and it was impossible to wash the grease off it completely. When he heard the question, Károly felt he was being deeply humiliated, and he didn't admit that it was his. He felt as if he was smelly and dirty himself, and that he had brought this dirt, this shame, from home. His parents lived relatively comfortably until the financial crisis. Then they got into debt, their business failed, and they had to sell their house. His parents' marriage broke up, and he lived with his mother. She feels this situation to be one of deep shame, and this sense haunts her, unchanging in its intensity.

Károly ascribed the burden of surplus meaning to the restrictions and mask-wearing: past and present telescoped together, and Károly experienced shame and exclusion as a present reality. He was not alone in this. Mask-wearing and restrictive regulations elicited many difficult personal experiences, and these individual experiences accumulated to make humiliation and exclusion a shared experience for large and small groups.

A Sense of Loss

Tamás (40 years old, a store manager) has been in therapy for two years (twice a week, on the couch). He describes this period as follows:

> This confinement is very difficult. Even going for a walk down the street has become an outing. But that too often makes me anxious: I watch people to see how close they are coming. You never know who might be infectious, who might be a threat. *Silence.*
> It's strange how work and being at home merge together. And therapy too: while I'm talking about myself, of these intimate things, the others are in the next room. You, and therapy, have come into my home. *Silence.*

I noticed something weird yesterday. I don't see how I didn't notice it earlier. The housing estate where I grew up is nearby. Lots of my childhood
memories came back. When I was a child, we could go to the end of
the housing estate. Beyond that was considered dangerous. *Silence.* We
were outside as much as possible. The atmosphere at home was really
oppressive then. (This was the time the parents divorced, the old home
that gave security fell apart, and he often felt lonely.) *Silence.*
Now I'm thinking of walking down the street. If someone comes, I go over
to the other side. Automatically. *Silence.* I remember when I was a kid
I always used to run to go to training. Mostly I got around by running.
Silence. Perhaps I felt that if I run, I'd be protected. *Silence.* There was
gossip on the estate. That a pretty blonde girl had disappeared on the
streets, and never been found. And there was a very fat woman, who
had twins. One day, they were drying their hair in the bathtub, and the
children got an electric shock. They both died. *Silence.*
Another memory comes to mind. I might have been 6 years old, when
I and my sister were sent to hospital. Perhaps it was measles? I didn't
see my parents for weeks (at least, so it seemed to me, I don't know
how long it really was). And I had to look after my sister (brief pause).
That's how it is now: I try to organize everything in the family: I earn
the money and protect everyone from the pandemic.

Tamás has lost his ability to orientate himself. He is no longer able to
distinguish between the threat from the external world and his own past or
present fears. The threat of the *here-and-now* brings the threat of the past
closer, the time when his parent's divorce led to the collapse of a world that
beforehand seemed safe. Everything came threateningly close. Spaces merge:
the therapy space is difficult to separate from the home space. Things are too
close, both physically, and even more so psychologically. The locale of the past
comes unexpectedly close – spatially, but even more so temporally: the housing estate which represented protection, but even within the protective shield
there was drama, and threats.

Changing Settings

Tamara (26 years old, an artist) has been in therapy for four years, with minor
breaks (once a week, seated). She logs onto the first online session from her
terrace, with coffee and cigarette at the ready. When I had asked her what
she thinks, what all this is about, she replies that perhaps she felt it meant
she too could shape the framework, not the therapist, as before. From the
next session, she sets up a setting suitable for therapy: she sits in an armchair,
she doesn't drink coffee or smoke, bringing only water to the session (previously she always asked for water before the session, then when the restrictions
kicked in and the jug of water disappeared, she seemed disappointed – the

water that I gave her was an important part of the session). After a while she arranges the reading corner (where she logs onto the sessions) similar to the way my consulting room is organized. But it's not conscious: in one of the sessions she's surprised to see simultaneous images of both her own room and mine on the monitor.

Dávid (48 years old, a financial specialist) came to analysis for two years, then for two years to therapy (twice a week, on the couch). In one of the first sessions, he logs on from a car. At the beginning of the session, he spends a long time looking for a parking space, and complains about the traffic, other drivers, and the government. Later he finds a parking space, but he cannot perch the telephone properly. It wobbles, and falls down. All through the session I feel dizzy, and the thought arises that it would be good to hold on – to the telephone, for starters.

Unstable (Internet) Connection

Gabriella (41 years old, a secondary school teacher) has been in therapy for one-and-a-half years (once a week, seated). At the beginning, she is worried the internet connection will be unstable. At the beginning of the sessions, she is very frustrated. Later she tells me she is angry at me in advance because I can't provide a stable internet connection. But in the initial period, this doesn't happen to us. However, a couple of months later, there is a time when the internet connection is unstable, and the webcam image freezes several times. Previously, she would have been unable to bear "jolt" of a couple of minutes, but later she puts up quite well with the multiple reconnection attempts. It is a little annoying, but it doesn't upset us. Although the internet connection is unstable, the continuity of the connection between us is restored. There is even an aesthetic aspect to the experience: the frozen image reminds her of an Impressionist painting.

Pets in the Therapy Space

As a therapist I hadn't made it clear to my patients what should happen to pets in the new setting. Initially it didn't even cross my mind to think of this. My own friendly dog, Mango, who always pokes his nose in, was shut out from sessions from the very beginning. The reasons were practical: I didn't want him to distract me, but perhaps there were less conscious elements too: when I look at Mango, I feel good, his presence is calming. So perhaps I was trying involuntarily to filter out these feelings that belonged neither to the patient nor to the relationship between us. Only slowly, over time, did I realize that everyone related to this differently. Some people let pets in, some shut them out. Then I started to think about what it means.

Ildikó (35 years old, a ceramic artist) has been in has therapy for three years (once a week, seated). For a patient living alone, switching to online work made no significant change to our relationship. The change of setting happened smoothly, and Ildikó seemed not to have noticed that anything had changed. She speaks on a monotone, and very rarely seeks out eye contact with me. After a while I noticed that her face sometimes comes to life and is animated and filled with love. When I asked what was happening, it turned out that sometimes her cat, Cirmi, also comes to the session, curling himself up on Ildikó's lap. Ildikó was able to say that she was pleased I had noticed Cirmi's presence without my having seen him. After this, we spoke a lot of her relationship to Cirmi, and how this adopted cat is the only being that accepts her entirely, just as she is. In Ildikó's case, the cat showed a part of the self (a part yearning for an ability to give warmth and love) that I would perhaps never have had the chance to meet if we *both* had not been jolted out of the customary setting.

Kevin (39 years old, a university lecturer) started coming to therapy three years before COVID. There was a long, slow process of rapprochement, the result of which was that we switched to analytical therapy shortly before the pandemic. He lives alone with his dog, Luna, whom he spoke of a lot even before the pandemic. His time is filled with work, so he has very little time for a private life. Initially the sessions show his anger toward his parents, and a sense of their absence. He has not yet had a long-term relationship, and finds it difficult to imagine allowing someone to get close to him. Usually it is he who leaves the relationship, if he feels it is beginning to be too intimate, or if the other is expecting too much of him. This desire to break off appears several times during therapy, but he is able to put this into words, and he is glad that he doesn't jump out of this relationship. I often feel his searching gaze directed at me: he watches my every reaction, just as in his childhood he watched his mother, to see what mood she was in. When we start working on the couch, he looks back at me, often at first, then more rarely, to see my reactions, or to see that I am there, that I am present. When we switch to working online, we agree that he would carry on lying down, and during the session we would switch off the camera. In the first couple of months, I often have the feeling that he is distant, that I cannot reach him. He often forgets the session. Then in October 2020 I notice Luna yelping, which I had noticed before too, but somehow I ascribed no meaning to it. I ask him whether this means Luna is with us too. After this he speaks at length warmly about Luna. As with Ildikó, a hitherto hidden part of Kevin comes to the fore and has a role in the therapeutic relationship. Shortly afterward, he unexpectedly asks me whether I've ever had a dog, or if I have one now. The question catches me off my guard, partly because it's unexpected from him (he never asked me personal questions), and partly because I don't share information about myself. But finally I reply: yes, I have a dog too. Kevin is very surprised: not that I have a dog, but that I shared this with him. Next session, he arrives punctually and says how much it meant to him that although I don't normally do it, I said something personal about myself. After this, the reason for the separation of the recent months becomes accessible: he was angry that he could not come to face-to-face sessions, but he felt the anger was unjustified: partly because "it wasn't my fault" things turned out that way, and partly because he didn't want to endanger our relationship. Although Kevin was present physically, he had separated in the psychological sense, he had left the relationship, and punished both me and himself. Thanks to Luna (and the fact that in the psychological sense I heard Luna yelping, and let my own Mango into the space), closeness was restored, and in it a hitherto hidden part of Kevin had a role – the part that was capable of intimacy.

9/11 and COVID-19 in Dreams

In the first phase of COVID, when we knew very little about the illness, the external world was dominated by uncertainty, unpredictability, and fear, and in the therapeutic space with our patients we tried to tame these feelings, which often overwhelmed us too, into something containable. Here are two fragments of dreams from this phase:

> **Klára** (45 years old, photographer, who has been in therapy for two years) says:

> I dreamed I was walking in the mountains with my parents. It was getting colder and colder. I look up at the sky and see two airplanes. One of them explodes and starts falling towards us. Nobody but me seems bothered about this. It's as if they haven't even noticed. I'm frozen still, I realize we can't run away. I wake up with a feeling of unbearable anxiety.

At almost the same time, **Eszter** (38 years old, a financial expert) brings the following dream:

> I'm in a big house, more like a castle, which is mine. I'm holding a reception. I notice that people are looking at me strangely. I realize it's because I'm eating striped grapes. There are more and more people in the garden, and I begin to worry they'll do some damage, they won't take care of my hamsters. I look up at the sky. The moon is beautiful. But suddenly I see airplanes falling, and I get a shock, because I know they are going to fall on us. I'm the only one looking up at the sky; nobody else can see the danger.

A couple of sessions later, **Klára** brought the following dream:

> I'm in a house in the countryside. The sun is shining, but the house is cold. I see my father, and I know he's going to die. I realize this is my inheritance. From now until my death, this is where I have to live. And

I know that I am alone, there's not even a town nearby. I walk through the rooms: there are large spaces, everywhere is dim and cold. Finally I get to the library, which is both familiar and alien, frightening.

Klára's father moved to Hungary from Transylvania at the age of 19. He met her mother (who is Hungarian) shortly afterward. Her father rarely spoke of his previous life, and did everything he could to integrate, even changing his name. In order to make a living, and for his family's sake, her father renounced his own aspirations (like Klára, he liked writing and photography), and earned his living with manual work. Klára saw her father as strong, somebody able to start again from nothing. She feels that compared to him, she hasn't accomplished anything. Associating with the dream, she says that she doesn't like the sunlight. For her, the house means that there is no choice, that she has to accept her inheritance, and live in it (or with it) until she dies. She must tend to what her father has created. She has an elder brother, but he is excused, because he has a family and children of his own, while Klára does not. Klára is not certain whether she has strength enough for this task. She is weak, while her father is strong: he was able to start again, to build everything up from nothing. The only warm place in the cold house is the library. Here she doesn't feel so lonely (Klára likes reading very much, and even writes a little. In the company of her books, she doesn't feel so abandoned). In the dream we see Klára's recurring basic experience: she has no right to live her own life, and frequently feels she is not really living. Although this dream can be understood and interpreted in the light of Klára's own life history, in the dream, through the subjective reality the current reality can be discerned: in March 2020, the fine spring sunshine (and warmer weather) was influenced by the threat of the virus, and fears (cold breezes).

Like Klára's, the dream of the other patient, Eszter, can be interpreted in the light of the family's past (Eszter is a third-generation Holocaust survivor): the grandparents lacked foresight, misjudged the situation, and did not flee Hungary in time during the Second World War. The reality of the present also appears in it: the welcomed guests someone familiar suddenly become an uncanny stranger.

Eszter's Dream (38 years old, financial specialist)

I had a really weird dream. I'm not sure I can explain it. It takes place in several places. I saw a friendly dog, but as it came closer, I could see all its parts. I mean its bones, its innards. It was a horror dog. A really shocking image. I thought: poor thing, he can't see. I think this was the most horrifying thing: he doesn't know, only others can see it.

Eszter's association was that the dog had been infected, and had become infectious. Nothing protects it anymore, but it doesn't know. It is very vulnerable. Alongside pity and deep sadness, a positive feeling appears: the dog doesn't let things get it down, it's playing happily, and trying to approach people. For Eszter, this duality is frightening: the dog's vivacity, while it harbors death within. The feeling of the dog is familiar to her: she often tries to behave as though everything is in order, indeed, she often doesn't notice if there's a problem, if she feels ill. This image (apparently everything is okay, full of life, while inside there is a serious problem) brings the family legacy, the transgenerational atmosphere of the family. Her grandparents, who survived the Holocaust, lived in the same household. They never spoke about what happened to the family, or shared their memories. While the family went about its business, there was the shadow of the past and the losses experienced.

Therapist's Experience: Snapshot of the Professional Community

After the general restrictions are imposed, most therapists switch to remote working. However, a couple could only imagine working as psychoanalysts in person, and so they continued like that, keeping to the safety protocol. The difficult thing for me was that I felt that there was less tolerance, less ability to accept other's attitudes. Some colleagues working in person interpreted their patients' (or even colleagues') desire to continue online as resistance. Other therapists considered it dangerous to hold sessions in person, and wanted it to be regulated by the society. In the community of psychoanalysts too, there appeared the same camps as in society, though much more subtly, and for brief, transitory periods: maskers and non-maskers, those who work remotely and those who work in person. Later, this polarization (in the analytical community at least) was resolved, and many individual solutions were accepted within the framework given by the regulations.

The Spirit of War

In April, as lockdown measures are tightened further, a general worry takes hold that there will not be enough to eat, and many people start hoarding. Bulk buying does indeed cause some items, such as toilet paper, flour, and yeast, to be in short supply. In the collective mood, the reality of the present (fear of infection) is for a short time overridden by the reality of the past (fear of dying of starvation, and a lack of basic supplies).

Gabriella (41 years old, a secondary school teacher) and her husband keep strictly to the lockdown, not even going to the shops, and meeting family only cautiously, outside. The day immediately before a stricter lockdown was introduced, Gabriella arrives slightly late at the therapy session. She explains that they have bought a new fridge, much larger than before. It transpires that in order to buy it, they went to a large shopping mall, one they haven't set foot in for a good while. We try to investigate what she and her husband began to be scared of, and why it should have happened right now. Even Gabi cannot understand the reaction, particularly the forcefulness of it, and we both feel it to be disproportionate.

Individual Crisis and COVID

Mária (35 years old, a sociologist) has been in therapy for five years (once a week, seated). She gave birth in March, just as more and more restrictions came into force, and anxiety increased in the external world. Although we had previously planned to finish therapy at the end of February, bearing in mind that Mária's anxiety was increasing as the birth approached (it was impossible to know what rules there would be in the hospital, whether her husband would be able to be present at the birth), we agreed to continue the therapy online. We would carry on with the therapy one month after she gives birth. Mária is not well. She complains of serious anxiety, of mood disorders. Although the birth went well, later the infant developed complications, and they spent two weeks in hospital. During this time, Mária feels constant and increasing anxiety. Although she feels helpless, she is constantly on the alert. This sense of alert and anxiety does not abate even after she returns home. In fact, it grows to be unbearable. Mária is constantly watching the infant's state, and even the baby's crying awakens deep anxiety in her. Pregnancy and birth is a particularly sensitive time, psychologically too, when the individual leans strongly on the external world, the other, for support. Although Mária was worried about giving birth earlier too (she wanted everything to go well, for the baby to be healthy), the anxiety was controllable, and it didn't overwhelm her. She was dominated by good feelings (looking forward to the baby). It gave a great sense of security that she had put great care into choosing the doctor and hospital managing the birth. But the unexpected threat caused by COVID-19 upset this delicate balance. Now it was uncertain what conditions the birth would take place under, whether the chosen doctor would be available, whether her husband could be present. She felt she was losing control and was left alone.

Various Reports on the Concept of Lockdown

Róza (37 years old, architect)

> I didn't think it would be so good not to have to go to work. Only now do I realize how much I have to accommodate to people. Here at home I can be myself. I'm patient with the children. I'm getting on much better with them than when I was going in to work. I'm more patient with myself as well. Now I have to face the fact that I put so much effort into maintaining my existence among others.

For Róza, the lockdown brought relief: being jolted out of the customary way of life awakened her to the effort she put into meeting others' expectations.

This experience, put into words in the therapy process, could be worked with later, and the change remained even after the lockdown was lifted.

Sára (36 years old, a chemist) has been in therapy for several years (twice a week, on the couch). She is married, and has two daughters. Sára's basic experience is that she doesn't fit in. For her, life in a community is a great burden. "As if I've always been like this," she says during therapy.

For her, lockdown brings surprising experiences. While previously she thought of herself as a boisterous, restless person, now she is surprised to notice how good she feels with the obligation to keep a distance. She was 14 years old when her parents emigrated to Hungary. The experience demanded that she constantly adapt and fit into the new world. She felt that she had to struggle to be accepted. Existing in a new country kept her constantly on the alert, in a state of tension. The compulsory lockdown order because of the pandemic was a relief to her, because the constant need to adapt to others was removed, though ever since she moved to Hungary, this had been a part of her life. Shutting out the external world gave her the chance to meet the inner world from before they immigrated.

Ferenc (26 years old, a financial specialist) grew up as one of three children, and recently graduated from university. Currently, he is a middle manager in a big corporation. He has a team of his own and he is responsible for them. He was proud of himself for fitting so well into the workplace environment, where they respect his aptitude.

He is taking lockdown very badly, and is confused. He feels it to be a step backward. It's hampering further development, and triggers anger in him:

> It makes me angry that I can't meet other people. It's fundamental to my being to be with other people. It inspires me and fills me with life. Under lockdown I am denied all of this. I moved back home to my parents so that at least I wouldn't have to shut them out of my life. But I experience this as a step backwards. I've moved beyond this, or I had done. I like being alone, but I like being with others too. I had got everything neatly sorted out. This virus really messed things up for me.

Ferenc is the youngest of the siblings. By getting the job, he experienced that he had finally grown up, and his parents finally treat him like an adult. At the beginning of the lockdown, he felt that since he is the only one of the siblings not to have a family, he should take care of his parents. But moving home takes him out of the role of an adult able to care for himself and others, and back to the role of child. His father left the village where he lived when he was a young man. He didn't want to continue his parents' country way of life. His parents experienced this as desertion, and later his father felt great guilt because of this. Ferenc's moving back home is difficult to understand in the *here-and-now*, in his relationship to his parents. However, in the light of his father's story, it becomes clear: his moving home can be interpreted as an unconscious attempt to correct a mistake. Ferenc felt he had to move back home: he unconsciously identified with his father, the planes of time telescope together, and he senses his father's experience in the past to be a present prompting.

Kinga is 40 years old, an engineer, and a mother of two children. In the first wave of the COVID period, she described a visceral feeling of being overwhelmed in the following words:

> I think of this virus as something that's always present, a constant threat. It makes me vulnerable. It makes me feel helpless. I don't know what to do with myself. It keeps me on edge. It's like it was lurking nearby and might strike me at any time. It gets me down. My stomach's already upset by it.

Kinga's grandparents fled to Hungary from a tyrannical regime. Initially they couldn't speak the language, and they lived in poverty. They felt forlorn in the unknown, new world. Her grandparents never managed to find peace in Hungary. Their sense of security in the world was undermined for good. Kinga is a young woman who makes her own living, and had been in control of her life, but in the uncertainty and threat of the COVID situation, she experiences feelings similar to those of her grandparents years ago:

> The worst thing is that I feel as though I don't know how I will get through it. I'm most scared of myself. I feel despair. What happens if I can't manage? When I'm feeling on top of things, I know that this is irrational, but mostly I feel this whole thing is irrevocable, that there's no way out.

Emma (39 years old, an HR manager) started therapy a couple of months before the lockdown. Recently, she has been showing continuous development. She started showing attachment. She was experiencing her feelings more fully. Her ability for self-reflection and mentalization developed markedly. In this still relatively early phase, a curfew was announced. After that, we held the sessions on Skype. The lockdown became more of a burden for the patient, and after her initial adaptation, she fell into serious regression. She lives with her husband, and during her sessions, he went shopping. Emma did not leave home at all, and she began to experience it as a kind of prison. Increasingly often, she burst into tears in helpless anger. A change took place between us too, in the therapy relationship. I felt that her attachment to me was gradually weakening. Her ability for self-reflection decreased significantly. Anything we built up in one session had disappeared by the next one (the "Kelemen the Mason" effect, Bakó & Zana, 2020a, 66–67, 2021a, 89–90). After several sessions of low efficacy, I gave up the mode of working I (or we) had adopted before the lockdown. I understood that the regression that had arisen as a result of this situation required a different approach. I listened to her. I empathized with her. I related to her as to somebody who is currently in crisis. I followed her emotional states, watching for what she needed in this situation. The work I was doing was not exploration. In this phase of therapy, I was far more active than in the previous, dynamically oriented analytic work. By now my own anxiety had increased too. I was increasingly concerned for my patient. I worried that I might lose her, because of the weakened attachment. I worried she might leave therapy.

Similar to other patients who previously had used the couch, with Emma we saw each other at the beginning and end of the session, but during the session we turned off the camera. In this regressive phase, I wondered whether to change the setting with Emma, and to work with the camera turned on. But I didn't do it. I felt that Emma's vibration would overburden me, that I wouldn't be able to contain either her, or myself. She was terrified of being infected and consequently of death too. She looked on everyone as a virus carrier, including her husband. She got no relief from anyone: from others or from herself. I saw her as a little girl who is unable to speak of what she is experiencing. Rather than calming, talking upsets her. As for myself, who was unable to redeem her from her sufferings, I saw myself as a bad mother. Fear of infection held me too in a sense of constant threat. Sometimes I had the fantasy that my own anxiety, which though unspoken was present in the therapy space, makes it difficult for Emma to reach out to me, to be able to trust me. I also had to think through how I relate to the threat caused by the pandemic, to death. How does this situation affect me? How is my own regression present, how does it appear, in the intersubjective space? Like everyone, I am affected too. With this constantly present threat, the security of the world around me had changed. Fear of death is familiar to me from earlier. It is a recurrent experience that the current situation called forth. In recognition of this, I reached for a method that had served me well before: I looked for a safe inner place that gives me strength and safety. For me this was an experience I had on a hot summer's day, floating in the warm sea. Living through this marine experience helped to lift me out of my own regression, and it helped me to regain my ability to contain.

I Don't Want to Hide: A Snapshot from a Non-therapy Relationship

Margit (77 years old, a retired teacher) told everyone she kept the rules, and stayed at home. "Why would I go outside," she said, "when you do the shopping for me?" One of her daughters found out by accident that for various reasons, her mother did regularly go outside the house. When she confronted her with this, Margit said:

> I don't want to be scared, to hide away. I take care. Honestly, I am careful. I'm not scared of dying. I don't want to sit at home worrying about when I'm going to fall ill. This way I'm experiencing that I am alive. I have no time to waste.

The Therapist's Loss and Grief

I suddenly learned that a very dear friend of mine had died, somebody I had spent a lot of time with in the world of Playback Theater. Zsuzsa was 65 years old, and a drama teacher. We didn't meet that often, but when we did, I always enjoyed talking to her. I respected her energy, the speed at which she lived her life. Zsuzsa was accepting of everyone, and was a role model for many. She worked as a teacher, but she set up a theater too in the secondary school. She was a genuinely creative partner in our work together. The news of her death reached me, but in vain: I caught myself trying to keep the experience at arm's length. I felt I needed a delay to be able to allow the pain, the grief, close to me. While my psyche was in turmoil, I sought out the whys and hows. It turned out that as so often, Zsuzsa had not taken her own health seriously enough: in this case, the symptoms of a "cold." By the time she went to the doctor, she had double pneumonia. She was put on a ventilator, but they couldn't save her life. She was one of the first victims of the pandemic. In order to soften the pain that overwhelmed me, I lengthened the morning dog walks to two or three hours. Meanwhile, I chatted to Zsuzsa. Her death brought back the experience I had when my grandmother died. I was 18 years old, living in a student hostel. My father left a telephone message with the porter of the hostel: "Your grandmother has died. Come home. The funeral is tomorrow."

I didn't arrive home until late that night, where a vigil was being held. Everyone looked at me when I walked into the room where my grandmother was laid out in state. I froze completely. My feelings vanished, even though I loved her very much. I couldn't weep, though I dearly would have liked to. Now, mourning for Zsuzsa, I was once more unable to cry. I wanted to imagine that Zsuzsa was alive, that she was with me on the morning walks. Sometimes I laid into her for not looking after herself, sometimes we ruminated, mused over shared memories, and planned the future. Sometimes we laughed, sometimes we were sad. I needed this "game," this playground I had created myself, in order not to be overwhelmed by grief. I had suffered many losses over the previous years. I felt that now it was too much: I couldn't stand it if I allowed myself to experience it in all its reality. By creating my own shared space and time for these experiences, I was able to retain my ability to listen to and help others. I went on these walks every morning. I got up early so that I (we) would have enough time. Morning became the designated time for this special grief. If during the day I was beset by despair, I could say to myself:

> Don't be afraid! It's all right! What you feel is normal. I'm here with you. You can allow these feelings and experiences to come to the surface now too. And tomorrow morning we will spend plenty of time giving ourselves over to things related to Zsuzsa.

This "trick" helped me slowly, over the course of time, to support myself and reach a point where I could experience grief. This is what happened when I was mourning my grandmother too. The frozen state I experienced at the vigil stayed with me for two years. It broke on a late autumn afternoon. I wandered into a Catholic church where there happened to be a funeral in progress. There was soft music. Two or three people stood around the coffin. The atmosphere was very moving. Suddenly I began sobbing, and this resolved the frozen state. I was overwhelmed by feelings once more. I felt sorrow, but this sorrow was a blessing. It freed me from loneliness. I was able to meet my grandmother again. Ever since then, I carry within me the love I experienced with my grandmother. Until then, I had been shut off from it. I knew that to mourn Zsuzsa's loss too, I needed time. I wanted to give myself that time. My imagination helped me to get a delay, so that I was not destroyed by sorrow. On the contrary, I came into contact with the rich, warm, colorful internal world that we shared together. It was with this strange experience of loss that the COVID period started. At the time we had no idea how long it would be with us, or of its extent.

Zsuzsa's loss, the foregrounding of unprocessed losses, and fear of the coronavirus, all met in a shared field. I had to support and contain others while meanwhile I too was uncertain, and emotionally burdened. Security, predictability, planability, and stability suddenly all disappeared, or were put into question. I had to find new points of reference in the world, which had become unsteady within and without.

The crisis lived through in the present affects/affected we therapists deeply too. We are part of the continually changing experience. We had to contain not only the experiences we lived through with our patients in the present, but also our own losses in the present and those called forth from the past.

May/August 2020

Conspiracy Theories Abound

Many theories are doing the rounds, theories about the origin of the virus. People are looking for (and finding) reasons, explanations, and a "culprit." One premise is that the virus escaped from a laboratory. Although specialists don't rule this hypothesis out completely, they consider it unlikely. The yellow press and social media are awash in assumptions about a "biological weapon," and there are many hypotheses about which power is responsible for the pandemic.

US President Donald Trump and Secretary of State Mike Pompeo initially hint, then in several statements claim, that they had "a significant amount of evidence that this [the SARS-CoV-2 virus] came from that [microbiology] laboratory in Wuhan" (Barát & Kemenesi, 2021, 82).

> Although the WHO and the American intelligence services denied it, in February 2021 the theory resurfaced, and when referred to in a much-cited study it spread through the yellow press globally. The author claimed that this virus was manmade, because no related viruses were known of.
>
> (Barát & Kemenesi, 2021, 90)

The first breakthrough in medicines to treat COVID came in June 2020. In Hungary, in this period there are several announcements that the drug favipiravir will be used. Meanwhile, experts remind the public that a drug or vaccine alone is not sufficient. There is no miracle cure, and efficient management of the pandemic requires attack on multiple fronts, from social distancing to vaccines, and drugs (Barát & Kemenesi, 2021, 113).

Temporary Relaxation, a Split in Reality

In Hungary, thanks to the very strict lockdown, and perhaps also to luck, the first wave claims relatively few lives. There is talk of whether the strict rules could be relaxed. The collective mood is changing too. Alongside the "take care of each other" mood of the first weeks, many other ideas gather strength in these weeks, and other realities start to unfold. Many still feel it reassuring to keep to the lockdown and the rules, but there are voices urging, and later demanding, relaxation. Another reality appears, that of those for whom the lockdown brought not security, but a deep financial uncertainty: for instance, those working in the entertainment or catering industries. Dissatisfaction is growing and people give voice to it openly. More and more often anger and aggression is directed at those keeping the rules: the mask-wearers, or even old people "who are the reason all this is necessary." There are more (mainly verbal) attacks on old people who do not wear masks, or don't keep the regulations: "we are suffering for them, and they don't even keep to the rules."

"I Wish It Were All Over and Done"

Márta is 23 years old and works in the catering industry. She has been in therapy for one year. Just before the beginning of the COVID pandemic and the restrictions, she split up with her boyfriend, and she also recently lost her beloved grandfather. She described her state like this: "It's like life has stopped everywhere, and I've checked out of everything too. I just want it 'to be over'" (Bakó & Zana, 2021b, 515). Although she kept her job, she experienced great uncertainty. She is worried that if the situation with the lockdown goes on for a long time, she might find herself without work. Márta took the spring period badly, with the lockdown. She became increasingly regressive and introspective. Her biorhythms are upset: she is sleepy during the day, unmotivated, and she can't sleep at night. She is dominated by loneliness and despair. Márta is stressed by the move to online therapy too. In the first two months, she is willing to connect only if the camera is turned off. She didn't cancel a session, but I felt that she was becoming distant, not just from the world, but from me too. In June, as the change in the external world was becoming palpable, and some rules were relaxed, the total lockdown was lifted, there was the promise of summer, Márta became increasingly irritable in the sessions, and then said she was dissatisfied with the therapy. She didn't understand why I didn't "open up," why we don't switch back to face-to-face sessions. Perhaps this method isn't the best for her. Perhaps I can't help her enough, I can't pull her out of this "shit." Anger against her ex-boyfriend flared up, while she also said she missed him, and desired him. She started to miss her grandfather again. She cried a lot. After she managed to express these feelings, she improved. Although she continued to find the situation wearing, she regained her vivacity and once more made contact with her feelings.

Péter (20 years old, a student) asked for therapy help in July 2020, because he felt the ground has disappeared from under his feet. The pandemic lockdown and restrictions had turned him inside out. Sometimes he experienced uncontrollable rages, and at others he was overwhelmed by emptiness, lack of motivation, and depressive moods. At the beginning of the lockdown, he and his girlfriend moved back to Péter's parents to save money on the rent. Péter previously had serious conflicts with his father, which is why he moved away from home at the age of 16. His father was sometimes an accessible, caring father who could be relied on, but sometimes he quite unexpectedly became hot-tempered and aggressive, which in Péter's childhood often spilled over into physical blows. His mother and younger sister offered no resistance and waited quietly for the storms to pass, but Péter stood his ground: he hit and kicked, and arguments often turned into fights. Ultimately, the abuse ended when he became a teenager and fought back so hard that his father took fright. More recently, their relationship has settled. When Péter moved home in March, there were no conflicts with his father, but his arguments with his partner Zsófi became steadily nastier. Péter's relationship with Zsófi had been working well for a year, and although they had arguments, they soon made peace and were able to talk everything over. After they moved into Péter's parents' home, the arguments became cruder. Zsófi accused Péter of physically abusing her, while Péter felt that she was also at her wits' end because of being cooped up, and that was why she was hurting and provoking him. This cost them their relationship (Bakó & Zana, 2021b, 515).

September/October 2020

Decisions

After the brief relaxation in the summer, in September the "numbers" (of those falling ill, and especially of fatalities) slowly begin to rise, and later, from October, even more so. Because too few tests are being carried out in Hungary (Barát & Kemenesi, 2021, 175), it is increasingly difficult to judge from these "numbers" how many people have actually been infected, and we are less and less able to measure the risk realistically. At the beginning of September, we still feel the relaxed mood of the summer, which gives more space, and the reality of the outer world (the rise in the rate of those falling ill) does not affect the collective mood that much. In this period, both of us are still offering sessions in the room, but if someone feels it safer, they can choose the online option. About one-third of patients choose to have sessions in person.

Not long after this opportunity for meeting in person becomes available, Zsófi (21 years old, a student), who had been coming to therapy about one year, telephones me before one of the sessions, saying she doesn't know whether to come in person. She wants to talk it over with me. She says she has had a slight cold for a couple of days, but she has no other symptoms. Previously I had agreed with everyone, including Zsófi, that if they have any symptoms, then we would have the session online. I remember this, and I'm inclined to say it, but in the end I ask her what she thinks of her symptoms. She replies that she doesn't think it is COVID. I tend to agree (I remember that at times of stress, Zsófi often has a cold), but at the same time I am very uncertain. Suddenly I wonder if Zsófi's question is about whether I would accept her even if she were dangerous. I ask her if she would really like to come. She replies yes, she would, if possible. Eventually, I agree that she can come. After the decision, I calm down. At the session, Zsófi is very quiet and introverted. When I ask what she is feeling, she says that she is worried that after the telephone call I regretted allowing her to come, and that I am probably worried she will infect me. And she was even angry with me, because previously I had said we would always decide together whether to meet in person or online, on the merits of the given situation. And this was not a shared decision. In actual fact I decide, and she is forced to accept my decisions.

T: Did you feel that I made the decision alone?
Zs: No. That's just it. I felt that I influenced your decision. That I forced my will upon you, and later you regretted it.
T: Is this familiar from somewhere?
Zs: Well, of course it is. *Silence.* On the weekend I was at home, but we had to wear masks, because Dad broke his leg riding his motorbike, so

we have to take care of him. It was a bit weird. It would have been so good to hug him, but we couldn't. At the same time, I started to feel that something doesn't square up. Then Mom said I could sleep there. At the same time, she and Dad were uncertain whether or not this was safe. In the end they left it up to me. I didn't actually want to go back to my flat. When I've got a cold, I don't feel good, and I just want to be at home, in my old room. In the end I went back to my apartment, but in a really bad mood. And I got more and more angry. But I should have been "grateful" that they offered me the chance of sleeping there.

For the patient, who had recently left the parental home, and is at the beginning of the process of separation, and becoming an adult, the weight of the decision becomes too much. The threat in the external world, her father's condition and vulnerability, and her own symptoms cause her to regress. She is angry with her parents because they don't sense that she is not now sufficiently strong or responsible to make an adult decision. She wants them to decide for her, even to take her in unconditionally and care for her in illness, like when she was little. She experiences something similar with me: instead of referring to our agreement and deciding the situation (as might have been expected), I draw her into the decision, and in doing so, like her parents, I place too great a burden on her. However, during the session, she is able to put all these feelings into words, and she becomes less tense. This situation is interesting from the therapist's side too: we went through a difficult, trying time with our patients and (as in this case) it was not always easy to orient ourselves or decide. Should I refer to our agreement and abide by the reality of the external world, or should I unconsciously mirror Zsófi's current inner state and not reject her desire for closeness? That was how I decided in this situation – whether the decision was right is a moot point. In this period, I often felt that (like her) I was constantly having to make decisions. And I was tired of it: it was difficult to follow the constant changes in the external world, to mirror reality for myself and for my patients.

Tamás (40 years old, a store manager) has returned home to Hungary from abroad. We agree in advance that after he gets home, we will have sessions online until he gets the test results, then if it's negative, he can come in person again. When he first comes in person, he says that the meeting was a success, but it was also very stressful: everywhere he went his temperature was taken, and security guards shouted at them not to get too close to one another. He tried to keep it all at a distance, thinking "I won't give into this madness," "I'm not scared," as opposed to those who are "paranoid" and terrified. At the second session, he mentions something I didn't know: because he was on a business trip, the compulsory quarantine didn't apply to him, and he didn't need to do a compulsory test either. But he did these, and at his own expense. I asked him what feelings this stirred up:

Tamás: These rules make me really angry. But I got even angrier, or rather more upset, that when I came back, Péter and my other friends didn't come over. But that was what we agreed. They said they wouldn't come over until I got the test result. I felt this was unjust, and hurtful. After all, as it turned out, that rule didn't even apply to me. *Silence.* I felt that they were saying a flat "no" to me. That they were rejecting me. I got angrier and angrier, and I was overwhelmed with helpless rage.

T: You didn't come here in person, and you didn't ask whether you could.

Tamás: Yes, because that is what we agreed.

T: But you felt it was unjust . . .

Tamás: Well, yes. *Long silence.* Because it turned out that that rule doesn't apply to me.

T: It's curious that this didn't come up in the previous session.

Tamás: Yes. I seemed to have forgotten it.

Tamás, who was overwhelmed by uncontainable emotions (anger, humiliation, a sense of being excluded) was probably trying to protect the therapeutic relationship by "forgetting" this feeling at the first session. At the second session, he was able to experience it against me, and put it into words, which opened the path to being able to process it and deal with it through symbolization. Although the patient's emotions are related to their own past, and previous experiences, they also reflect the current collective mood: anger and frustration are growing palpably at societal level, and society is no longer helping to modulate or contain the emotions that overwhelm the individual. Rather, it amplifies them. The rules, as the regulatory functions of society, no longer provide a point of reference to the individual.

Anna (32 years old, an interior designer) started coming to therapy just before the beginning of the pandemic (twice a week, on the couch). She is recently divorced, and she raises her 1-year-old daughter alone. The only help she has is from her parents. She can only work if they look after the child, but they live with her elderly grandmother. In the first lockdown, the period from March to July, in Hungary the restrictions work, and a full-scale pandemic is avoided. At the same time, the rules are very strict, and convey the message that everyone should stay at home, that we should "take care of each other." In this period, Anna experiences marked anxiety, and is very aware of every somatic symptom. She shut herself away, meeting nobody outside the family, and is highly judgmental about people irresponsible enough to leave home. In the second lockdown, although the actual risk is far greater (the infection and mortality rates rise steeply), the lockdown measures are more lenient than those in the spring. Although Anna is still careful, she lives far more freely than in the spring period. She meets acquaintances (taking precautions and wearing a mask) and she sees her family too. Fear of both becoming infected and infecting others is lower in this period compared to the first one.

Virus and Projections

Kamilla (36 years old, a teacher) has been in therapy for six months.

> When I'm having a difficult time I often dream of Oszkár. I dreamed of him again last night. I've realized now that if I dream about him, it means I'm in trouble, even if I don't experience it that way. This is a recurrent dream, where I go back to my past. Oszkár was the only man I loved. In the dream I'm with him, safe and secure in love. I wake up completely refreshed. I toy with the idea of telephoning him and meeting up with him in real life too. Of course, I won't do it, because I'm worried he would reject me, and I'd fall apart completely. *Silence.* I realize I'm scared! I'm scared of the virus. And everything. Everything else it brings. I'm wary of other people. But perhaps here too, I'm most worried that if I get the virus, I'll fall apart. I'm afraid of my own reactions. I'm worried that I'll give up, that I won't fight, that I'll be weak. So I try to keep myself distant from everything and everyone. And most of all, from the virus. Of course, it's not like an old lover, or an abusive family member, who I can actually avoid. The virus is an invisible enemy, who's always on my track. Haunting me, ever-present . . . Spooky!

Kamilla's father was an alcoholic. When he arrived home drunk, her mother hid away with the children. Often she fled to the grandparents to avoid the abuse. For Kamilla, keeping a distance from others is a familiar struggle, which for her represents both an escape and being left alone.

The Meanings of the Setting

Barbara (36 years old, a kindergarten teacher) started coming to therapy shortly before the pandemic, and was very much looking forward to being able to come to a session in person again. Yet when in September I suggested she could come, she chose to have the session online. When I asked her what was going through her mind, she said:

> It's interesting, but it doesn't bother me at all that I have to wear a mask. This way I feel you are safer. *Brief silence.* Perhaps the mask doesn't just protect us from the virus. It's easier to be with people anywhere. For instance, I feel better on the bus too. My face is half-covered, and I don't feel as vulnerable to other people's stares. Perhaps it is easier for me to hide.

Only later was she able to say that although she wears a mask everywhere, she would prefer not to have in-person therapy. That is why she chose the online session. She also noticed that although to begin with it was very difficult to switch from in-person to online sessions, gradually it brought liberty: she was able to talk freely about topics she had not been able to previously. Like Károly (see Mask and Shame), for Barbara, wearing the mask acquired extra meaning, but in a very different way: for her the mask represented protection in the psychological sense, a chance to hide, to keep her distance. In this phase of therapy, it was difficult for her to imagine that the deepening closeness and trust between us was a genuine psychological reality, and was not subject to changes in the outer real world (for instance, whether we are wearing masks). She was worried that if we put the masks back on in the physical sense, then it would go back on in the symbolic sense, and we would become distant again. Barbara's and Károly's cases are interesting because they demonstrate how the same external event (e.g., distancing, or mask-wearing) can be ascribed many very different meanings. They both live in the same external reality, but Károly and Barbara's internal realities, the ways they experience the situation, are radically different.

Szilvia (61 years old, a primary school teacher) started coming to therapy about six months before the pandemic (once a week, seated). In September, she requested not to switch back to in-person sessions, because she felt that online she finds it much easier to open up. She is able to talk about topics she could not otherwise mention, or only with great difficulty, for instance, issues of intimacy or sexuality. During the in-person sessions, so far the focus had been mainly on the problematic relationship with her adult son, her chronic illness, and her professional identity, but in the online sessions, these topics were gradually replaced by questions relating to men. Earlier, sex had been completely absent from her marriage, while she had had several extramarital relationships, mostly with married men, and with them the sex had been wonderful. Currently, she is getting to know several men via dating websites, and although she thinks she longs for a long-term relationship, she gets involved in brief, mainly sexual relationships. In her case, the online space made it possible to portray parts of the self (such as the seductive little girl) that previously hardly had a role at all. Like Barbara, Szilvia felt proximity to be fragile, and for her it was safer to experience growing closer, a deeper intimacy, through an online relationship with a physical distance.

Responsibly–Irresponsibly

Géza (48 years old, an engineer) has been in therapy for one year. Like Barbara, he chooses the online sessions. When I ask what lies behind his decision, he replies that perhaps he assumed that I would prefer this, that I would feel safer. This function was not unusual: in this case too, Géza tried unconsciously to guess the other's expectation or desire, and to behave accordingly. Three weeks later, Géza catches the infection, and although he has a rough time, he does not go to hospital. It transpires he caught it at a wedding planned a long time ago, where many people were infected, some of whom died. Looking at events in retrospect Géza perhaps wanted to protect me from infection: he presumed (not without reason) that I am "cautious," while he and his partner tried to live a "normal" life. He feared not for himself, but for old people, his parents, and for me. In his case, through the change of setting, we were able to give words to transference feelings that previously were not available in the therapy.

Samu (40 years old, a sociologist) started coming to analysis four years before the pandemic. In the fall he opted to come to therapy in person.

> I was thinking how odd it is that I've been working online for a long time, but I come to you in person, even though I could choose to do this online too. I have a sense of trust, that you are taking care of us. That's how I felt in the past too. At the beginning of therapy, it took some time for me to trust you. Today there's no question about it. The fact that I feel you are taking care of us both makes me more aware too. I take care of myself, and thus I take care of you too. I don't go to places where the threat of infection might be higher. I don't want to get ill and endanger myself and my family. If that did happen, then I'd go into quarantine for two weeks. I'd only meet you online. It's good to remember that we are mutually responsible for each other. Interestingly, this eases my anxiety. My sense of responsibility has grown. I think this situation has made me more mature.

As in therapy, so in supervision sessions too, difficulties related to the pandemic come up. In October 2020, a 50-year-old therapist asks for a consultation where, deeply upset, he speaks of his patient's irresponsible behavior:

> After the summer vacation I agreed with each of my patients that I would work in person for as long as possible. And we agreed that for this to work, we need to take care of one another. If any of us, or anyone in our environment gets COVID, or suspects, we will inform each other and switch to online sessions. So I was shocked when one of my thirty-year-old patients said, just incidentally, towards the end of the session, that her boyfriend had COVID. I froze completely. I was scared. I was thinking: I'm bound to have caught it from her. I was gripped by panic, and meanwhile I forced myself to keep calm, not to show it. I could hardly wait for the end of the session. Even now, I don't know what I should have done, or what of this I should take back into the session. I totally fell out of my role. My fear was much greater than my professional commitment.

In the time of COVID, the therapist has an additional burden in having to contain the reality of the crisis (which changes from day to day), and even the actual risk of infection. In this situation, the therapist expected himself to be able to contain the patient's aggression in the hitherto customary manner. This risk and threat was not merely symbolic, but the patient brought it right into the therapy space. In the technical sense, in defining the boundaries, he had taken into account the reality of the external world, that there was a danger "out there." But when put on the spot, he was unable to hold to it, to signal to the patient that she might be infected, and was endangering him by coming to the session. He tried to cling on to a false therapist role, while because of the real danger his ability to contain collapsed. We could look on this as the collapse of an inner therapist role: the therapist became incapable of behaving authentically and tried to repress his feelings, to deny his fear, his anger, and all the while he was no longer able to reflect on these feelings.

Dreams and the Transgenerational Atmosphere

Álmos (a 37-year old agile coach) is a third-generation Holocaust survivor, and has been in therapy for two years. Currently, he is working abroad, and there are many conflicts at the workplace. He asked for therapy to have the space to think about who he actually is. He presented the following dream:

> I'm playing ping-pong with a friend in my room, and he tells me he has just had a lovely baby daughter, but he's getting divorced and leaving his daughter too. In his family this is normal, after all both sets of grandparents, and his parents, did the same thing. He says all this with melancholy, but he's not devastated. Meanwhile another ex-schoolmate of mine appears. He is grossly obese, and slovenly. He's brought spaghetti bolognese to eat while he watches us play ping-pong. He reaches into his left hand pocket and as if it were the most natural thing in the world, sprinkles a fistful of cocaine onto the bolognese alongside the cheese. Then he sets about gobbling it up, like a pig. Meanwhile he says he's aware of his drug addiction. We have to accept it, it can't be changed. After that, I'm at some training course for doctors, with my girlfriend in the middle of the woods. The scenery is beautiful, a large wooden house in the woods, with a parking lot. First the trainer tests us to see how fast we can get the cars out of the garage in case of danger. I'm not very good at this . . . After that I'm hiking in the forest with my girlfriend, it's beautiful, but I'm nearly shitting myself with fear, because we know that a brown bear is wandering around somewhere. If it sees a human, it will kill them. After a long hike my girlfriend spots the bear next to a tree about two hundred metres away. We both start to run helter-skelter back to the wooden house, where people are wandering in and out, oblivious to the danger. The bear starts running towards us at a horrific speed. When we get to the wooden house, they're issuing certificates of attendance at the training course. We realize the certificates are in my rucksack,

in the car. So before I hide in the wooden house, I get in the car to get my rucksack, with the certificates, cards, and stuff, for the training program. Meanwhile I'm terrified the bear will come. So I start to park the car, but I'm really slow and clumsy (I'm surprised at myself), and I understand why the trainer started with maneuvering out of the garage. People are still wandering in and out, with no idea of the danger they are in. My nerves are in shreds, but soon I get into the building.

Álmos speaks very little, if at all, of the pandemic. However, like the bear in the dream, the threat is present nonetheless, like a stalker constantly at arm's length. He knows very little of the family history. What he does know is his grandfather's vacillation about whether or not to come home to Hungary from the camp, or to settle in another country. In the end, he came home, but his ambivalence about this decision ran through his whole life.

External and Internal Spaces in Dreams

Tibor (42 years old, a social worker) has been in analysis for four years. He brought the following dreams:

First dream

I can't work out where we are, in my home or in your consulting room. I'm in my usual place, in the armchair. It's as if you were there, but at the same time you're not there. I start looking around, because I sense you aren't present. I look up at the ceiling, and I realize I've never looked at it before. There's an animal on the ceiling. It's weird, because although I'm there, it's as if we were online, because I zoom into it. I see a crocodile, with its mouth open. Then I'm outside in the lobby, where there are masses of people, including a visiting nurse and battered children. I know they're all waiting for me (Tibor is a social worker). But your family is there too, a man and children. I think how strange it is, your husband looks just as I imagined him. I go into the bathroom. Although it's homely and I'm alone at last, I feel I shouldn't be there. Then I go back to the room where the session is, but you're not there. But your therapy notes are there. I peek at them, but I don't understand them. At the same time, I realize that you've been there all the time.

Second dream

I'm speaking to my mother on the phone. She says she's rented my old bedroom out to you so you can hold your sessions there. I get very angry when I hear this. My mother lost her temper and shouted at me, she said it's too late now, you're already there holding sessions. I go home and sure enough, my old bedroom is full of patients.

Tibor's strongest feeling about the crocodile was amazement: that he had never noticed it, because probably it had always been there. It doesn't scare him, rather, it gets him curious: is it harmless or dangerous, imaginary or real? Like Márta, for Tibor too it was difficult to regulate the relationship distance in online space: sometimes he feels that he comes too close, dangerously close to me, or even to his own feelings. Sometimes he feels the other, the therapist is too close (to his childhood bedroom, his unconscious, to his alarming feelings). In the dream, feelings familiar from before crop up: uncertainty, doubt, whether he's in the right place, whether he is allowed to be in the place where he is, or would like to be. But this dream might also reflect a deeper, quasi-psychotic fear, which depicts the individual reality permeated by the *here-and-now*, external reality: fear that the boundaries (internal and external) weaken, that he can no longer know who or what is dangerous; whether the danger is without or within; when we get too close to each other, and to our feelings.

The Positive Effect of COVID: A Snapshot from a Non-therapy Relationship

Ottó (45 years old, a chemist) has been at home a lot since the beginning of the pandemic. Even in the summer period he was working remotely, although he could have gone into work in person. Before the lockdown period, he lived a very active life. He really enjoyed having company. During the months he spent at home, he realized that he was very suited to a quieter, more withdrawn way of life.

> I discover myself to be an introvert, really. During lockdown it often occurred to me that I'm basically an introvert, but my life forced me to be extrovert. And I was. But now I feel that this is the world for me, when I can retreat from the world, I have time, and allow myself to turn inwards, to mourn. I'm grateful to COVID for guiding me back to the real me.

November/December 2020

Numbers on the Rise

In late October and early November, the cases of sickness and fatalities rise sharply, and we are in the thick of the second wave of COVID-19. In December, Hungary has the third-worst figures for COVID deaths in the European Union. The health service is under extraordinary strain, and health workers are overcome with tiredness, tension, and a feeling of helplessness. Many of them break down at the sight of so much suffering (Barát & Kemenesi, 2021, 201–209).

The collective mood changes too. As one patient put it: "The magic of the situation disappeared." Increasingly, in sessions, the dominant characters are tiredness, a feeling of emptiness, psychosomatic symptoms, and sleeping disorders. In this period conspiracy theories spread like wildfire, and more threatening emotions appear both in the outer world and on the "stage" of therapy, as shown later in a vignette (Klára, 45 years old, a photographer). At societal level, the tensions between generations, and anger, were stirred anew, exclusion became stronger, racist tendencies gained traction, along with populist propaganda, and intolerance at societal level. Solidarity faded, and destructive tendencies (splitting, projection, scapegoating) grew. Meanwhile, social and political events in the world at large trigger strong emotional reactions. In Paris, a secondary school teacher who spoke about freedom of speech in a lesson is decapitated. In the United States, after the death of George Floyd in May 2020, the Black civil rights movement (Black Lives Matter) flares up again. In Poland, a strict anti-abortion bill (later to pass into law) is submitted to parliament. Meanwhile, in Hungary, at governmental level and in the collective mood, there is growing intolerance to any kind of otherness. Shortly beforehand, during the COVID pandemic, and under the state of emergency imposed to manage the crisis, a bill was passed that made sexual transitioning impossible, and by writing into the constitution the tenet "the mother is a woman, the father is a man," legislators made it more difficult (practically impossible) for same-sex couples to adopt children.

A Fairytale but Not for Everyone

In October 2020, in the name of safeguarding children, a member of parliament organized a performance of shredding the book of fairytales *Meseország mindenkié* (published in English as *A Fairytale for Everyone*). The purpose of the book was to sensitize children to all manner of otherness, including homosexuality. Destruction of a book (which has in itself for generations been a metaphor for intolerance, non-acceptance, terror, and intimidation) reflects the collective mood of this period: what was previously unthinkable can now not only be said, but actually done. Not only is society haunted by undigested, brutal feelings that shade the collective mood, but more space is given to actual action, to physical violence (see later, Case Vignettes from Society, November/December 2020 Winter).

The External World Crystallizes in the Community of Psychoanalysts

This is a personal snapshot of a moment of dilemma, showing how difficult it is to make a decision, the right decision, when we ourselves are caught up in a historical event, the process of which is ongoing. As the tension caused by the pandemic grew, in this period we experienced that there was increased scapegoating in society, and the question arose in us: do we need to act, and if so, when? At the same time, we felt that typical of this period was a prompting to some kind of action, in the place of reflection.

The shredding of the book *A Fairytale for Everyone* (published in Hungary by Nagy, 2020) triggered tensions in society that were apparent in the community of psychologists, and in our narrower milieu of the Hungarian Psychoanalytical Society. A separate closed group started to exchange correspondence about this issue. There was no question of us disagreeing about discrimination or book shredding, but there was serious debate, often with heavy emotional overtones, about what role we psychotherapists, or as the society of psychoanalysts, as a whole, should have in such a situation. Several people reasoned that our association should take a clear position in society. We cannot stay silent, and we should take an official stand when a minority group (in this case the LGBTQ community) is seriously attacked. There are some historical situations (e.g., terror, dictatorship, oppression) when an attitude of neutrality is unsustainable, even at the level of the association (Braun de Dunayevich & Puget, 2019; Hollander, 2019, 16, 22). Others cautioned that the increasingly crude controversy pouring out of media into society was pervaded with politics and appeared to be manipulated: behind it may lurk the deeper social tension induced by the pandemic. Thus, the controversy surrounding *A Fairytale for Everyone* was an integral part of the game of social division, in a different garb. In this period, the questions that came up in our association cropped up in professional societies in other countries too. In international professional forums and conferences, we noticed that although the problem took on a different guise, many associations were facing similar challenge, and asking the same question. The analyst's approach, which gives preference to reflection over action, faces a serious challenge in situations when a mere attitude is not sufficient, when concrete action is necessary. When does this point come?

The Therapists' Own Experiences: Where Is the Wolf?

For me the debate was extremely interesting and relevant. However, emotionally it became a burden in many respects. This was when I felt that, somewhat similar to the scenes of mask-wearing in shops (see March/April 2020), thinking differently is difficult, or even unacceptable. My own subjective "then-and-there" experience is reflected in my contribution to the debate:

Dear All,

Let me start by repeating what another colleague closed with: it's very good that in this forum we can share ideas about these difficult, complex, and emotionally upsetting issues. With almost every post I read, I've felt that something in me resonated, that at some level it reflects my opinion too. But this also expresses my deep ambivalence. While on the one hand

I have a growing wish to express some kind of solidarity – to condemn all forms of explicit and implicit racism and exclusion on any basis. On the other hand I feel the pressure and complexity of this, and another voice in me grows louder, telling me that in the end my "tool" is reflection, the understanding and mirroring of the whole process (in therapy, or in any other professional forum). What really struck me was the Little Red Riding Hood and the wolf metaphor one of us used. Although I more or less understand, and I assume every one of us understands, what we are in, but this simile really helped me to be able to be able to express the ambivalence I am currently struggling with. Partly, I would like to convey that Red Riding Hood can come to me [for therapy], but the wolf can come too. They, moreover, are the main characters in a fairytale. Red Riding Hood always brings the wolf with her, and the wolf brings Red Riding Hood. I have no problem with this in therapy. Indeed, as a matter of fact I enjoy it when the wolf comes out of the forest. But what can I do with Red Riding Hood and the wolf on the street? That's a much more difficult question. If wolves roam the streets at night, and even strut around boldly during the day, then I'm uncertain. I start to get scared, I retreat and withdraw – or I arm myself. Who knows . . . At any rate, the characters of both Red Riding Hood and the wolf lose some of their nuance. The question for me now is whether I am (whether we are) still in the "fairytale," where the wolf can be, indeed should be, understood, and contained, or in reality where a (real) wolf might tear Red Riding Hood limb from limb before my very eyes. In the former case, I'd rather reflect; in the latter case, perhaps action should be taken (by expressing solidarity, for instance). The pressure for some kind of action is great, too great for me, the pressure to take a stance one way or another. In the midst of this I am slow, I digest these things slowly, I'm still struggling with the tricky dilemma of "reality vs. fantasy" – which unfortunately does indeed entail the risk that the moment will slip me by.

Katalin

Tihamér's words, which he wrote shortly after the discussion in the forum, take the metaphor of the wolf, and he portrays this period through the metaphor of a children's game:

The lamb is inside, the wolf is outside, or is the wolf inside?

The rhyme "The Lamb is inside, the Wolf is outside" and variations of it (with the wolf perhaps inside the sheep's pen) well illustrate the state we have been experiencing in the COVID-19 pandemic. Initially we experienced that the virus was out there, in the world. Far from us. Although it was a threat, with sufficient distancing it wasn't that depressing. It was enough to work and hold therapy online. It gave us a sense of security to stay at home as much as possible, or all the time. In this case we don't meet the wolf, and so we are protected from it. If we behave like good, clever lambs, we might avoid injury and destruction. This was aided by governments taking measures such as curfew and lockdown. We were protected. It wasn't us who had to decide. We didn't have to shoulder the burden of this responsibility. But in the second phase of the pandemic, there were no longer measures like this. Responsibility became ours: Should we wear masks or not? Should we hold sessions online or in person? Should we meet friends, parents, children? Should we go on foreign holidays, or even inside the same country? We find out about the rising number of people who have died from this virus. Did they die because they were already chronically ill, so people without underlying conditions are protected, and people with conditions are at risk? And is it just them? Am I at risk too!? Or not!? Who is putting me at risk? How far am I putting myself in danger when I go to the shops, when I hold sessions in person, meet someone, or simply live, go out of my house? Is the wolf already inside the house? Have I brought it in, because I want to live, and sometimes I go out? When will it attack me? What signals are there that it intends to strike? If my throat tickles, if I have a slight cough, if I'm cold, is that the virus? It's here already!? I'm anxious, I'm uncertain, I'm scared. I sense that danger is close at hand. I can't see it yet, but I feel it in my gut. It's like when I can't see in the dark, but my imagination fills the cavernous darkness with frightful beings and feelings. I have created an atmosphere where I hold myself in check. I become a prisoner of my imagination. I can't see the wolf, I just feel it in my gut, in my body. In the third phase of the pandemic, when more people die, even people who lived close to me and/or were emotionally close to me, the fear is even greater. It can easily mushroom into terror. My sense of reality weakens. I have to work harder and harder so as not to live in constant anxiety. The wolf is inside the house. It threatens me. I always try to face it down. The nights are a torment. I can't work out if it's bitten me. Perhaps it has? The atmosphere that I live in is constantly present. I want to go about my business, but I can only do so if I restructure myself again. I seek out my friends so that I can stay in reality, or at least close to reality. I know the wolf is inside the house. I think over how I can keep it in check. If I take vitamins, will that protect me against it? But it brings some relief to allow the idea of death into my consciousness. I think: "If the wolf bites me, I might die." I reckon with this. I settle my affairs. Anything might happen! I know I have to live like this for a while yet. I accept all my thoughts. I know that in this situation all my feelings and thoughts are valid. I hold myself, so that I can hold others too. I contain myself, in order to be able to contain others.

Online versus In Person

Many differing attitudes appear in sessions in this period: some stick to in-person sessions, others switch completely to online work, and many choose a hybrid solution. The two of us adopt different attitudes: while Tihamér held most sessions online with some patients in person, from November 2020 to June 2021 Katalin worked exclusively online.

Fear of Exclusion

Andor (33 years old, a trainer) is an assistant to an international training center. He has been in therapy for years. He feels that he's fallen into a trap. In spite of the global pandemic, the international training center wants to hold the program in person. The trainees can choose between online and offline modes, but he can't. A young professional, he is very wary of being infected, but he feels that he has no choice. The only thing he can do is resign himself to the situation and take part in the program, endangering himself. Although this was not an explicit expectation of the instructor, this was how Andor interpreted the situation. He was worried that if he brought it up, he might be excluded from the training program. This fear was so strong that he didn't even try to float the idea of online participation with the instructor. Although he feared being infected, this present danger was overridden by a much greater fear: that of being excluded, shut out. His grandparents were repatriated because of their ethnicity, and they experienced that as being driven shamefully into exile. Unconsciously, Andor avoids any situation where he might experience similar treatment. In his case, the current crisis called forth the psychological memory of an age-old family trauma, and the fears of the past (the possibility of being excluded, stigmatized, judged) merged with the reality of the present, reinforcing it, as in the case of Eszter, who came from a family of Holocaust survivors (see March/April 2020).

Should I Stay or Should I Go?

András (50 years old, a media professional) comes from a family many of whom perished in the death camps. A sense of threat, of being in danger, has become a basic element of the family's psychological reality. Before the pandemic, András decided to leave the country, because be judged the situation in Hungary, the collective mood, to be dangerous, and he persuaded his family of this too. He wanted to flee the country before it was too late. His decision was determined by the family's ever-present reality (the transgenerational atmosphere), which was pervaded by a fear of death, a sense of being under threat. Ever since childhood, he had fantasized about what would have happened if his grandparents had made the right decision, if they had trusted their feelings and left the country. When he left, he experienced his own decision as a corrective. He made a wise decision, one that his ancestors should have made decades ago. Living abroad wasn't what he expected. András experienced isolation, loneliness, and disappointment, which the pandemic and its concomitant restrictions only served to sharpen. Although he realized his desire for the corrective move, which he had been toying with for decades, it failed to bring relief, because it was related more to the reality of the past, not to the current reality, his own *here-and-now* desires.

Róbert (53 years old, a middle manager) decided to move abroad a couple of years before the pandemic. When he made this decision he was 50, his partner was 55, and their child was 13. Over the last few decades, the couple had made a good living for themselves in Hungary, with a wonderful home, good jobs, and a sound financial footing. In spite of this, the desire to change was defined not by wanting to go somewhere, but by wanting to flee from somewhere. Róbert initiated the move abroad. In the months before the move (which coincided with the outbreak of the pandemic), he started to feel worse and worse. His mood changed, and he became withdrawn. He watched the news anxiously. He was horrified by hatemongering posters plastered all over Budapest:

> I don't want to live and bring my children up in a world where this hate is present. My grandparents made the wrong decision when they didn't move abroad to escape persecution of the Jews, although it did occur to them. They paid for that with their lives. I don't want to hang around for that.

Unprotected

Amarilla (36 years old, a sociologist) has been in therapy for about one year. In this period, more and more often, she has told stories related to the difficulty of putting up with loneliness, of being alone. These stories came mostly from her childhood, and then she shared recent experience with me, one that had happened to her a couple of days previously:

A: I'm fine now, but if you had seen me yesterday you wouldn't have recognized me. Ádám [her husband] left home in the morning. His friends had asked him to help repair their car. I reckoned it would take a couple of hours. I was expecting him to phone about one o'clock to say he'd left, he'd do the shopping and would soon be back home. I was fine until one o'clock, I had stuff to do. At two, I started to get tense. Usually he texts me. I didn't want to call him. I hate his friends, and I didn't want them to tease him because of me. From three o'clock I didn't know what to do with myself. I got more and more angry. There was anger and desperation in me, side by side. I was overwhelmed by fantasies: he's died, he's been killed, he's with a woman, but he lied to me that he'd gone to his friends. I couldn't stand it any longer. I telephoned him. I shouted into the phone "Where the fuck are you?" I thoroughly laid into him. He wasn't angry. He knows me. He said he was going into the shop right then, and hung up. I was beside myself. By then it was dark outside. I didn't switch the lights on. I sat in a corner. All I could do was shout and weep. The tension was unbearable. I felt I would go mad unless it stopped. I thought he would never come home again. He'd punish me, he'd go and sleep at his parents'. I knew I couldn't stand it. I planned how to kill myself if he left me alone. I don't know, am I managing to convey the state I was in?

T: It's frightening even to listen to it. It must have been terrible. You must have felt very lonely!

A: I'm sure I would have killed myself if Ádám hadn't called in the meantime. I answered the call. He asked me to put it on the loudspeaker. He spoke to me continuously. When he arrived, he put me in bed. It was good that he took the whole thing seriously. That hadn't happened for ages. I'd got really tired.

T: Is there anything familiar to you in all this?

A: There was a time when this feeling was an everyday occurrence. It was when I started to go out with boys. *Silence.* If I know when the other is going to arrive, I don't get this feeling. If it's open-ended when he's going to come, if it's "I'll be there later," then my security vanishes, as if my sense of time disappeared. I have a feeling of infinity. I'm coming apart. I'm falling down somewhere. There are no footholds, or handgrips. I'm swallowed up by the depths, by time. I'm destroyed. I lose all control. What I can say now is that it's not just me that disappears, it's the other too. There's a point I get to from which there's no return.

In this period there's a growing sense of uncertainty in the outer world, a mood of "not knowing when or if it's going to end." For Amarilla, the external world no longer reflects security, it no longer holds her, so when her husband "disappears," she has nothing to cling onto and slides back into a disintegrated, regressive state familiar from the distant past.

Attila (36 years old, an architect) has been in analysis for two years. He tells of how he was recently very upset by a documentary that showed the working of anatomical laboratories and pathology departments. He can't rid himself of the images and the feelings that the film left in him. It showed the work of a medical examiner with great naturalism. One of their tasks is to remove parts of the body, for the sake of medicine. Attila's association with the film is that a person becomes an object, and loses his human aspect. In relation to this, he recalls a childhood experience, when he was in hospital for months, hovering between life and death. His memory is that he wasn't scared of death, but everyone else around him was. The metaphor of the pathology department (in which there is utter helplessness, hopelessness, and subjection to the external world) reflects not only Attila's own internal reality, but the experience of the community.

Klára (45 years old, a photographer) feels overwhelming anger toward all immigrants after the Paris attack (see Diary November/December

2020 – Numbers on the Rise), but at the same time she feels this is disproportionate and feels it important to emphasize how she condemns all kinds of
generalization. What is more (she adds), as a matter of fact she is half "alien"
in Hungary too, because her father was an immigrant. Klára grew up in Hungary, and assimilation caused her no problems (at least apparently) until now.
She is astonished at the force of her feelings. She experiences helplessness and
anxiety, and says that the most difficult thing is that she doesn't know who
to be angry at. Uncontrollably strong feelings and emotions shoot through
her, and they are difficult to link up to her own life history, and perhaps even
to the past of her own family. She experiences feelings in the collective mood
(anger, destructive emotions looking for a group to be a convenient scapegoat) as if they were her own, while the anger is also directed against herself,
the "immigrant" part of herself.

During this period, I conduct some occasional crisis consultations. Some of
these were paid for, and there were some "pro bono" cases.

Elena, a Ukrainian student of 23, came to Hungary three years ago to
study. Alongside university, she worked in a restaurant to make ends meet.
Although the first few months were very good, even then she experienced
what she calls culture shock. She only had one distant relation in Hungary,
a mentally feeble elderly woman, who doesn't even recognize her. Currently,
Elena is in a bad emotional state: she's crying a lot, and feels lost and lonely.
Because of the COVID situation, she hasn't been home for almost a year. She
often has migraines, which at her current workplace they make allowances
for. When she was living at home, she had to work even when ill, there were
no excuses. Here in Hungary, she is concerned that although they are kind
and polite, that's just a veneer: if she doesn't "deliver the goods" and she creates more problems than a Hungarian, they'll let her go. She becomes more
and more terrified that they'll fire her and she'll be forced to "go back where
she came from": for her, this is almost equivalent to a death sentence. She
had similar feelings earlier, when she had to apply for her residence permit
in the immigration office. The procedure was far from transparent and very
drawn out, and all the while she felt vulnerable and helpless. Integrating in
new country, local customs, adapting to a different culture, and struggling
with bureaucratic hurdles were all a great burden to her. Knocked out of her
customary environment, she constantly and intensely monitors her surround-
ings, and she translates the signals she picks up: what does kindness actually
mean here? Will I be safe? The pandemic amplified her already familiar feelings to an unbearable pitch: vulnerability, helplessness, a sense of being lost,
and loneliness. It was increasingly difficult for her to determine which feelings
belong to the present, the *here-and-now*, and which to the past, the there-and-
then. Elena loses contact with time as well, and submerges in a timeless state
of frozen hopelessness. She loses her belief that this state will one day come
to an end.

Tímea (25 years old, a student) is a third-generation Holocaust survivor. She came to therapy with issues of sexual identity long before the pandemic began. The threat of the pandemic, and the increasing tensions in society grow to an almost psychotic level in this period. She is concerned that because of her sexual identity she will be shot and left to fall into the Danube – not just her, but her family too. For her, this threat is real in the *here-and-now.*

Splitting Appears in Online Sessions and in Dreams

Shortly after we move back to online sessions, **Tamás** (40 years old, a store manager) starts the session by saying that he fully understands the therapy consulting room is closed, and he's not angry at me for that. Then he continues:

> The difficult thing is that while I'm trying to live normally, "as if the virus didn't exist," you can't get away from it. I'm angry, I think it's unjust that while some people can work safely from home, I can't, even if I wanted to. *Brief silence.* Perhaps it's envy? *Silence.* A few days ago I got very angry with my accountant. I got into such a temper it surprised me, and even frightened me a little. He has done the accounting for me for years, and I'm always very polite to him. I think it was humiliating for me that he sees the details of my life. And now I suddenly realize that he is actually a paid employee.

Márta is a 23-year-old catering worker. For a couple of weeks now, we have been online again. Before the session she messages that we should speak on the telephone, not on Skype (she had made the same request in the spring, when she was in a state of collapse).

T: What do you think, what does this relate to now?
M: Well, that the flat is a mess. *Brief silence.* Though I can set the camera up so that you don't see it, but I do. *Silence.* It's weird that everything takes place in the same room. This is where I work, and hang the clothes out. And this is where therapy happens. It's as if I allow myself things that would otherwise be forbidden. And later they'll be forbidden again. *Silence.* So right now, everything and everyone is shutting up. I think I'm concerned it will stay like this later too. People will get used to it, and we'll stay like this. *Silence, then with great feeling:* "I'm fucking sick of it. I want it to be over already!"
T: You're very angry at the virus, which you feel is squeezing out everything.
M: There seems to be nothing else.

T: I'm thinking about what it means that you asked to switch off the camera today. What's the mess that you can see, you are in it, but I can't see it. You are left alone in it.

M: Ah, that, yes. I think I'm concerned that the same thing will happen as in the spring. That I fall apart.

With the camera turned off, Márta and I are together in the therapy session, yet in two separate worlds: she sees something I cannot (the mess, the overwhelming, threatening feelings) – or she only lets them show in a very controlled, filtered manner. We are not in the same reality. I can see what the camera allows me to. By turning off the camera, the patient unconsciously shows her desire to shut out from therapy the thing that disturbs her, that is too much (the mess). She wants to exclude (split off) these feelings, but this comes at a price: she is left alone with them, and this shows in her fear of falling apart, of disintegration. Márta's case well reflects the then-and-there reality of the outer world. It is as if we lived in two worlds: one world has the cautious and the COVID deniers, and in the other world are the anxious and those longing for a "normal life." The inhabitants of the two worlds do not understand one another, because they have no shared language.

Szonja (43 years old, an elementary school teacher) has been in therapy for three years (twice a week, on the couch). After switching back to online sessions, she brings the following dream:

> I dreamed that after the session Skype kept on running, and you stepped out of the virtual world. We chatted in the living room, as though we were friends. My husband was there too, we all chatted together. It was a weird feeling. I felt you were too close, you could see into my life. When I was going to therapy in person, it was different. Then I could decide how much I tell you about myself, about us.

Szonja's dream also shows how easily the boundaries of the self are blurred in an online meeting (see Trauma and Self). Naturally, the experience has a real aspect, linked to the external reality: in the sessions we do indeed see into the space where the other lives. Previously, this had only appeared in therapy at the level of fantasy. In the more relaxed periods caused by the crisis, concrete reality and inner reality are difficult to tease apart: the patient's fear is not just that I can see into the living room, but that I can see or penetrate into her feelings, and that she can no longer regulate this.

"People Don't Respect Each Other Any More": Social Snapshots

In this period the time bands are introduced again: between 9 and 11 in the morning, only people over 65 can enter a shop. Hateful comments appear on social media, many people feel their freedom is being restricted because of the "wrinklies." As one patient put it: "People don't respect each other any more." As emotions grow stronger, so they seek, and find, a target.

A woman patient of 50 or so told of a scene that seriously frightened her:

> Yesterday, as I was going home, a man of forty was preparing to get off the tram. He was already standing up. He was holding the strap, and more and more often he was looking long and hard at a well-dressed woman. Her face was covered by a mask, she had a hat on her head, and practically the only thing visible was her eyes. She was minding her own business, simply traveling. When the tram stopped, the man stepped towards her, and totally without warning, he said: "Wretched Gipsy." Then he got off. The woman looked round, totally dumbfounded, as if to say "What on earth was that all about?"

In the same period, a young student told of the following experience:

> An elderly woman traveling on the bus kindly asked a middle-aged man to pull his mask up over his nose, because only then would he be protecting her and the other passengers. The man took off the mask and put it in his pocket. He looked hatefully at the elderly lady, and then spat at her.

These increasingly frequent accounts of such experiences in therapy bring up the therapist's own related experience:

> I'm waiting in line at the gas station. In front of me at the cash register is a family, and behind them are three people waiting to pay. As well as paying for the gas, the family order hot dogs. One of the people waiting is increasingly impatient and starts complaining. "Why not go and eat in a restaurant? Why are you holding up the line?!"

The anger and frustration the man exuded was disproportionate and incomprehensible given the situation. Hiding behind his mask, the man seemed to have become impersonal, and capable of expressing aggression inappropriate to the situation. Although he was apparently reacting to the given situation, his behavior and feelings did not reflect the *here-and-now* reality. These social vignettes reflect not only a lowering of the individual's capacity to tolerate frustration; they also point to damage in society's unconscious containing and transforming function. The community is no longer able to tame and regulate the feelings that overwhelm the individual, or even to protect the individual from attacks: in the best scenario, they are passive, and mute (the silent witnesses on the bus or tram, who by extension become victims of the aggression themselves) or in a worse case, the undigested feelings may become generalized and overwhelm a group of individuals. The number of infections and fatalities continues to rise. But there are enormous differences in how people relate to this, as if we were not living in the same reality: many are cautious, as in the first period, while other behave as if there were no danger. One patient brought the simile that it was like in Harry Potter, when people heard more and more news of Voldemort's return, but the Ministry of Magic was paying no attention to them. Voldemort is an apt metaphor, not just for the concrete threat of the virus, but for the threat overwhelming society at that time: we have first-hand experience of it, but it's difficult to pinpoint. It is as if we wished to ignore it.

Different Attitudes: A Split in Reality

Though we are living in the same external reality, in this period radically differing attitudes grow in power – virus deniers, avoiders, cautious folk, those at risk, those envisaging the end of times, etc.

Erzsébet (40 years old, a trainer) is married with two children. During the pandemic, she "lived freely." She made a deliberate effort to meet others, and went on lots of trips. They took in a dog so that they could go out to the street even after the curfew.

> I won't allow myself to be intimidated. It's important to me to feel free. This virus misery is the work of politicians, so they can restrict people's freedom. Well, they're not going to restrict mine.

In order not to feel herself restricted, Erzsébet denies the actual danger. **Jenő** (40 years old, a social worker) expressed a similar feeling:

> Actually there is positive side to the way I experience things (says Jenő sarcastically). As we discovered in therapy, I'm prone to live through awkward situations by distancing them from myself, whatever happens. True, this means that often it's as though I'm present behind a glass screen. It's the same now, with the virus. It's as if it doesn't actually endanger me. There's a benefit to the therapy, that I'm suspicious of myself, and I ask "Is that really how things are?!"

Barna (28 years old, works in the film industry) experiences intense fear within, but shows hardly any of this to the outside world:

B: All round me, everyone is experiencing this situation differently. I don't know how to relate to it. I try not to be scared. It's difficult to form my own opinion. I notice myself trying to adapt. Perhaps assimilate is a better term. I take on the other's feelings.

T: What is the benefit to you in this?

B: Perhaps that I don't need to bother about what I actually feel!

T: What do you feel?

B: What I feel is one thing, and what I show is another. I'm scared, but I don't know what to do with that. I'm scared, but I don't know who to turn to. It's good that in therapy I now dare to talk about this. I got out of the habit of asking for help long ago. I just put on an act. It helps me to disappear, but not to exist. If I don't exist, I'm not scared. Someone that doesn't exist doesn't have feelings. That was good when I was a child, when my father was rough with me, with us kids, and with my mother too. *Barna remains silent for a while, looks down, and continues.* Someone I knew well has died. The virus destroyed his lungs. It occurred to me that it's like when my father struck my mother, and I went and hid because I was scared. That's what putting on an act is good for. You can disappear, so the virus doesn't notice me, it won't harm me. Maybe I can avoid being "struck."

Mihály (50 years old, a store manager) is married, with one child. When he speaks about the pandemic, he does so with emotional distance, as if it had nothing to do with him. He says that people he knew well have died, but he says so without feeling, simply conveying a fact. When he speaks of this, his body is tense, his facial expression is rigid, his voice monotone. When he speaks about work and his tasks, on the other hand, he is enthusiastic, the narrative becomes full of feeling, gestures, and his features and his voice are infused with life. It's as if there were two worlds totally separated from one another. In the world where the pandemic rages, his feelings are non-existent, split off, while in the other world, the everyday world in the old sense, his feelings are disproportionately amplified.

Arnold (70 years old, a retired pharmacist) has two sons and seven grand-children, and he meets them regularly.

> If I have to die, then the best way is to be surrounded by family. I don't want to miss even one week when I meet them. We're very careful, we use masks. The meetings are out in the open. I get tested regularly, and so do the others. If there's any suspicion, then we postpone the meeting.

The patient is trying to keep up contact with reality: he watches the outside world, he is careful, and able to correct, and re-plan. At the same time, he knows that in order to maintain his stability in this loose, constantly changing, uncertain world, he needs his close relationships, and he doesn't want to lose them.

Antal (60 years old, an entrepreneur) is married with three children. He listens almost exclusively to news that tells of the losses. In his conversations, he talks again and again of the threatening, deadly nature of the virus, and the victims. Although he "goes out into the world," he does so with great trepidation. During the pandemic, complaints he already had previously have become more pronounced, such as indigestion and hypertension. The sense of threat is an integral part of his life. He is now unable to distinguish between the threats from the outer world and those from within, and a constant sense of threat becomes a fundamental experience for him.

Zoltán (58 years old, an economist) and his wife have not set foot outside their apartment since the pandemic began. Since then, their only contact with their children and grandchildren has been online. They experience the threat as constant, unpredictable, and fatal, and this experience does not change or adapt to the current external reality even when we have more and more information about the virus and potential risks. For them, safety is given by a strict constant quarantine, and they don't understand how people who meet up can be so irresponsible as to endanger themselves and others. For this couple, the outer world is so threatening that the only way to reduce the completely overwhelming anxiety is total separation.

Rita (32 years old, an artist) and her family decided of their own accord to stay at home for a week, to reduce the risk of infection. The only exception to this was therapy, because at home it was difficult to find a separate space for the duration of the session.

When Rita arrived for therapy, I had very strong somatic reactions. My throat tightened, and I felt tension in my stomach. I experienced the situation as cloistered, under threat. I felt like I should run away, that I was in danger. I hadn't felt like this until Rita arrived, so I started to observe her behavior, and her body language. Her posture was full of tension, her movements gave the impression of somebody who has lost their way. Meanwhile, her eyes sought out my gaze, as if she were reaching out to grasp onto something.

The masks we were wearing robbed us of the ability to reduce this bodily feeling. The mask covered the previously normal facial expression I welcomed her with, and by the time she got to the armchair, she had lost contact with me, and passed into a lost, disintegrated state. While Rita was looking around in desperation, she began to speak. Her speech suggested a desperate desire to cling on to something: at the same time, it was difficult to understand what she wanted to say, and the narrative disintegrated too. She felt this too, and several times she asked whether what she'd said was comprehensible. We couldn't work out what was happening, what had happened since the previous session, when she had left calmly. The patient said:

> The whole family were at home for a week. I felt that I was suffocating, that I couldn't stand this confinement any more. That I had to move out. *Silence.* The worst thing was that that's not like me. I love my children and husband.

When Rita's mother was a child, she was harassed sexually by her stepfather. Rita believes her awkward relationship to femininity and motherhood is because of her mother. Although her mother did everything for her, she seemed never to have been present. Her face was inscrutable, void of feeling, frozen. In the period preceding this session, she had been working on the effects of her mother's trauma projected on to her, understanding them and teasing apart what belongs to Rita, and what belongs to her mother. As we understood later, she arrived at that session with feelings that even she felt were alien to her, whose origin she did not understand, which aroused guilt in her, and confused her. She arrived at the therapy session in this regressive state and was looking for a refuge, something to cling on to. But the same experience was played out between us: behind the mask (which previously had no special significance) in the regressive state not only did my face disappear, but the previous secure relationship did too.

Later she described the experience like this:

> It as if sometimes, in my normal life, suddenly there flashed in another emotional state, another me, another world. I'm helpless against it. That must be what it's like when you're possessed by the devil. I know there's no such thing, but all the same.

The voluntary lockdown and the feeling of being shut away has distanced her from the outside world, from current relationship realities, and invokes the hitherto successfully repressed feelings that she kept at a distance: a sense of being in danger, threatened. She passed to an almost psychotic state in which past and present, her own reality and her mother's, outer and inner reality are all in one psychological space. She felt that she had to escape, but her husband and children were stopping her, which triggered aggression toward them.

> I don't know what I have done. Whether I've hurt them. I don't know what's really happened.

In this world shut off inside and outside, Rita's sense of reality is damaged too, and she can no longer separate reality from fantasy. In this seriously regressive state, she returned to a very early coping strategy: splitting. Not only did her split-off feelings emerge, the anger because of her mother's absence, but so did her mother's split-off traumatic feelings and experiences.

Dream from This Period

Tamás (40 years old, a store manager) has a daughter, a young teenager, and she gets infected. Within a couple of hours, Tamás falls into a desperate, disintegrated state and cannot quite grasp what he is really scared of: he is not worried about what the illness will do to his child or family, but he senses an abstract fear, which is unbearable. He brings this dream:

> My daughter and my wife are each in a very small Formula One racing car. They are being chased by the police, who eventually stop them. My wife (who had probably been drinking) escapes, but the police get my

daughter. I try to help her (probably I'd been following on foot). My daughter can hardly stand up, she staggers around as if she were stoned. The police question her, and I try to salvage the situation. I'm petrified that things will turn out badly. I wake up with a start.

Later he remembers that the previous day they had watched Formula One together (which they don't normally do). It was just when Grosjean had his accident. His car hit the barrier and almost exploded. It turned into a ball of fire, and it was several tense seconds before it was clear whether the driver could escape from the car. Then he remembered an experience he had had as an adult, when he was operated on for a perforated appendix: just when he got home from hospital, he accidentally switched on the TV (not a habit for him, he remarks again), and it was showing the airplane colliding with the Twin Towers. In the dream, being stoned reflects Tamás's current inner state: as if he were disoriented in space and time due to the effect of drugs. The size of the Formula One car (very small, they can hardly fit in) reminds Tamás not just of being confined at home in lockdown, but the prolonged restrictions and vulnerability related to the virus situation, ongoing since March. The virus has entered their home, which is now no longer safe and more like a prison. "The virus might be in any of us," he says, "we are shut up with it." Tragedy may strike at any minute – the explosion, as in the case of Formula One, or in the case of the Twin Towers.

COVID and the Transgenerational Atmosphere

Máté (64 years old) is one of the top leaders in a big corporation, and recently retired. He found the switch very difficult, so he asked for therapeutic help shortly before the pandemic broke out.

> I read things are getting worse. As a matter of fact, I'm glad. *Here* (in Hungary) they only take things seriously when there's a crisis. It really annoys me that *here* human life isn't important. We sacrifice the elderly, the sick. The weak are dropping like flies. *Silence.* I got really angry yesterday. I went to see my mother by taxi, and the driver took her mask off, saying that she couldn't drive in it. I had a choice: I could have got out. But there was a huge traffic jam, and I knew I'd never get there. And who knows if it would be any better if I called another taxi. So I stayed. On the way back I got another taxi, the driver had a flashing mask, and sprayed perfume not just on the taxi, but me too, as a kind of protection. In the evening of course I started to get more and more anxious. I hoped I hadn't "killed" my mother by going to visit.

The patient is a second-generation Holocaust survivor with a very ambivalent relationship to his mother. Although it's a huge chore for him, he speaks to his mother on the phone every day, and regularly visits her even during the pandemic. In order to see her in person, he has to forsake a great deal: he cannot meet his friends, and he too lives a shielded existence. His relationship to his mother is dominated by alternating feelings of anger, deep frustration and guilt, and anxiety. In his case, the current crisis (on a personal level: the pension, fear of old age, and in the external world: the pandemic) amplifies the effect of the ever present family transgenerational atmosphere. The internal conflict of "I mustn't kill my mother" (which is a reversal of I could kill my mother, my mother kills me) finds an object in the external world: the meeting, and being close might actually harbor danger. Not only are the external and internal realities too close, but the reality of the present (the pandemic situation, and managing it well or badly) and the reality of the past (the Holocaust) telescope together, making orientation difficult: How much should I be scared, and of what? Who or what am I angry at? Surreal, grotesque events in the everyday world, such as the second taxi journey, fall under the dark, threatening shadow of the past.

Pál (33 years old, a top manager) is a first-generation intellectual who works at a multinational. He has been in therapy for four years (twice a week, on the couch). He is very ambitious, and always tries to come up to expectations. He has a high-ranking job, and that "makes him who he is." To him, the fact he got this far means that he's a responsible adult, who doesn't need his parents or anyone else. But for a while, work hasn't been bringing him pleasure, and he is continually overworked and under stress. That is why he started therapy. Slowly the idea took shape in him that he could resign, give himself a couple of months' free time, partly to rest, and partly to work out what he really wants to do. Eventually, in November 2020, after a long internal struggle, he writes his letter of resignation and applies for a course in photography (something he'd always longed to do). He gives his letter of resignation to his boss, but the boss talks him out of resigning, saying that the timing is really bad, and with the pandemic he won't find a new job. People are being laid off everywhere, and people should be "glad they've got a job." In the end, Pál does not tender his resignation but he is very disappointed, and doesn't understand why he couldn't stick to his resolution.

A couple of weeks later, he manages to understand better what happened:

P: To begin with I was organized and confident, and told him my reasons. But when my boss began to argue (he said things such as not to be hasty, not to decide because of a momentary mood, lots of people are losing their jobs, I should be grateful I've got one, all workplaces are the same anyway, etc.) I began to feel like a sulky kid who's obliged to listen to the reasoning of the clever adult. I felt I ought to justify it, but the only reasons that came to mind were emotional, which I felt to lack seriousness, to be ill-considered. *Silence.* I suddenly realize now that this conversation happened on the day when the lockdown became stricter. The day before I'd sat in a restaurant with my mates, but the next day all restaurants were closed. *Silence.* And everywhere all you could hear, was the outside everything is terrible, dangerous. I knew this is amplified by the media, still, perhaps it began to affect me. And company communication had the same message: when we complained we couldn't stand the pace, the answer was that everyone is in a difficult position, the company too, this is a crisis, and we have to put up with it together. I felt that I leave now, it would be running away, if I resigned.

T: Because it's a crisis. As if there were a war, and you were deserting.

P: Yes. I think I'd be ashamed of myself. What would they think of me? It wouldn't be adult behavior. After all, "these are hard times, we have to put up with them."

Pál's father worked hard to build up a family business out of nothing, so ever since childhood Pál heard that all this was being done for the family, he sacrificed everything for them. Pál was only praised if he got top grades at school. Other times, his father looked straight through him. When he graduated, and then found a well-paying job (the first one in the family to do so), his father was very proud of him. When he mentioned how he wasn't content, how he was overworked in the office, his father said: that's what it's like being an adult. It's no better anywhere else. Through a long process of self-discovery, Pál became able to express his own desires and needs, and came to a realization that he has a right to live a different life. In his case, the newly independent *me* is still fragile, and vulnerable to the effects of the external world. In November 2020, the reality of the external world starts to have a stronger effect on the individual, suggesting "there's a crisis, we have to grit our teeth and bear it." The company adopts the wartime rhetoric used in government communication and spreading through the media, which chimes in with the patient's family legacy: Pál feels that his duty is to perform better than usual, because "we're in trouble," it's a war situation. There is no place for his weariness, or his feelings.

Károly is 35 years old, an economist. His wife gets COVID, and she is very ill for several weeks. Károly experiences increasing anxiety, and fears he might be left alone with his 2-year-old son. As his anxiety increases, so unconscious defense mechanisms grow. With increasing desperation, he tries to rid himself of the unbearable feelings, projecting them onto the external world. He is angry with people who don't take the quarantine and lockdown rules seriously, like he and his family have always done. He experiences the quarantine situation as humiliating, as though he was being stigmatized. In his case, it is clear that feelings that are familiar and have long been dominant for him (anger, exclusion, humiliation) are projected onto any present situation, regardless of the *here-and-now* reality: previously, he was implacably angry against people who were "too cautious," who refused to meet them, who restricted him when going shopping. But now he is angry at people who are "not cautious enough" and expose him and his family to all manner of infection.

He experiences the feelings of exclusion and humiliation, which have haunted the family for several generations, as a present reality. His case also demonstrates how the transgenerational legacy, the transgenerational atmosphere, can permeate the present: the anger and shame of many generations seeks out a target object, and soon finds one in the *here-and-now*. The undigested emotions feeding on exclusion and shame are deflected from the "cautious ones" on one day to the "careless ones" on the next.

Zsuzsa is a 41-year-old kindergarten teacher with two children. She started therapy at the beginning of the COVID pandemic, and expressed her feelings as follows:

> Since the beginning of the virus pandemic, I've been thinking of my grandfather often. When he returned home from forced labor he was given a job mending the roads with another ex-army officer. One day he brought home a flier. Somebody must have reported him, because the secret police came and found the burned paper in the stove. My grandfather went to prison and the whole family was in danger. They were all stigmatized as enemies of the system. My grandfather "brought home" the danger, the problem, into the family. This feeling of being in jeopardy is here with me too. Maybe too much so. I'm worried I'll infect my family, so I haven't seen my parents for months. I don't want to put their lives at risk. I know, this might even be seen as normal. The interesting thing is that I have this deep sense of guilt, as if it had all already happened. It's kind of surreal. I'm even scared to think about it, because my grandfather's story slides together with my fantasies and fears. This freezes my thinking completely. I try to keep my head down, so I don't harm anyone.
>
> (Bakó & Zana, 2021b, 515)

Bianka (28 years old, an economist) started coming to therapy (once a week, seated) at the beginning of the pandemic, mainly because she still hasn't got over a breakup. She is still very sad, although it is two years since they split up. She starts after the lockdown has begun, so we commence therapy online. In the fall she comes in person for a couple of weeks, but we are forced to return to online sessions again, because she goes abroad for work. I was surprised by the contrast that I felt between her online and face-to-face presence. In the online sessions, I almost always perceived her in the same way: as tired, enervated, and sad. When she appeared in the consulting room, it was as if I were seeing a different person, a vivacious, pretty young woman. When we return to online therapy, she slips (or we slip) back into the previous presence. Although the location, the country, changes (in the first period of therapy, Bianka is living in her parent's apartment, and later she is abroad in a rented apartment), I perceive hardly anything of this, as if these meetings were beyond space and time, almost incorporeal. Although they split up over two years ago, the patient gives the impression of someone deeply in mourning. In the first period of therapy, we speak only about the relationship. Her current life (work, friends, the pandemic in the outside world) barely gets a look-in. This well reflects her internal reality, which in this period is filled by the past and mourning. My feeling is that Bianka is not living in the *here-and-now*, but somewhere else, in the past, with only faint glimmers of the present reality. In her childhood, she always heard that for them "family comes first," and she felt it too. Her parents put the family's (the children's) interests before all else. They put aside their own needs, and spent all their money on helping their children to study abroad. Bianka did everything not to disappoint her parents. She studied hard, and got her degree. But all the while she was haunted by a strange feeling of being alien: she always felt an outsider everywhere. Listening to her, I feel that it's as if everything she experienced happened not to her, but as if she was telling the story of a film or a dream – someone else's dream. I wonder whether this has anything to do with her own life, and if so, to what extent. Later the patient's family history unfolds. Her paternal grandmother, who still lives with them in Budapest, is a Holocaust survivor. She came from a poor family, and before the Second World War learned how to make corsets. In 1938, at the age of 16, she fell in love with Bianka's grandfather, who was 18, and came from a rich Christian family. During the war, her grandfather hid her grandmother, who lost much of her family in the Holocaust. After the war, under the communist regime, the grandfather was persecuted because he was from a noble family. He lost everything, and couldn't even get a job. The grandmother became the breadwinner, and in her small shop she made corsets and swimsuits. Her mother's family lived a comfortable bourgeois life before the war. After the war, the area where the family had lived for generations, which was Hungarian, was awarded to another country, and the family had to decide whether to stay, or to leave behind all their assets and move to Hungary. They decided to move, but on the train journey they lose the two suitcases that had all their remaining belongings. They arrive penniless to start a new life in Hungary, the grandfather finds his feet and accepts his new life (he becomes a shop assistant), but the grandmother never gets over the loss: she never takes a job, she struggles with recurrent depression, and constantly ruminates over the past. A struggle to survive (whether successful or not), a new beginning, fitting into a new world (or failing to) becomes prevalent in both branches of the family. Perhaps the most surprising thing for me in Bianka's therapy was that while everyone in our environment was talking about the pandemic, the very strong reality of the external world, this was barely present at all in the patient's own world, her internal reality. Nor was where she was living, which country, or what was happening around her. The experience of the past, the transgenerational atmosphere, is so strong, in her case so forceful, that even a very prevalent powerful *we*-experience is unable to override it: the family fears not the pandemic, but falling into poverty. Bianka's own internal psychological reality is constant: the dominant emotions are sadness, despair, alienation, and loneliness, as if she were constantly hauling a great weight around. These feelings were present during the happy years of her relationship, as a kind of shadow-reality, then since the breakup they have taken up all the space.

The Transgenerational Atmosphere in a Dream: The Therapist's Own Experience

I'm at an open-air market with a girlfriend. We're both wearing masks. We wait in line, chatting freely, and we feel good. The woman in front of us in the line suddenly turns round and bawls aggressively: "Why on earth can't you keep a distance?" The mixed emotions of aggression and fear emanating from her struck both of us deeply, and we fell silent. I too was overwhelmed by irritability and anger. At a rational level, her behavior was incomprehensible, because we were keeping a distance and wearing masks. The distance we were not keeping was not distance in the physical sense. She was probably riled by the friendly chat between two intimate friends.

That night I slept badly, and several times woke up with a headache. I had a dream:

> I'm in Paris. As well as the customary good feelings there's a little tension in me, but basically I'm in a good mood. There are several of us, perhaps the members of the supervision group, who I have a friendly relationship with. I'm not sure about most of them, but one person appears clearly: Klári, one of the older generation of supervisors. We buy tickets in the metro. I want to buy several (a carnet of ten), because I have the idea we'll be travelling a lot. Klári tells me not to buy that many, because she has plenty, and I should take some of hers. She no longer needs them. *This is a break in the dream, the mood of the dream deteriorates, and the other people slowly disappear.* Then I'm in the theater. I don't remember there being many of us. I think that here it's just me now. I crawl over many floors, up a winding staircase, and there are long, packed, rows. Nobody is wearing a mask. We're standing close together, and I'm getting more tense. I step into the auditorium, which is a conglomerate of several dim halls on different levels, its structure is confusing. The stage and the auditorium blur together. It strikes me that I wouldn't go to the theater at home. I find my place (the ticket and the number on it, 3C, are very clear in my memory), I calm down a bit. They left a lot of space, and we are sitting far from each other. But as the performance begins (or the beginning draws near) there are more and more people around me, on chairs they've pulled up, they're sitting on the floor, lying there, the crowd is all

over the place, overwhelming. I leave my place and look for somewhere with more air, at the back. I find a place at the back on a wooden bench. It's less comfortable than the original upholstered seat. Slowly there are more and more people here too, but less than in my "own" place earlier.

The play hardly features in my dream. Sometimes there are glimpses of it, but it's more like a circus act: the actors are acrobats on high, and they do dangerous exercises and jumps on the ropes. The performance attracts my gaze, but it makes me tense and suggests danger. My attention is increasingly taken by my environment. I watch the people sitting next to me, with interest, but also with fear, on the alert. They aren't watching the play either, they are living their life, as if they had settled down in the auditorium for the long term. Next to me appears a teenage girl. I don't know when she appeared. She's alone. A song makes her weep bitterly. Somehow I know she's an orphan, perhaps she lost her mother, and she's crying because the song brought up this loss. I'd like to caress her, to hug her, but my body goes stiff. I think of the danger, and I'm scared of getting closer to her. In front of us is a mother with a small child on her arm. She stands up and moves away from the weeping girl.

I woke up with deep anxiety and a sense of guilt. It's dawn, and I have a bad headache.

The dream has two particularly emotionally strong episodes: the first, when Klári says she'll give her tickets to me because she no longer needs them. It's then I realize that we're not going on together. The other is at the end, when the orphan girl appears beside me. In the dream she's familiar from somewhere, but I don't recognize her. Next day it comes to me: she is Ágika, who would have been my aunt, but she was killed as a teenager in Auschwitz. I was told many things about her sister Éva, who was born after the war (who died at the age of 21 from ovary cancer, and whose parents mourned her until their dying days). Conversely, I only saw one picture of Ágika, a sad little girl with a bow in her hair sat at the piano. But I was never told anything about her, and I didn't dare ask. The dream image (everyone distances themselves from the crying girl) condenses the traumatic world of the past (the Holocaust) and the present (the pandemic), and feelings of being abandoned, excluded.

The Period before Christmas

Extremes

In Hungary, we are going through the second wave of the pandemic. Even though there is no drop in the number of infections and fatalities, the pre-Christmas mood overrides this: many people are breaking the rules, and the shops are choc-a-bloc.

Klára (45 years old, a photographer) lives with her partner. They have been taking precautions for months, hardly leaving their home. She begins the session saying that she has caught a slight cold. Then she continues by saying that for days she has been anxious, scared that she has caught the virus. On the weekend someone lent them a car, and making the most of this, they went shopping in IKEA and the hypermarket AUCHAN. There were masses of people, the pre-Christmas crowds. Looking back, she doesn't understand how they could have been so irresponsible, given that they are so cautious, and that everyone knows she's a hypochondriac. The most perplexing thing for her is why they both began to get anxious afterward, when previously this risk hadn't been apparent to them (Bakó & Zana, 2021b, 525–526).

Acute Crisis during the Pandemic

Marcell (37 years old, a middle manager) came to therapy ten years ago for years. Now he asks for help from his ex-therapist for an acute crisis. He tells of an appalling family trauma which he felt he was unable to process alone. His mother lived with Marcell's 92-year-old grandmother, and they had a very good, close relationship. During the pandemic, the grandmother was admitted to hospital. In this phase, because of the pandemic, there was no hospital visiting, which both Marcell's grandmother and mother experienced as a great tragedy. The operation was successful, and the grandmother was taken to the convalescence ward. But the ban on hospital visiting was still in force. The elderly woman pleaded with her daughter to take her home, and the daughter asked her mother to stay there a bit longer. She hoped that the physiotherapy would improve her condition. The next day Marcell's mother got a telephone call from the hospital, to say that the grandmother had died. She had hung herself. Marcell's mother felt terribly guilty, and hardly ate anything. She lost 15 kg (30 pounds) in a month. She did her work, but she was in torment. One month after his grandmother's death, Marcell got a telephone call from his father, saying his mother had been admitted to hospital with a stroke. This was when he asked for therapy help. The restrictions put in place because of the current COVID crisis upset the delicate and very rigid equilibrium over the generations. Neither the grandmother nor the mother survived the temporary separation.

The Therapist Changes Room

In this period, I move to a summer house in the countryside for a couple of weeks. I didn't signal the change of location to my patients in advance. I gave them (us) the freedom to connect to the reality of the previous session, or for the change to come up in the therapy space and acquire meaning in the *here-and-now*. Some of them didn't react to the change at all, and the change of location had no relational meaning, while for others the change of setting became meaningful, and we worked with it.

Márta (23 years old, a catering worker)

M: Are you somewhere else? *Silence.* Well, I'm in quarantine. I was with my cousins on the weekend, and it turns out they are infected. It's not as bad as in March, I'm just worried that my social skills are atrophying. I won't be able to go and meet people even when it's allowed.

After this Márta speaks at length about how ambivalent she is about her job. She doesn't know whether she wants to go back there when this restriction is over. I ask her what keeps her there. Perhaps there's something she likes at the workplace?

M: *Long silence.* This is off topic. Just now, I thought you looked over at someone.
T: As if I was paying attention to something else? Or someone else?
M: Yes. I had the feeling that while I'm suffering you are not even listening to me.
T: You feel that nobody understands you, nobody is really listening to you. Not even me.
M: Yes. For instance, I had this feeling last time too, when you said that you feel that I'm interested in people.
T: And that's not true?
M: I don't give a shit about people.
T: Everything's shit, and you felt even I didn't want to hear that. Perhaps it was too much for me?
M: Yes. *Silence.* Another thing that came to mind about the room was that perhaps I was envious. While I'm here in quarantine, cooped up, you can travel freely.

At the next session she says that the previous session had knocked her out, for at least a day. She felt impoverished and excluded. At the same time, she feels we got close to something. She felt the turning point was when at the previous session she said, "I feel that you're not listening."

After the session she had the following dreams:

In the first dream we are in a session but not in the usual room. And someone else is there, Anna, from the restaurant (Anna is a waitress she has a fairly good relationship with). I feel that you and Anna are communicating over my head, as if you were gesturing to each other, but this is my session. I get angry and interrupt: "Hello, I'm here too!"

The second dream also seems to start in a session, but I realize that you're sleeping in your own bed. It's as if I were in hospital. I'm sitting next to you. You sit up, and it turns out you are wearing a nightshirt. That's very strange. I notice how thin your legs are.

All I remember of the third dream is that I'm sitting on a sofa, and words start pouring out of me. And I cry a lot. It feels good. It's a relief.

In relation to the dreams, we return to Márta's early experience, when her younger sibling was born. Because there were complications, her mother had to spend a couple of weeks in hospital with the little sister. Because she was small too, she didn't understand where her mother had gone and then when she came home with the little baby, why she didn't pay attention to her. The current crisis calls forth Márta's early experiences (fragility, easily taking offense, the other might disappear). She experiences these in the everyday world, and brings them into the therapy relationship too.

Mária (35 years old, a sociologist) speaks about the approach of Christmas and her related doubts:

M: My husband doesn't want to meet the family at all, but I would like to. The problem is that it's no use asking them to wear masks (that way we could be together no problem). Even though they promise to, afterwards they "forget." I keep having to watch, to ask them, and it's really tiring and frustrating. The problem isn't just that they think differently about the virus, but that they don't take into account what we feel, what we'd like. *Silence.* You're in a different place. *Silence.*
T: Where do you imagine me to be?
M: That you're in one corner of a big group room. Perhaps there are others there too. But it's possible that the space is empty.
T: What feelings does it bring up?
M: Anxious ones. As if others were watching.
T: As if there were someone, or something else in the space. As if there were something that is here between us, but we don't speak about it?

An excerpt from the next session:

M: After the previous session I had the feeling that not just the location was different, but so were you.
T: How was I different?
M: You seemed to be more relaxed. *Silence.* I had a dream, too. We're in that room, in person, but the room isn't like I imagined it last time. It's a weird-shaped room in a peasant cottage, full of furniture. It's dark and gloomy, but not a homely dimness. It was like a consulting room, but was not. It resembled a living room. There were two armchairs opposite each other, a coffee table, but these were in the middle of an elongated room, like a passageway. Suddenly my mum was there too. Then I noticed the folder you make notes in. Then it suddenly

changed to my own e-book reader. First I thought this means that we're reading the same thing, we have the same knowledge, but then I suddenly realized that the content is different.

T: What is the feel, the mood of this room?

M: It's not homely enough, not safe enough. I don't understand, something is unclear. Now the dream comes back: the two of us are chatting, but not in a therapy situation. The area around the castle district [in the center of Budapest] appears, where you normally do the therapy. That's where I went to kindergarten too. Only those who live there can go to this area. That's where you live too. You invite me in and show me a room where there are dishes and chalices. You say that it's got holy water in it, and if I pour it on my neck, then all my troubles will pass. I'm astonished, and sad, because apparently I won't be able to come to you any more, if our thinking is so different. I say what I think about this (the holy water), and you pull a face, you're indignant. This facial expression is familiar, at the same time it's not. I've never seen an expression like that before. *Silence.* And after that, there was an even more frightening dream. In the same room, behind you on the wall, there's a mirror. I can see myself in it. I try to wriggle to a position where I can't see myself. I realize that it's not actually a mirror, but a shiny surface that gives a distorted reflection. The distorted image bothers me. I don't want to see myself like that, and I'm scared of how you might see me. The gloominess is really disturbing.

The news is full of countless stories, both real and fake. One of them is that many doctors with other specializations will be "called in" because soon there won't be enough specialists to treat the patients.

Anna (32 years old, an interior designer) gives this reaction to me being in a different location:

A: Is something wrong?

T: What makes you think that?

A: I was alarmed when I saw you. Perhaps because you are in a different place.

T: Where did you think I might be?

A: In hospital. My first thought was that you'd been called in, because things were so bad. Then, that perhaps you were ill. . . . *Silence.* I'd got used to the previous place. There's a bookshelf behind you, and I often look at the books.

The "new usual" place (my room, where she recognizes the books on the bookshelf) had become important to the patient. It represented security in this uncertain, constantly changing situation. When uncertainty grows in the external world, she too becomes increasingly sensitive to these signs, and ascribes a meaning to any change. For her, I, the therapist, reflect the external world, and watching me she tries to gauge how bad things have got.

Events in Society: Vaccines and Projections

This period is that of the "vaccine wars." Countries and companies try to shout each other down as they make their bids. It's extremely difficult to sift through the trial results, and impossible to compare the effectiveness and safety of the vaccines. At this point, there are no published results regarding the Chinese or Russian vaccines, unlike the vaccines from Pfizer, Moderna, and AstraZeneca, so at the time how effective and safe these vaccines were was a question of guesswork (Barát & Kemenesi, 2021, 194). Christmas 2020 is drawing near, the lockdown is increasingly irksome, with a lack of information about vaccines, fantasies about them begin to appear.

Mariann (30 years old) is a single veterinarian. She works in a private practice. Lately, she has been complaining of overwork, tiredness, and burnout. She says that everyone is frustrated, irritable, and lots of people have lost their livelihoods. Meanwhile, far more people are bringing her their animals than usual, and she can't cope with all the work. Lots of people are adopting dogs because of the curfew (which doesn't apply to dog-walkers) and she's worried about what will happen to these dogs when the pandemic is over. Lots of people want to neuter their animals right now, just before Christmas, and she can't understand this either. That reminds her of the vaccine: lots of people talk to her about this, sharing their fears and asking for her advice. Even she doesn't know what to think, and these questions reinforce her own uncertainty and anxiety. She doesn't want to have the Russian vaccine; instead, she'll wait for the other one. She says that many people are scared of vaccination altogether. They won't get vaccinated because they're scared they'll have a microchip implanted. She doesn't believe this, but, well, who knows. . . . One of her friends is always taking his telephone apart because he's worried that he's being listened to. Someone else she knows puts masking tape over the phone camera. She doesn't believe this . . . but then again, who knows.

Isolation and Regression

Dia (40 years old, an interior designer) has been having serious digestion problems in recent months. She explains this by saying that because of the virus her life has become increasingly stressful, and her future at work is uncertain. She has a lover, but meets her partner less and less. Her social sphere has shrunk too.

D: I'm having an antisocial day. I miss my parents and my friends. Every day has the same rhythm. My life is boring and monotonous. I feel like the world has abandoned me.

T: The world?

D: My parents never call. We only talk if I call them. It's the same with my friends. I'm cooped up. Because of my illness I can't eat what I want.

T: The things that brought you joy have disappeared.

D: Completely. My life is sort of timeless. Sometimes a memory flashes by. I was asthmatic as a child. I was often in hospital. I didn't like it at the time, but even that was better because at least there I could see other people who suffered the same way as I did. Now I don't know how others are suffering, or if they are. I live in a closed space. My only constant, reliable relationship is therapy, you.

Dia is isolated, and in this inner world, distanced as it is from the outer world, in which past and present, the internal worlds of *me* and not-*me* telescope together, she loses her points of reference, and she cannot imagine how others live, or what they experience.

Szilvia (61 years old, a teacher) has been working online only for a month. Her younger daughter, who in the first lockdown was living with her, has recently moved in with her boyfriend.

Sz: I think I'm basically all right. I feel fine at home. I try to pay plenty of attention to myself, to my own feelings. But a tiny thing made me very anxious, and I don't really understand why, especially the intensity of it. Here in the village for years now there's been a move to decorate the windows before Christmas. It's someone different every day. Everyone knows whose turn it is when, and you can walk over and admire them. This year I volunteered too, I thought it would be nice to decorate my house. But when I saw the first two decorated windows, I started to get nervous. I thought it was a mistake to volunteer, I can't do anything as pretty as that.

T: Who are the people that decorate their windows so finely? Who lives there?

Sz: I always imagine a very attentive mother, who cooks tasty food and cares for the whole family.

This story gave a way in to Szilvia's feeling of loneliness: although she feels all right at home, she is alone. It also shows that in the village, for mothers, appearances are important. It's important what others think of them. There's a lot of emphasis on the yard being tidy, that the clothes be neatly hung out. Nobody could know of family problems ("they didn't hang them out in the window," as the saying goes), and the patient's life is haunted by taboos. Holidays and the run-up to Christmas can bring up a feeling of loneliness anyway, and this is amplified by the pandemic restrictions. For Szilvia, reaching back to traditions and customs (decorating the windows) shows an increased desire to belong to a community: an uncertain individual, feeling lonely, in a crisis situation, tries to rely on the holding capacity of the community. Her desire to join this initiative reflects this, and her anxiety shows her familiar fear that something about her might slip out (through the window).

Lost Time

Hugó (30 years old, a psychologist) has been in therapy for about two years. He came with the problem that although he has a good job, he cannot find the right partner. During the pandemic, he has become even more isolated:

H: The virus has stolen a year of my life. During this year I could have been looking for a partner. But the way things are, I can't. A first date in a mask would be daft. You can't see any of the girl's face, her reactions.
T: You don't know what she thinks of you, whether she likes you or not?
H: It's almost like a blind date.
T: Like when two people who can't see, who are blind, meet.
H: The difference is that because of being blind they develop other forms of perception, while for me I'm just barred from seeing.
T: Instead of love at first sight, there's the feeling that "if I can't see her, I'd rather not meet her."
H: Something like that . . . but this will be a wasted year anyway.

For Hugó, who even beforehand found closeness difficult to tolerate, the appearance of masks made it impossible to approach a potential partner.

Amarilla (36 years old, a sociologist) had this to say about the distortion of time, and the telescoping of temporalities:

The fact we couldn't move freely took me back to my childhood, when I was in hospital waiting for my parents to come and get me. "They said: 'Tomorrow,' but I thought that tomorrow would never come."

Dreams from This Period

Eszter (38, a financial specialist) had been complaining in earlier sessions that she couldn't decide whether she was ill or tired. Perhaps she had headache, a sore throat, but she wasn't convinced these were actual physical symptoms. (In this period, several patients who do not normally somatize told of similar experiences: they couldn't decide whether the symptom they felt was physical or psychological in origin.) In the sessions she complained of general tiredness and being out of sorts. She had a dream of which she remembered very little:

E: I'm in the elevator, taking out the trash. On the second floor a man gets in. He's young and he doesn't have a mask. I don't have one either, after all I just popped down to take out the trash. I'm tense, and worry the man infected me.

T: What feelings do you have about the dream?

E: The first thing that comes to mind is anger. I don't understand why a young man should get in the elevator on the second floor when he could walk.

T: Have you felt anything like this recently?

E: Yes, now I come to think of it. I got really frustrated this week. I asked for an appointment with the gynecologist, but it turned out they wrote it down wrong. They marked me down for an online consultation, and I wanted to meet in person. It cost me a lot of time and energy to go there, and I couldn't even get what I wanted to done. What's more, when I was leaving, I bumped into the doctor I would have gone to, in the elevator. He offered me his hand to shake. Perhaps he was embarrassed that he didn't take my appointment. I responded in kind, but also I thought that now I might be infected, and when we got out, I quickly disinfected my hands.

T: The doctor you went to set you at rest, to be safe, ended up putting you at risk.

E: Right, and afterwards I dreamed about the elevator!

The feelings in the dream (anger, fear, threat, frustration) are very typical characters of this period. In sessions it is very difficult to identify what belongs to the patient's past, to their inner world, and what belongs to their current experiences.

A fragment of a dream from one of the next sessions:

E: It's as if I were watching a dance exercise, a round dance. After the rehearsal we sit in a circle. Somebody I know is there, and says things that I think she shouldn't. They aren't other people's business. They're inner secrets.

T: First you speak of "them," dancing, and afterwards of "us," as if you were part of things. It's as if it's not clear whether you are present as a participant or as an onlooker.

E: Well, yes. Actually I don't know. *Silence.* Well that's nothing strange to me. When I was small, and I heard arguments. And although I was there, it's as if I weren't there at all. And how many times have I felt this, at home, and at work too.

This "I'm outside and inside" feeling elicited many associations for me. The pandemic comes to mind, the current crisis, where we are both participants and onlookers. But even my role as a writer, as in this book I record the mosaics of external and internal reality, I am simultaneously a participant and an observer, a witness to events.

January/February 2021

The Period When the Vaccines Appear

Ábris (50 years old, an artist) was previously a pandemic denier. But in November last year the virus attacked his system, and he had pains he'd never experienced before. He didn't take the first symptoms seriously, and suspected it was a cold. Later his condition became more and more serious, he was admitted to an intensive care unit, where he nearly died. He spoke about this later in therapy:

> When the muscle pains came, I was terrified. I couldn't move. I waited for days for things to get better. In the end I was admitted to intensive care and put on a ventilator. Later I found out that fortunately I didn't have double pneumonia. I was lucky. Actually I still can't grasp what actually happened to me. Three months of bitter struggling. I'm still very tired, and breathing is difficult. What I really want to do is tell everybody: this virus is no joke! All the while I was thinking, I've still got stuff to do. I can't die.

Brigitta (34 years old, a full-time mother) lives abroad with her husband and their 2-year-old child. Her husband goes out to work, while she stays at home and looks after the child. She took the first year of the COVID pandemic well, but now suddenly feels a strong desire to come home to Hungary with her child, even without her husband.

> I'm suddenly fed up of everything. It's become unbearable being with just the child all day, in a country I don't like that much. I've hardly met any adults for a year. My husband had it good. He went to work at seven in the morning, and worked until six in the evening. I was left with no support. I didn't even care what would become of our marriage. I was simply suffocating in that cloistered world.

In this period, although vaccines are becoming available, it is uncertain who will get which vaccine, and when. The relief so badly longed for never actually comes, and the internal world of many is dominated by a feeling of "I can't stand it any longer."

Suspected COVID

One of my patients, who I had met in person the previous day, informed me that a member of his family had a fever with a suspected COVID infection.

After that I canceled my personal meetings until it was clear whether or not my patient had been infected, and perhaps I too.

I texted my patients:

> Due to suspected COVID infection I would like to hold tomorrow's sessions online.
> Best regards,
>
> (name)

The following day Mándok (40 years old, university lecturer) spoke of the great fear he experienced. He was worried we would never meet again. After the text message, he expected my family to inform him of the sad news that I was on a ventilator and the chances of my surviving were low. The patient was beset by anxiety during the 24 hours until we met. It didn't even occur to him to ask about my state, and frame what had happened in a realistic context. He experienced helplessness, a paralysis. He became passive. In his imagination, I was already dead. He reckoned that the reason my family didn't tell him was because they were in a state of shock. He started to mourn too, but mostly he was sorry for himself. His experience was that once more, he had lost something (somebody) that was important to him. Mándok's grandparents were repatriated because of their ethnicity. For a long time, the family hoped that they would escape this fate. The head of the family was an important official, and this gave them some protection. Meanwhile, they heard about the forced labor, and this nightmare appeared in their imagination, and finally came to pass: they too were repatriated. The family lost all its assets and its livelihood. But the greatest loss was the loss of sense of security in the world:

> We can lose anything, at any moment. When I got the text, it was a familiar experience, one I expected, because I come from a family that loses things. At last I start to trust, and of course I lose the trust.

The patient was able only temporarily to contain his feelings after the text message. Although he was able to symbolize his anxiety to some extent (he was able to "dream" the death of the therapist), his ability to calm himself, to regulate his emotions, was damaged. The current experience took him back to the past, and the reality of the present was overwhelmed by the family's legacy, the transgenerational atmosphere (you can't trust the world, anything can be lost).

"I Don't Want to Exist at That Price"

Ida (42 years old, a doctor) is married with two children. She has been in psychotherapy for three years. She's finding it increasingly hard to put up with being confined indoors, and the lockdown. One session, she says that before the therapy session she began to read a book that deeply upset her. As a result, she is still perturbed now, at the beginning of the session. The book is a series of confessions from the parents of seriously sick children. Reading the stories, she felt deep sympathy for the parents. She begins to cry several times while she speaks of it. It's clear she was deeply touched by it. After 15 or 20 minutes, she says, rather angrily:

I: I don't want to be like this. (*Cries. There is both anger and pain. She looks helpless. She falls silent, then for a few minutes stays immobile*).
T: Like this?
I: So weak, vulnerable, someone who loses their cool after reading a heavy book.
T: You don't want to be someone at the mercy of their emotions.
I: (*After a brief silence and pause for thought*). Yes. You could put it like that.

Lockdown and Post-traumatic Working Through

Beáta (36 years old, an HR manager) and her family lived life in the fast lane before the pandemic. They had hardly any time together, they all had things to do. Mostly they ordered food to eat at home. The parents often worked at weekends, and the children did sports or had private tuition.

> Finally we are operating as a family again. We've had two difficult weeks. Initially it seemed utterly hopeless trying to make something normal out of this lockdown chaos. The first days we just improvised. We just tried to survive. We could hardly wait for the day to be over. Everyone was at home, and both my husband and I were working from home. The kids hand online schooling. Even the teachers didn't know what to do with this situation. Everyone was frustrated and nervy. At the end of the first week, we agreed things couldn't go on like this. My husband was fantastic. He suggested the four of us sit down and draw up a daily/weekly plan. Each evening we discussed how the day had been for each of us. If necessary, we changed the plan. Now we cook almost every day, and we eat together. It would be good to carry this over to the time when we return to "normal life."

Lockdown Dreams

István (33 years old, electrical engineer) has been in therapy for one and a half years. He was born into the third generation of a repatriated family. January was very difficult for him. He had lots to do at work. He's going to a training program with an exam at the end. He's worried about the pandemic too. István was prone to disintegration before, but he didn't understand why or when it happened to him. Since the beginning of the pandemic, he has steadily become more introverted. This withdrawing from the outside world gave him an opportunity for him to see what was going on inside. In January, he is surprised to note that what is grinding him down, and confusing him, is tiredness and exhaustion. He is becoming vulnerable. His body is constantly tense, and he is losing contact with the world. He brings this dream:

> I rushed down into the basement of an extremely dilapidated building. It was like a hospital. I tried to be as invisible as possible. It seemed as though I'd fallen into a trap. Eventually I find a window. I get to the roots of a tree, and it holds me captive. In the distance I see others, but I don't go towards them, because they seem dangerous too. I go back to the basement. There are masses of slippers there. I looked at them because I don't have any. I think: I'll take a pair. But I'm scared that I'll get some infection, some virus, and that will drive me mad.

For István, this state of flux, with exhaustion and threat, is a mixture of the reality of the past and the present: as the descendent of a family who experienced forced labor, for him it is very threatening that "mental illness" appears in the outside world, and in this topsy-turvy world the individual is no longer safe.

Győző (52 years old, agronomist) has been having recurrent dreams for years, and doesn't know what to make of them. Typically, the mood of his dreams is that he cannot get into contact with other people. They don't see him, or don't hear him. They take no notice of him. He suspects the dreams are connected to the death of his father. In the lockdown period, when we are shut up for long periods, the dreams occur more frequently. One night he dreams he is in a village, surrounded by people. He tries to talk to them, but they don't stop, they don't look at him, and they don't react to his words. He becomes desperate, and sad. This feeling calls forth a childhood experience:

> It's like when I was a child, when they forbade me to go outside the yard. My father's family was aristocratic. Under socialism, they lost everything. He was always embarrassed when he went to the people who used to work for him, and who to this day call him "Master Lacika." My father forbade me from playing with peasant kids, or "mixing" with them. Of course, I longed to play with them. As if it was them who had excluded me. It was terrible, depressing, dreaming for years that I was excluded. I felt that it had something to do with my life, but I couldn't connect it to anything.

Lockdown and being cooped up called forth Győző's childhood experiences, and also provided an opportunity for him to be able to identify feelings (often alien to him) that had haunted him throughout his life, such as exclusion, loneliness, or as he put it: the child was given a name.

The Therapist's Own Experiences: The Vaccine

The previous day, as soon as the opportunity arose, I registered on the site opened by the government where you could request the vaccine. The next morning I see there are several articles about whether the government handles the data safely, what it does with them, and whether contrary to earlier promises we cannot choose which vaccine to have. I was a bit annoyed about this, but (at least at the conscious level) it didn't cause me much headache or anxiety. I soon decided that if they offer me a vaccine I don't trust, then I wouldn't allow them to inject me with it. The next night I dreamed we were being examined, and put on a list, with a great many people. Although I felt this to be humiliating, at the same time I noted that they weren't actually treating us badly. But I knew they would take us to Auschwitz. I asked somebody to say at least what year it was. He replied: 1930. In my dream I started sobbing desperately, because I knew what others didn't: that the war would last until 1945. It was impossible to survive in Auschwitz until then. Then I woke up.

In my dream, my own reality and the uncertainty over the current situation (the threat of the pandemic, my mistrust in the current government) merged into my grandparents' reality, the memory of the Holocaust (the external world tries to destroy me), signaling the distance between conscious and unconscious experience. This case of mine was not the only one: vaccines and the tighter control over private life caused disproportionate, irrational anxiety in many people.

Mária (35 years old, a sociologist) starts the session by saying that although she's had the vaccine, after the initial joy she felt increased uncertainty and anxiety again. We still can't see "when all this will be over." Previously, she had hoped that everything would "come to rights" by the summer, but this hope is starting to unravel, and there is the fear that perhaps nothing will ever be as it was. Because her husband hasn't yet had the vaccine, they are still living a rather secluded life, not meeting anyone. As if they were stuck in a state of uncertainty, in helplessness. At the same time, she has doubts over whether the strict isolation they have been living in for a year now is actually necessary. They don't meet their family, or only taking many precautions, but meanwhile others are living their lives. The patient brings the following dreams:

First Dream

I had a really strange dream. I dreamed I had to go to prison. I don't know why. The prison was more like a hospital: everything was sterile and white. I'm late. I try to hurry, but I get lost. I can't find the way. This place is like a labyrinth. There are security guards everywhere. They aren't threatening, but they're not helpful either: they're completely neutral. I try to get information from them. They give me directions, but I end up in the wrong place. I'm more and more anxious that I'm going to be late.

Second Dream

Soon I have to leave on a spaceship that will take me to the Sun, where there is life. I'm late, and I have to pack quickly everything I need for the journey. Not just for me, but for my daughter too. On this journey, she is coming with me (in prison I was alone). This expedition will last six years, and the way back is the same. In a flash it comes to me that we have to spend time there too, and Kriszti (the daughter) will be an adult by the time we get back. I'm in despair, you can't prepare for that. A feeling of unbearable confinement and anxiety comes over me. Suddenly my brother appears. He says not to worry, because there will be Wi-Fi, so at least we can have therapy on the way. I feel that now even that won't help. I can't stand it that long.

Snapshots from Non-therapy Relationships from This Period

A 70-year-old man who regularly meets his children and grandchildren says:

I'm not scared. Who knows how long we have to live. I don't want to spend the remainder of my life not meeting my loved ones. What I say is: dying with family is the finest way.

A 50-year-old man says:

I was in the playground with my grandchildren. Several people weren't wearing masks. I told them it was in everyone's interests for them to wear masks. I thought they were going to lynch me. It was astonishing for me to see how antagonistic we became in the blink of an eye. The atmosphere got so bad that we had to leave. I didn't want to argue in front of my grandchildren, but I was angry, and ashamed at myself for my cowardice. I felt I ran away.

A 70-year-old man says:

A few months ago we moved into our summer house by Lake Balaton. I listen to the radio a lot, to keep in contact with the "outside world." We hardly go out anywhere, just to the shops. I'm confused. I don't know what comes from the outer reality, and what comes from this confinement. Everything has become surreal. It's like when my parents told me about the war years. The family moved to the countryside. The war raged around them, but they went into hiding, just like we are doing. There's a danger, and there isn't.

March/April 2021

The Third Wave

Vaccinations have started, and a wave even stronger than the first is developing. The number of cases of illness and fatalities rises sharply. Meanwhile, pandemic fatigue is beginning to set in and determine rebellion against protective measures. This triggers growing tension, in society, and also between friends and in the family.

Eastern Vaccine, Western Vaccine

In January 2021, when vaccinations began (in Hungary), the "eastern" vaccines without European licenses trigger strong emotions throughout society: many reasonable doubts and many scare stories circulate, and the "collective mood" changes almost every day.

Titusz (35 years old, businessman) has a chronic illness. In January he lives relatively freely, and he goes running. Several times he says that he will definitely wait for the "American" vaccine. He follows the news regularly, and he has decided to wait because this is the most reliable. When the virus variants appear, he experiences very strong anxiety, and withdraws into voluntary quarantine for weeks. In this same period, the vaccination of the public picks up pace. His GP calls him and offers him two options: he can be vaccinated the following day with the eastern vaccine or two days later with the American vaccine. The young man answers "Vaccinate me with anything I can get as soon as possible." He justifies his decision saying that the anxiety had become unbearable, and he wouldn't have been able to stand even two days under such tension (Bakó & Zana, 2021b, 531–532).

Snapshots from Non-therapy Relationships from This Period

A **40-year-old woman**, who doesn't know how long she'll have to wait for the vaccination, says:

> This lack of contact is enough to make me go mad, and the fact I don't know when it'll be over. Until we get vaccinated we're hardly going out of the house at all. We don't meet anybody. It's beginning to be unbearable. The world has become empty. Our life has been like this a year now, and who knows how long it will last.

A **woman of nearly 70** is invited by her GP to go the next day for a vaccination with the Russian vaccine.

All night I couldn't sleep. I didn't know what to decide. I asked my husband to help. For instance, we could both get vaccinated. He said he would leave the decision to me. Let it be what I want. I went to the doctor in tears, and said to him that I was scared of having the vaccine, and scared of not having it. In the end I didn't have it. I don't trust it: only Pfizer. So it's more lockdown for me.

A 70-year-old man who is otherwise very critical of the governing party tells enthusiastically that he has been vaccinated, and how well organized it was. He seems liberated, like somebody who has been snatched from the jaws of death.

A woman in her 70s is very scared she will be infected. Whenever she can, she talks about this anxiety. and to whoever, including her cleaner, who is in her 40s, and pacifies her, saying:

Don't worry Klárika, it's not just old people who are dying from the virus now!

In a group of friends, a **65-year-old woman** delivers her opinion on vaccination:

I'm against it because these modern vaccines contain microchips that can be used to manipulate people.

It was interesting to see that this remark, with its paranoid contents, did not trigger stronger reactions in the group. Everyone was accepting; nobody said it was nonsense. The last snapshot is a good illustration of the extent to which it is dependent on the current collective mood what a community designates to be normal or abnormal. Because this content (they implant a microchip into us) is part of the *there-and-then* reality of the external world, it does not necessarily signal the current psychic state of the individual so much as the mood of the group.

The Scapegoat

Szilvia (61 years old, a teacher) has an elder daughter, and she and her boyfriend get infected. Her daughter has been vaccinated, but she is at risk because she has a chronic condition. The 85-year-old mother of the patient, who was recently with them, also catches the infection, and is admitted to hospital.

Sz: I'm very angry with Gábor (her daughter's boyfriend), because he "brought the virus home" to the family.
T: So apparently you feel that Gábor does not belong to the family?
Sz: Well, yes. Perhaps I really do feel that he's not good enough for Timi. *Silence.* But I'm very angry.

T: I wonder who you are angry at.

Sz: Sighs. I can't be angry at the Chinese, or at the government. But I'm angry at people who don't keep to the rules. That's how we've got to this state. We didn't keep them either. We met without masks. That's why I'm angry.

Szilvia's mother didn't think her daughter's first husband was "good enough," which led to countless conflicts and contributed to the divorce. In the present, the patient begins to see Gábor as foreign, an intruder, someone bringing danger to the family – whereas she actually likes him. At the family celebration, they agree together not to wear masks, but when there's a problem, Gábor becomes the scapegoat. He is excluded from the family, and he becomes the one to get angry with.

As the pandemic gets more serious, many institutions remain closed, including schools and kindergartens. The day nurseries can stay open. One weekend there's a technical glitch and the central IT system is down. As a result, there is chaos in the vaccination centers: many who had an appointment miss out on their vaccination, while others who didn't have an appointment, manage to get the jab. Meanwhile, news spreads on various forums about where and how to jump the line get a vaccination.

Anna (32 years old, interior designer)

Today I finally took Marcsi (her daughter) to the day nursery, but I'm very unsure about whether it was the right decision. Perhaps I'm putting her in danger, or my parents, or the nursery nurses. Several of them are elderly. It's so difficult having to decide. *Silence.* On the weekend several people called me to go to the vaccination center, to see if we can get the jab. The plan was that if someone gets a text (a confirmation of the appointment), they would forward it to us, and by showing it we too could get vaccinated. I just can't decide. Partly I really wanted to get vaccinated, but party I felt that it's unfair on those people who are next in line. *Silence.* It strikes me that in 1944 probably this is how they waited in line for a Swiss visa. Those who didn't wait in line and trusted for the government to protect them, they died.

"You Can't Make a Mistake"

Gabriella (41 years old, secondary school teacher) teaches in a private secondary school. During the session, she tells in detail about how much effort (for instance, introducing new technology) she puts into meeting the pupils' expectations, and thus the parents' who pay a lot of money to have their children educated. At the same time, the pupils are increasingly frustrated and dissatisfied. They probably feel they aren't getting enough. A couple of minutes before the end of the session she says:

G: At the moment I feel that therapy isn't giving me what it did before. Nothing's changing. I'm just as tired. I'm sleeping worse and worse.

Perhaps I need something different from you, or something more. We should think about what.

T: *I feel exasperation and helplessness, I feel that recently I made huge efforts to help Gabriella understand what she is going through, and though sometimes she is relieved, later she is dissatisfied again. The fact she says all this in the last few minutes heightens my helplessness and exasperation: she gives me the tension, but not the opportunity of understanding together what's going on between us. I pause a little, then I say:*

Perhaps we are experiencing something similar now here together, which is familiar to you from everyday life. It must be difficult when things that you cannot give are expected of you. Probably you feel continuously that others expect more and more of you. You do more and more, but there's no sense of success, and you are increasingly tired and helpless.

She starts the next session by saying that her stomach hurts a lot, and her reflux symptoms have returned. Her husband is constantly anxious too, worrying about his elderly parents. They aren't meeting anyone to avoid infection. Then she speaks about work again, where she feels she cannot let up, because "later there could be a high price to pay for any small error."

T: What does this bring to mind, that you "can't make a mistake"?
G: Well, firstly, what I said the last time. That the whole set of statistics has to be calculated again because I slipped up at the beginning. It took a week of my time. *Silence.* Now I think of the family history. If my grandfather hadn't stepped out of the line at that particular moment, then he too would have been shot into the Danube. Or if my father hadn't been so resourceful, then he wouldn't have come back from forced labor. *Silence.* The other branch of the family was much less fortunate. Many of them were killed, the business was confiscated. We never got it back. The lesson they learned was that if you're not extremely careful, it's very dangerous.

The uncertainty of the pandemic intensifies the already present transgenerational atmosphere: we always have to be on our guard, be prepared. We can't let up, we can't make mistakes, because in the present, that might cost the patient's life.

"We're Not Scared!"

Tamás (40 years old, store manager)

Tamás: I'm fed up with other people's neuroses, I don't want to take them on. (*He falls silent for a long time. I feel the emotion in him, and the tension grows in me too. Finally I speak:*)

T: What happened?

Tamás: There we were, the usual crowd. And I really did hear something, a throw-away comment, that someone had fallen ill, but I simply didn't pay attention. *Brief silence.* Perhaps I didn't want to hear it. *Silence.* The main thing is that we really didn't think about this, and we went to a party for a weekend. Later it turned out that that certain someone did actually have COVID. Later my wife admitted that she didn't want to spoil the mood, she didn't want us to have to cancel the visit. She knew how important it was for me. *Silence.* For a couple of days I haven't been myself. It worries me a little, but I don't think we should overreact. (*Silence, meanwhile I wonder if it might be COVID*). And what really bothers me is if anyone asks: "But it's not COVID, is it?" (*what a good job I didn't ask . . .*) It's as if I were under suspicion. As if they were saying that we are irresponsible. *Silence.* Lepers.

Like many others, Tamás has lost his ability to orient himself: he cannot decide how far to be careful, in what situations, what is allowed, and what isn't. He tries to banish anxiety and fear, to split them off, hiding behind an attitude of "we are the people who aren't scared, who don't subscribe to this nonsense." He tries to keep distance from a sense of guilt, and at the same time he experiences exclusion, suspicion. The much deeper and earlier feeling of shame colors the *here-and-now* reality, and thus he is overwhelmed with uncontainable anger and shame.

Magdi (58 years old, a teacher) left her husband a couple of months ago, during the pandemic, and asks for therapy help.

From time to time a nameless anxiety comes over me. I sense that it's connected to the current situation. To COVID. I listen to the news. The number of fatalities is dreadful. I already feel that it's pulling me down, into the depths, but I can't not listen. It's not good that this has become my only contact with the outside world. With reality.

When the children left home, Magdi felt that there was no reason to stay with her husband. Since then she has spent much time alone, and she will be alone during the approaching Easter holidays too. When she thinks of this, she becomes very melancholic:

Nowadays I'm thinking a lot of my mother, who I don't think I ever saw happy. I was conceived in mourning. My mother's first child died of some infection at just a couple of months old. A couple of months after Péter's death, she got pregnant again. That was me. Here in therapy I've come to understand her deep sadness, and the distance between my husband and me. Now I understand better why I have a "frozen" reaction to the pandemic. For sure the virus is threatening too, after all it ruined my mother's life, and mine. Not this virus, but another. But they're both terrible. I withdraw, as if I were hiding from it and saying "You can't find me, you won't kill me." While I shut myself away from others, it's as if they have left me. I'm left on my own, just as I've lived my whole life: with my mother, but without maternal love. Am I doing the same with my children? It's worrying to think that . . . (*She struggles with tears. after a while she cannot hold them back and breaks into sobbing, while saying repeatedly:*) I didn't want this! I didn't want to be this kind of mother!

Vanda (42 years old, a lawyer) has been in analysis for two years. Vanda's parents lost their parents very early on, when she was a child. Vanda's life has been haunted by the fear that some trouble, or tragedy, can happen at any moment.

One afternoon I noticed that I was anxious waiting for my husband to come home. This was surprising to me, because so far I'd experienced the opposite. I don't go out all day, so I was waiting anxiously for him, like the Messiah. At last I won't have to be alone. Now, when my husband came home, I avoided him. I didn't go to greet him. I didn't kiss him. I acted like I was hard at work. My husband always respects that. He kept his distance too, and went to bed early. I was half listening to where he was going, but I didn't approach him. When I went to bed, I thought about whether to go into the bedroom or to sleep in the living room. It was just like when we have a big argument, and I'm very angry at him. In the end I went into the bedroom, but I hardly slept a wink all night. I wondered what the problem with me is. What's my problem with my husband, after all we didn't argue about anything. Then I realized: I'm scared of him. I'm scared that he brought the virus home. He runs a business with his parents. He meets lots of people, so there's a high chance he might get infected, and infect me too. I kept my distance from him instinctively. I was ashamed to talk about this to him. I hardly dared admit it to myself. That day he left early in the morning, but in the evening when he came home, he confronted me with my fear:

"What was wrong with you yesterday?" he asked.
"I was tired," I said.
"I don't know what to do so that you're not scared of me. I know
    you're worried I'll bring the virus home. I worry about that too."

In the end we decided he could sleep at his parents' for a week, then we'd see. It was good to talk this over. It didn't actually resolve anything, but the pressure and the shame, that I'm terrified of the virus and of my husband, as a potential carrier, that has subsided for a while.

Márk (36 years old, a company director) has been in therapy for three years (twice a week, seated). He arrived in therapy saying that he'd like to be a better father than his father had been. Currently, he is in a marital crisis. He and his wife had gone to the kindergarten where they plan to enroll their child. Márk is very agitated as he tells of the experience:

> We went in to where the children were, and there was the teacher and two parents as well. Neither the teacher nor the other two parents, nor the children were wearing masks. I had a mask on. After a while, my wife took hers off. I was angry at them, and got more and more frustrated. I actually wanted to tell them, we're in an enclosed space, wearing masks is obligatory. But I restrained myself, because the relationship with Zsuzsa is conflicted as it is. I don't understand her behavior, because she was the one who wore a mask even when it wasn't obligatory. It made me angry that she allowed herself to be affected by others so easily. On the way home I told her: "You acted as if you wanted to play up to the teacher, so that they take Barna into the kindergarten." She got so angry with me that she stopped on the side of the road, and shouted at me to get out the car. I got out, because I was angry with her too, for being so irresponsible, for making compromises.

For his wife Zsuzsa, the *here-and-now* reality of the small group (the immediate environment in the kindergarten, where we don't wear masks), and her desire to be accepted, overrode the threat very much present in the external world, and even her own fears. The patient was overwhelmed by his own feelings and fears, and was unable to understand how from one moment to the next Zsuzsa steps out of their shared reality and adapted to the reality of the given environment, "going over to the other side," leaving him stranded.

Dream from This Period

Eszter (38 years old, financial specialist) continues to be cautious and wears a mask. In this period, she only meets people outside. At the instigation of her partner, who very much wants to go somewhere with friends, they go hiking. Many more people than expected go on the hike, and this arouses some tension in Eszter. In the car her tension and anxiety rise, because one of the friends isn't wearing a mask, with the excuse that they don't have it with them. All through the hike she feels that the others are coming "too close," they aren't keeping a safe, obligatory distance. Although she tries to relax and get to know new people, she's very frustrated when the person she is talking to comes too close. When they stop for a picnic, everyone sits in one group, and only they sit slightly further apart. Meanwhile, she feels she is being excluded. For the patient it was difficult, practically impossible to achieve in this situation what would for her have been safe and comfortable. She felt this "pressure of the group" to be so strong that she couldn't "play the eccentric." While she couldn't protect her own personal space (either in the car, or later in conversation), she couldn't "play the eccentric," in actual fact she got increasingly frustrated and (if not physically, then psychologically) distanced herself from the others, until she was left alone. This story contains a feeling very familiar to her: fear of being excluded. At the same time, the story is not just about the patient: feelings of exclusion and fear of it run through the whole of society. She starts the next session by saying that she feels ill. She doesn't know if it's COVID, but she's very scared. Several in the group have caught COVID since the hike. She brings the following dream:

> I'm in a very dictatorial state, it's like North Korea. Somebody has to be allowed to pass through the checkpoint, and I'm there too. I get in contact with the leader, probably Kim Jong-un. I write to him on Messenger, and all the while I'm more and more scared. In the reply he sends an Indian telephone number. Nothing else. I call the number, and the person is allowed to cross the border. At the same time I feel I have lost. I cannot break free, I belong here. I've become a traitor. Then I'm with a boy in a hotel, and we hear the police coming. We barricade the door, but they break in. They capture us, and we have forty-eight hours to respond to the charges. If they don't, they'll execute us. I know I don't stand a chance.

T: What feeling is most dominant in you now that you have recounted the dream?

E: A constantly growing fear. And total despair.

T: Who do you think has to be allowed over the border?

E: It comes to me now: that's me too.

T: As if the price of freedom were that you had to sacrifice yourself, a part of yourself?

E: Er, yes, that's a familiar feeling.

The current crisis (fear of being infected or being eccentric) calls forth not only Eszter's previous experiences, but the traumatic experience of earlier generations, the sacrifices made (and not made) during the Holocaust, and the deep sense of being excluded from the community of humans, a wound unhealed to this day.

Csanád (41 years old, a doctor) has been working remotely for almost a year. A couple of months ago, he brought a dream where he is running away. He is the third generation of a repatriated family. The grandparents were classified as class aliens, they didn't get good jobs, and the children couldn't go to university. For the family, the reality even today is that the authorities see everything, they monitor you, and they are a constant threat. The decrees and restrictions made in the pandemic reinforced the family's fears. Csanád is increasingly worried that online he is being watched and monitored. He presented the following dream:

> There's another rule: you have to pull a plastic bag over the mask, as an extra layer. There were three of us who didn't do it, and they caught us. They took us to the police. Immediately they put us in a cell, we got eleven years, without a trial. The other two didn't take it too seriously. But I did. Meanwhile they let us out for a couple of hours. While I was wandering around the city, I thought: I should escape. I couldn't think of anybody that would hide me. I knew I would go back to the cell. I thought: there are cameras everywhere anyway and they know where I am. I'd be found out for sure, what's the point of hiding. Eleven years will pass eventually. Maybe it'll be shorter.

Rituals Are Overturned

One of the most shocking consequences of the pandemic crisis, is that customs and rites that have been with us for centuries (such as visiting the sick, funerals, weddings, school graduation ceremonies, break-up ceremonies at school) were overturned. The unthinkable became a reality: schoolchildren didn't go to school. There were no graduation ceremonies, so an era, in the symbolic sense, was left without closure. There was warp in time, order and continuity was broken. Individuals who lost their orienting ability often reacted disproportionately or incomprehensibly: for instance, caution was overridden by the conviction that a wedding, a funeral, could not be missed.

Snapshots from Non-therapy Relationships from This Period

János (52 years old) lost his father in February. His sister Veronika wanted at all costs to be at the funeral, she felt that she ought to be at the funeral to say goodbye to him:

> My sister, who lives in Germany, can't come home for the funeral because of travel restrictions. So she asked us to postpone it until she can be here. She said that if it didn't work, it would be a burden for her, she would feel her relationship with Dad lacked closure. Actually, I was happy to oblige. I realized how important it was for me too, that she be present.

Jácint is about to celebrate his 51st birthday.

> Last year I made lots of preparations for my fiftieth. I was born in March. I had a plan for who to invite to the party. I thought it would last two

or three days. The pandemic put an end to that. I thought, never mind, I'll celebrate it this year. It's sneaky but it's worth it, I thought, but the virus blocked this year's too. I'm really disappointed. I wanted so much to celebrate together. Such a big event you can only experience together. That's the way to do it. This way, it's as if time had stopped. It's really sad.

Olga (27 years old, a student) was in her first year at university. She was really looking forward to university life. She spent a long time thinking what to do, and finally chose a program to be a special needs teacher. For years she saved money so that she could live like a "real student."

When we started the year, we met once on Margit Island [a large park in central Budapest]. I thought the whole year would be like that. Since then there's been nothing. Teaching is online. There was no freshers' camp either. I wondered about whether to postpone a year. I didn't, but I've become really listless. This isn't what I wanted.

Late April/Early May 2021

A New Reopening Begins

More and more people are getting vaccinated, and in parallel with this, the restrictions are slowly being eased.

Vera (29 years old, an artist) has been working at home since the pandemic broke out. She goes out into the "dangerous world" very little. Her relationships, her living space, have all shrunk.

I'm like a bird whose wings have broken and who spends a year in animal hospital. Now it could fly away, but it doesn't know if it's still able to fly. *Silence.* I've become very uncertain in real life. One day I went to meet two people I know. At last we could sit out on the patio of the cafe. The whole time I was there I felt bad. I "flew" back home to my nest as soon as I could. And I was relieved to get home at last.

Petra (26 years old, a catering worker) worked in a catering establishment before the pandemic. For a while she got a fraction of her regular pay, then in fall 2020 she was laid off. Since then, she has been living on savings, and her parents help her out financially.

Because of the virus I lost my job. Because of the lockdown, I've lost myself. The vaccine doesn't help. With the virus and this confinement, I've lost something for good. My sense of security has disappeared. There's no hope I will ever get this back. I feel I'll never be able to find my way back to the old me.

Salamon (51 years old, a teacher) comes from a family where the grandparents were repatriated. He has lost his sense of security. He feels unable to make decisions, and is scared of the consequences.

I feel mistrustful of the whole world. I don't trust myself to make good decisions either. I can't predict which of my decisions is good, and which is risky. You don't find out immediately, only later, years down the line. It's like the Chernobyl catastrophe. We didn't know there was fly ash in the air and that it endangered everybody. That's how the virus is too. It could be anywhere, in the air, or on our clothes. The virus is an invisible enemy. We only notice it after it has wounded us. That's why I've become mistrustful and suspicious. But not just me. This madness has become normal. I see the same thing in many people.

Pál (33 years old, an executive) still has his job, and he earns well, but he begins to be more and more scared of falling into poverty. One of the things he is worried about is not having a pension, because he is not saving enough, and in his old age he might become homeless and die of hunger. This feeling dominates him so much that he starts saving every last penny. He brings home toilet paper from work. He eats and even showers at his family's, at friend's homes, to save money.

This Vaccine or That One

Mária (35 years old, a sociologist) gets a Western vaccine because of her chronic illness, but her husband is offered the Chinese vaccine, which after much hesitation he accepts so that he can at last get out of the house. "Any vaccine is better than getting sick," he says. To begin with, she is glad of the opportunity, but soon she is overwhelmed by powerful anxiety and guilt: she got something better than her husband. She is better protected. If they go outside (which she now wants very much), then she is endangering her husband, and in her imagination he might even die of it. Her negative feelings and anxiety are reinforced by the fact that the "others" (family and friends) did not accept the Chinese vaccine, but decided to wait for the other vaccine, or to pull strings to get it. Mária feels that she and her husband are losers, because they accepted a "second-rate" vaccine.

Dreams from This Period

While Mária and her husband are living a confined life, and only meeting people in the open air, the other members of the family are taking less care, and meet up. She's very much looking forward to her parents getting the vaccine, and they can meet at last. Her mother is offered the Russian vaccine, which she doesn't accept. Mária becomes very anxious and worried for her parents, but other feelings appear too, such as envy of those who don't take the restrictions as seriously, or anger toward her mother who didn't take the first available vaccine.

In this period she brings the following dream:

> There are lots of guests. We are all together, and nobody is wearing a mask. I'm more relaxed too. I'm not wearing a mask either. Suddenly I realize what's going on, and also that the others seem not to perceive the danger. I'm left alone.

The carefree, liberated mood of the beginning of the dream changes suddenly when Mária realizes that, merging into the collective mood, she has forgotten the danger. Her relief disappears, and the family feelings of anxiety, anger, and loneliness become dominant. Her dream also reflects the current collective mood: while there is still a serious threat in the external world, the containment of it is increasingly difficult – even at the group level. More and more people are not keeping to the guidelines, and organizing "secret" meetings. The chasm between the "cautious" folk and those "longing for freedom" grows further.

Zsigmond (40 years old, middle manager in a big corporation) comes from a family where the grandparents were repatriated because of their ethnicity. One night the police came and took the whole family. Certain loud sounds, noises, or even the slamming of a car door, or a period of overwork, provoke strong somatic reactions and a nameless anxiety in Zsigmond:

> I've come here today very tired, tormented. All night I couldn't sleep. I heard disturbing noises. I didn't know where they were coming from. Several times I got out of bed to listen. I couldn't work out what it was. I even went outside to see if there was a noise source below us, above us, or next to us. Several times I tried to shut the door so that it wouldn't come in. I was struggling against something invisible all night. It seeped into my home, into my mind. My wife just lay there sleeping as if nothing happened. I got stomach ache. The next day I had such a bad headache even painkillers didn't cure it.

Eszter (38 years old, financial specialist) had three consecutive dreams:

First Dream

> I'm at a waterfront festival, and there are more and more people. Suddenly, I throw the glass of wine in my hand at someone else's face, and he dies. I'm utterly shocked at my own murderous passion. I don't understand.

Second Dream

I'm walking with a young man by the seaside. There are more and more people, we start to walk away from them. We are running from the people, the crowd, but they run with us. I realize they are fleeing too, we are fleeing together. The road is underwater now, so we can't see where we're stepping. If we step in the wrong place we might sink, but we have to run faster and faster.

Third Dream

A puppy is shut in a room. He wails to be let out, but I know there's a monster in the room too. I want to save the puppy, but I know that if the monster gets out there might be unforeseen consequences: it could kill me, and others too. I can't decide what to do.

The central feeling of the first two dreams (tension increasing to erupting point) is linked to the crowd of people. The unbearable tension results in unexpected aggression, or desperate flight. In the second dream, the path covered in water is a good metaphor for the uncertainty experienced not only by Eszter in the *here-and-now*: although we move, running, forward, we don't know where the path is taking us, or what dangers it holds. Even the path is not safe: it's easy to make a wrong step and sink. As we interpret the third dream fragment together, we begin to see the patient's fear of her own feelings (such as aggression), from the monsters inside that she is scared to show, and let out.

Attila (36 years old, a photoreporter) has a very ambivalent relationship to his career. At the end of April, he brings the following dream:

I'm in a postapocalyptic world where people live in the forest. I don't know what can have happened. Perhaps it was a war, or even an invasion of aliens from outer space. There's no fighting now, but the world isn't what it was. Something has changed irrevocably, something difficult to put into words. Suddenly people are dashing somewhere, and I run with them. But I'm not one of them, I'm the photographer, whose job it is to record events. But when I try to do this, I realize I have no equipment, I have no tools. Without equipment, a photographer is helpless. I'm not a photographer any more, but a civilian, just one in a helpless crowd. The most difficult thing is that I don't understand.

Attila's strongest feelings about the dream are his incomprehension, helplessness, of being without means. For him the camera provides protection: he can be present at events (be it an occasion with friends, like a wedding, or an official assignment, like recording a catastrophe) while at the same time he keeps a certain distance not only from events, but from the others, the "civilians." The camera equipment helps him to process events in the outside world; it has a kind of transforming function. In defense of his identity as a photographer, he is capable of bearing witness too, recording and telling narrative of the most brutal events. The dream portrays the patient's feeling that in this period he is left increasingly without means, and his customary coping (processing) strategies are no longer working. He loses his ability to distance himself from others, to draw a distinction, and merges with the civilians, a mass of people who for him are threatening. He changes from being an active eyewitness to a passive victim.

Snapshots from Non-therapy Relationships from This Period

Luca and **Lóránd**, a couple in their 60s, both had the first vaccination. Luca has also had the second. Before the pandemic they traveled a lot, and they were looking forward very much to returning to that way of life.

> Just a couple more weeks (says Luca eagerly) and Lóránd can travel too. They will set out for the big wide world. Of an evening, we like to get out the world atlas, pick a place we'd like to go, and in our imaginations we're already on our way. Lórand and I know how childish this game is, but for the time being it's fun, it reduces our frustration.

Rudolf, 45 years old, had two divorces behind him when he met his current partner. He traveled a lot, and was hardly ever at home. In the time they spent together, they traveled much and were often out together in society. They'd been living together for two years when the pandemic situation changed everything. They both started working from home, and rarely went out.

> Andi is very pretty. I was proud to take her everywhere. It was good to show her off to my friends. Since we've been shut up at home, it turns out we are two very different worlds. I'm bored with her. In my previous relationships I shared a company, an enterprise, with each of my wives. I don't have that with her. I realize that it was my self-esteem that married her. I'm certain that when the pandemic is over, I will divorce her.

End of May/End of July 2021

"The COVID Bubble Has Burst"

In Hungary, the government links the "reopening" to the number of people vaccinated. This creates a mood similar to a sports event: we rush to get the desired result, we cooperate, etc. Those reluctant to get vaccinated become an "enemy," and health care workers performing way over their capacity become "heroes." When the desired number is reached, the miracle really happens: the restrictions are quickly and drastically reduced. People flood into night clubs and restaurants. Many plan summer vacations. Almost from one moment to the next, the collective mood is one of relief, of liberty from the restrictions: the previous fears of many people disappear almost without trace. People are thronging the streets, sitting on restaurant terraces. It seems as if everything were back to normal, as one patient put this feeling: the COVID bubble has burst. At the same time, the feelings of anxiety and tension that were prevalent for so long have in many people been replaced by feelings of tiredness, exhaustion, low spirits, and emptiness.

The Therapist's Own Experience: "Being Jolted Back"

While shopping at the market I notice that something is bothering me, I feel uncomfortable. I suddenly realize that I'm bothered by the closeness of others. All distancing has gone. The person behind me is standing so close I can almost feel their breath on my neck. Shortly afterwards I watch the Champions' League on TV, and see packed stadiums: sixty thousand people sitting, standing, cheering, shouting, rejoicing, all in close proximity. In this period I begin to shift back to personal meetings. When I arrive in the consulting room for the first time after several months, I get a strange feeling. Partly it's as if I hadn't left that long ago, and partly it's as if I hadn't been here for ages and ages. I notice that every clock says a different time. They stopped at different moments. At one of the first sessions, I involuntarily follow my patient's gaze: I look up at the ceiling, where I notice a cobweb. The story of Sleeping Beauty comes to mind: as if we were awakening from a long slumber. But are we awakening to the same world, or has it changed in the meantime? In one of the sessions, my patient is sitting opposite me and we are wearing masks, but during the session we almost forget this. At the end of the session as we stand up to take our leave, I have a bizarre feeling: Joker's grin is projected onto my patient's masked face. I wonder to what extent this is about me: am I trying to make the danger disappear? Or the feeling that it's strange for me too, to return to face-to-face meetings, while at the same time I want things to be like before? To what extent is it about my patient, that he finds aggression unacceptable, both in others and in himself? Or to what extent is it about the external world, that people are trying not to notice the danger anymore? Or all of these at once . . .

Meeting In Person Once More

György (68 years old, a retired lawyer) has a chronic illness, and for over a year, since the beginning of the pandemic, he has not been to the consulting room in person. Although it wasn't easy for him to switch to online therapy, he got to like it, and felt that it was no worse than meeting in person, although he was very much looking forward to the first face-to-face session. At the second in-person session, toward the end of the hour, he said he was disappointed and frustrated at the end of the previous session, but he can't understand why. In the end, we manage to pinpoint two small circumstances that upset

György in the last session. The first was that although *there-and-then* he was unaware of it, he noticed that I was making fewer notes than before. I picked up my pen once and then put it back down. He felt that what he was saying was no longer interesting, he's no longer exciting for me. The other point was that I didn't accompany him out when he left, although I used to previously. Then, when he stepped out the door, he felt that things weren't like before: I'd changed. Because I had no sense of anything lacking after the previous session, I tried to recollect what my patient must have felt. Then I realized that I did indeed take far fewer notes in the online period, and this habit stayed with me in the in-person sessions. For me that meant that my way of working had changed a little: I allowed myself more dreaming and reverie, and spent less energy trying to give words to feelings during the session. In that particular session, another *here-and-now* circumstance was a contributory factor: outside it was 35°C (95°F). Before György, there had been two patients who were still not vaccinated, so I had been wearing a mask. Although I felt I was concentrating, the heat and wearing the mask meant I was indeed a little weary, slightly less concentrated than usual. Over what was nearly a year and a half, I had lost the ritual of saying goodbye in a couple of cases: while I go out to meet every patient, there are differences in saying goodbye – some of them I escort out, and some of them I say goodbye to in the consulting room. I shape this relationship jointly with the patient at the beginning, watching how they feel most at ease. In György's case, I was a little uncertain when he came back, but (more instinctively than consciously) I felt that he liked to go out alone. But for him it was upsetting that I couldn't remember this aspect of our relationship, which was mainly something bodily. Minor bumps and jolts like this happened with others too ("how was it again?"), but these brought no break in the relationship; it remained continuous. Yet for György, whose father had left the family early on, these enactments were filled with meaning: Is our relationship continuous, or has something broken, am I not the same as I used to be? Do I not listen to him as I used to? His case sheds light on another interesting aspect: in the first in-person session, he reaches back not to the previous online session, but to the much earlier memory, of our last in-person meeting almost a year and a half previously.

Teréz (42 years old, a book publisher) has been in therapy for a year, but because she started during the pandemic, so far we have only met online. When she arrives in person to therapy for the first time, she is clearly very embarrassed. She talked all through the session, hardly giving me a chance to join in. The next time we met, it transpires she felt this too. She arrived with a serious list, where she had reflectively written down what she experienced:

Teréz: I felt very strange. In the online space I felt I was completely safe with you. I trusted you completely. I spoke of things I had never mentioned to anyone, almost uninhibitedly. When we met in the flesh, this disappeared completely. I was very embarrassed. I can't remember what I said, only that I kept on and on talking. Looking back, it's as if I didn't let you get a word in. I practically delivered a monologue.

T: What do you think alarmed you?

Teréz: When I came to see you, it was forty degrees [104 degrees F]. I was thinking about what to wear. Because of the heat the only sensible thing was a light blouse. Even then I felt it wouldn't be good. I tried something else. I changed clothes several times, but the heat didn't leave me much choice.

T: You chose the summer blouse, but it was a bit like you were going on a date.

Teréz: I was embarrassed. What would you think of me?

When she was a child, her father had sexually abused her. During the years' therapy, we had talked much about this. In the "sexless" security of the online therapy space, she spoke honestly about this, with emotion and feeling. The first in-person, "flesh-and-blood" meeting, the light summer blouse, and the desire to please, completely confused her. It brought back the maternal judgment, the sense of shame: a girl shouldn't attract attention.

Nóra (22 years old) is a student studying abroad. She started therapy shortly before the pandemic, saying that although she likes life abroad, she misses her family and is very homesick. Her homesickness was heightened by the fact that because of restrictions, it was a long time before she could visit. At the end of June 2021, she finally had the chance to come home, and came in person to the next session. She said of her impressions:

N: It was really strange coming here. It's terribly hot. When I left, it was 12 degrees. (*At the time the temperature in Budapest is 35 degrees C, 95 F*). And it was funny that first I wanted to come in a summer dress, but in the end I came in trousers. I noticed this, I thought I'd say it.

T: What might this be about?

N: I think I feel more protected like this.

T: Something frightening?

N: Well, everything is strange and frightening. When we came from the airport there was a huge traffic jam. Dad didn't talk to me, all the way he was swearing and honking the horn, getting angry. I'd forgotten about that. And this incredible heat. It's sultry. And the dirt. Everything seems dirty.

Ilona (41 years old, an accountant) contacted me in the first phase of the pandemic, but initially she said she would come to therapy if we could do it in person. Later she contacted me again saying that because we didn't know when we could meet in person, she'd like to start therapy online. From June 2021, when we can meet in person, she said she'd like to continue online for a while, because it was easier to organize her life that way.

T: What feelings do you have about meeting personally, and going further away from home?

I: Well, it provokes a lot of anxiety. It's now I realize what a good life I've had over the last year. I ought to meet loads of people now, and I already feel the anxiety growing in me. *Silence.* But the interesting thing is that I'm anxious even about the meetings I usually like. When I'm there with them, then I enjoy them.

For this patient, who was anxious in social situations, the social distancing was "good," and helped her to avoid meetings she didn't want. Returning to "normal life" shocked her into realizing how anxious she had previously been at what seemed like everyday life. The pandemic jolted her out of her customary ways, it was like waking up from a dream: as if she saw life from a completely different, unusual viewpoint. The jolts, and the wonderment can move people forward, and can instigate growth.

Gabriella (41 years old, teacher in secondary school), who, since the beginning of the pandemic, has not been to therapy in person, announces that after she becomes protected, she is not prepared to communicate with anyone on Skype. Even to therapy, she will only come if it can be in person. She and her partner are planning many events. She complains of sleeping disorders, chronic tiredness, and a strange sense of emptiness, which she doesn't really understand: as summer approaches, there is less and less work, and soon they will get their "old lives" back. She and her partner lived the deep anxiety from day to day, and adopted even more draconian restrictions than were absolutely necessary. As she put it: "We'd had enough of anxiety, that was all." For her, the anxiety was too much, unbearable. She was no longer able to contain the tension, the uncertainty, and this inner feeling overlapped with the mood transmitted by the outer world: society was no longer able to contain difficult feelings, fears, and caution had a place in life. Although many people, including Gabriella, managed to free themselves of difficult feelings, but alongside splitting appeared another feeling, more difficult to link to an object: tiredness, and emptiness.

Snapshots from Non-therapy Relationships from This Period

Orsolya (33 years old, a therapist):

I see a lot of people without masks these days. Some of them look just as I imagined them without a mask, and some of them are surprising. It took me a couple of meetings to link up the two images.

Zalán (49 years old), a doctor colleague, tells of what a difficult situation he is in, and he doesn't know what the best solution is. A camp is being organized for children with celiac disease, and he is the camp leader. Given the pandemic, there are strict rules for anybody (campers and organizers) attending the camp. For the adults, vaccinations are compulsory. Not long ago a coworker showed him an exchange on messenger showing that a couple of the organizers are trying to get fake vaccination certificates because they don't want the vaccine. He is in a serious dilemma: partly he feels that the others have a right to think differently, and he should listen to others' opinions. On the other hand, he feels it is his responsibility to enforce the rules, and to care about safety.

Nimród (33 years old) is a soccer fan. Two years ago, he was found to have an unknown immune disease. He bought a ticket for the Hungary–Portugal soccer match. When his friends asked him if he wasn't worried about being infected, he replied:

> It's a once-in-a-lifetime opportunity to see Ronaldo live. It's worth any risk. Anyway, sixty thousand people can't all be mad!?

Lenke (68 years old) traveled a great deal in the time before the pandemic, and after the restrictions were lifted, she bought one flight after another.

> I've got to make up for lost time. Over the last year and a half I could only plan. I felt as if I were in a restaurant where the table is stacked with delicious dishes, but I can't eat them. Now I'm going to devour them!

Enikő (53 years old)

> This whole thing, with all these restrictions, was a pointless fuss. Some will profit from it. They're the ones behind it all. It's the money. Finally this hysteria is dying down.

Bálint (40 years old) arrives to meet a group of friends, and doesn't know the protocol for greeting, so to avoid making a false move, he asks the others, whom he hasn't seen for a long time:

> Can we hug? "It's compulsory," says one of the women, and goes towards him. The others did the same. Even those who shortly beforehand had been more distant in greeting the others.

Petrik (52 years old) listens to the news every morning: how many have died, how many have fallen ill, how many are in hospital, and on ventilators. He follows this not only on Hungarian news portals, but on the international media too. He keeps in touch with everyone online. He has retreated to live in a summer house in the countryside. When he goes shopping he keeps to all the rules, but the feeling that he might have caught the virus keeps him scared for days. For a while he has indigestion and finds it difficult to fall asleep. Although the threat in these period is falling, and restrictions are being eased, in him the sense of threat goes on unchanged. For him the outer world is still threatening.

End of July 2021

Uncertainty

In Hungary there are practically no restrictions, and masks need only be worn in hospitals and health care institutes. There are no travel restrictions, and mass events can be held irrespective of size. But from other parts of the world, there is disturbing news of new virus variants and new illnesses. There is much uncertainty over how protected the vaccinated are, and whether further vaccinations are necessary. Some seem not to acknowledge the new threat. Many people go on vacations abroad, while others fear there may be another wave and new restrictions, starting in the fall.

Has Fear Disappeared?

Gabriella (45 years old, secondary school teacher) says that all her fear has vanished. Soon she will go on vacation abroad, and she is very much looking forward to it. Although she knows the fall may bring difficulties, emotionally she doesn't experience them. Now she is living for the present.

Mór (40 years old, a trainer) has been coming for several years to therapy. He is from the third generation of a repatriated family. His entire life he has felt as if under constant threat, and he asked for therapy to address this anxiety. During the pandemic, he and his wife lived a secluded existence, withdrawn from the outside world. In July, when there are hardly any requirements in Hungary, and wearing a mask is not compulsory, they continue to wear masks, and avoid public places. They live their lives in fear:

> One day my wife and I talked of how our reality must be different from that of those around us. They are behaving as if everything were okay, as if there were no virus, no danger. They live liberated lives, traveling, going here and there. We still see the danger, and we live accordingly. Sometimes, if I'm alone, and I'm the only one wearing a mask, I feel strange. If I'm with my wife and we're wearing masks, I feel less awkward: we reinforce each other.

Xavér (32, a translator) is an American who arrived in Hungary in the weeks immediately prior to the pandemic. He earns a living doing translations. He works to a tight schedule, and the translations take several months. He doesn't know many people in Hungary, and because of the pandemic he could only meet them rarely:

> I put up with confinement fairly well. I had no problem with the half-and-half reopening either. Interestingly, at the beginning of the summer, I went into slowdown mode. Now I could go and party, go to events, go abroad,

but I don't have any energy for this. I can't pick up the rhythm of the new situation. I'm incapable of it alone. I heard a psychodrama group was starting, and I hope that others will be in a similar situation to me, and we can help each other.

Ignác (59 years old, IT specialist) has come back for a second tranche of therapy. He approached me again because of the ordeal of the pandemic. He works as an IT specialist. He takes on projects that last for several months. As soon as he finishes them, he takes a journey, either a long one or a short one. He prepares for these journeys very carefully, studying the geography, the sites of the country, and even the literature and art. Sometimes he takes friends with him, or children from a previous marriage that no longer live with him. He forged this lifestyle during his earlier therapy. But with the pandemic travel restrictions, this carefully constructed life became impossible. This state knocked him completely flat.

> The problem is not just that I can't travel, but that I miss the months-long preparation that preceded the journey. It's unbearable for me. I'm worried I've lost my balance so much I might do something stupid. That's why I want to come to therapy again, so I can regain my safety, my trust in the world.

Gréta (35 years old, a sociologist) is a single woman who has been in therapy for two years, mostly online. In the period before the COVID pandemic, she lived several years in Belgium on a Ph.D. scholarship. She had a wide group of friends with whom she partied and traveled. She came back to Hungary before the pandemic travel restrictions, because she feared that later she wouldn't be able to come home:

> The confinement was actually useful for me. That was the year I managed to write my doctoral dissertation. I reckon if there had been no restrictions, perhaps I would never have got this far, or only years later.

Now she is planning to go out to her friends from mid-August, and they will travel to Australia together. She grew up in a family of intellectuals, where study counted as something very valuable. The parents expressed this as a serious expectation, and put it before all else. Gréta sometimes accepted this, and sometimes rebelled against it. She thought that writing the dissertation was a symbol of being deprived of freedom. She managed to survive the confinement of the pandemic in a creative way, which surprised her too:

> I feel that by finishing my PhD, my rebel phase is over. Up to now it was as though I was discussing this with my parents. But I realized that this is my own business with me.

Later she said that the threat posed by the pandemic and the many fatalities confronted her with the fact that she had behaved childishly with her parents:

> While so many people are suffering and falling ill and dying, my little struggle became ridiculous, insignificant.

Snapshots from Non-therapy Relationships from This Period

Forty-two-year-old man

On the internet I read that in spite of the reopening, the number of those treated in hospital has increased 1.5-fold. This really scared me. I thought it was over at last, but apparently not. The terror comes back.

Thirty-seven-year-old male musician

I missed the audience. Over the last year I made music at home, but it's nothing like doing it in a team. I feel that remote working suffocated my creativity. It was tough. I need time, lots of time, to find my way back to where I was. Now I feel it's almost impossible. I'm forcing myself. Maybe it'll work.

Thirty-two-year-old woman

I'm going to be wearing a mask for a long time yet, for sure. It's not easy, when you're the only one wearing a mask. Nobody looks at me as if to ask why I'm wearing it, but I feel that if nobody else is wearing a mask, it affects me negatively anyway. It's as if only I can see what they can't. But I'll carry on, though I'm tense in spite of myself.

Fifty-four-year-old woman

From the moment I read that you don't need to wear a mask, I took it off. It was like getting a great weight off my chest, and coming up for air. It was a liberating feeling.

Twenty-eight-year-old woman

I'm certainly not getting vaccinated, because people say it can cause infertility. I haven't had children, but I want to. I don't want to deny myself the opportunity. Better safe than sorry. I'm doing what I can.

Closing Image: How Will the Fireworks End?

We stopped keeping the diary at the end of July 2021, because after that we needed to move on to the next phase of writing and editing the book. Meanwhile, the pandemic was far from over – indeed, fall and winter 2021 was a difficult, confusing time in both the outer and inner psychological senses. In fall 2021, we experience a pandemic wave stronger than the previous one, with the delta variant, which spreads more efficiently than previous virus variants, causing sickness and death, but there are hardly any restrictions. The long-awaited miracle (that vaccines would bring liberation from the virus) did not happen: many people did not take up the vaccine, and some people got infected even though they were vaccinated. Uncertainty, exhaustion, despair, and disappointment are the dominant feelings of the collective mood. As the closing image of the Diary, we have chosen one last snapshot, which was recorded outside the period the Diary was written: December 2021.

Mária (35 years old, a sociologist) had spoken in previous sessions about how she was thinking of going back to work, but it was difficult to imagine being distant from her daughter, and entrusting her to a day nursery. Another central topic was related to the pandemic: recently, she had been living freely, she had lost her fear, and trusted that the vaccination would protect them. Now, however, she started to be anxious again, although it did not penetrate everything, as it had done before. At the beginning of the session, I ask her permission to use in the book the dreams and fantasies that she brought. She gives her consent, then continues:

> Interestingly, I've brought a dream that would fit into the book. Or rather two dreams. One is fairly short, and is connected to what we were talking about last time. I'm there in the kindergarten with Kriszti, and I can't imagine leaving her there. But it's not a bad place, the folk there aren't bad – but the situation is inconceivable. The second dream is far more complex, and it really upset me. It was as if my age was constantly changing. Sometimes I was in the present, sometimes I was my daughter's age, and sometimes I was Kriszti herself. It starts with me in therapy, but we are on the telephone or on Skype. Like the first phase of the pandemic. I'm on edge and tense. I feel that all is not right in the world. Then you say that we should try something else, some non-verbal method. Then there's a break, and we're at a face-to-face session. I seem to be Kriszti's age, you're holding me in your arms, and pacifying me. Then I'm at home, in my current home, but my parents are there too. Here I'm an adult again. We go out to the balcony to look at the fireworks. I've always been very afraid of fireworks. Loud, unexpected noises are very difficult for me. While I watch the rockets being shot, I start to crouch down. While I watch the rocket fly high up, I get smaller and smaller, age-wise too. At the end, I'm the size of my daughter. This is frightening, and I cry. Dad takes me in

his arms and pacifies me. That's a good feeling, and I calm down. Then suddenly I am Kriszti, and my husband is holding me in his arms, trying to pacify me. Then the dream switches again, and I'm an adult. I'm worried that I've caught COVID, and so I have to do a quick test. For the test, I have to prick my finger, but I'm scared the needle will go too far in. I don't manage the first time, then when I try the second time, I wake up.

Mária brought several associations to the fireworks. She remembered that when she was about 5, she heard her uncle say that the epidemic had come. She was terribly frightened. She though it was the plague. It was probably some banal influenza epidemic, but to this day she remembers her fear. Perhaps the most anxiety-provoking part of the dream is when the firework shoots up high, and she waits in fear for the explosion, while she gets smaller and smaller. She doesn't know how it will end: Is it a mere firework, or an atom bomb, that soon will destroy the whole world? The most frightening thing about the sounds and noises is that they are unidentifiable: we don't know what they mean, but they suggest a sinister outcome, a catastrophe. Mária's dream is a condensation of the world of the pandemic, which calls forth her early experiences: the unidentifiable, frightening sounds, and undifferentiated feelings of early, perhaps intrauterine, life, inexpressible in words, separation anxiety, the security of being held, the experience of merging with the mother, and the fear of separation from her. At the same time, her dream and associations contain the present and past of all humankind, shocking experiences and fear put into words, or left unsaid: destructive epidemics, natural catastrophes, the terrors of war, and catastrophes that might end the world (the history of humankind). The extended time before the explosion, Mária's experience of growing smaller and smaller, is a condensation of each person's existential anxiety, the experience of unpredictability, and insecure existence: we cannot know what is coming next, while we wait to see how the firework will end.

Note

1 The following articles may help the reader to better understand the Hungarian social context: https://verfassungsblog.de/hungary-and-the-pandemic-a-pretext-for-expanding-power/; www.fairtrials.org/news/impact-COVID-19-rule-law-hungary-and-poland

References

Bakó, T. & Zana, K. (2018). The Vehicle of Transgenerational Trauma: The Transgenerational Atmosphere. *American Imago*, 75(2), 273–287.

Bakó T. & Zana K. (2020a). *Transgenerational Trauma and Therapy. The Transgenerational Atmosphere*. Routledge, London and New York.

Bakó, T. & Zana, K. (2021a). *A transzgenerációs trauma és terápiája. A transzgenerációs atmoszféra*. Medicina kiadó, Budapest.

Bakó, T. & Zana, K. (2021b). COVID and Mass Trauma: The Atmosphere as a Vehicle for Group Experience. *American Imago*, 78(3), 515–538. www.muse.jhu.edu/article/837107

Barát, J. & Kemenesi, G. (2021): *Vírusvadászat*. CSER Kiadó, Budapest.

Braun de Dunayevich, J. & Puget, J. (2019). Állami terror és pszichoanalízis. *Imágó Budapest*, 8(2), 24–35. [English source: "State Terrorism and Psychoanalysis," *International Journal of Mental Health*, 18/2 (Summer 1989) 98–112.]

Civitarese, G. (2021a). Heart of Darkness in the Courtyard, or Dreaming the COVID-19 Pandemic. *Psychoanalytic Psychology*, 38(2), 133–135.

Civitarese, G. (2021b). Experiences in Groups as a Key to "Late" Bion. *International Journal of Psychoanalysis*, 1–27.

Eigen, M. (2007). Preface. *Psychoanalytic Review*, 94(1), 1–1. https://pep-web.org/browse/document/psar.094.0001a

Ellman, L. P., Nancy, R. & Goodman, R. N. (eds.) (2017). *Finding Unconscious Fantasy in Narrative, Trauma, and Body Pain: A Clinical Guide*. Routledge, London and New York.

Faimberg, H. (2005). *The Telescoping of Generations. Listening to the Narcissistic Links between Generations*. Routledge, London.

Ferro, A. (1992): Two Authors in Search of Characters: The Relationship, the Field, the Story. *Rivista di Psicoanalisi*, 38(1), 44–90.

Ferro, A. & Foresti, G (2008). "Objects" and "Characters" in Psychoanalytical Texts/Dialogues. *International Forum of Psychoanalysis*, 17(2), 71–81.

González, F. J. (2020a). Trump Cards and Klein Bottles: On the Collective of the Individual. *Psychoanalytic Dialogues*, 30(4), 383–398.

González, F. J. (2020b). With Fellow Travelers to Nodal Places: Reply to Dajani, Doñas, and Peltz. *Psychoanalytic Dialogues*, 30, 424–431.

Goodman, N. R. & Meyers, M. B. (2012). *The Power of Witnessing: Reflections, Reverberations, and Traces of the Holocaust – Trauma, Psychoanalysis, and the Living Mind* (Chapter 24, pp. 301–318). Routledge Press, London.

Hartman, S. (2011). Reality 2.0: When Loss Is Lost. *Psychoanalytic Dialogues*, 21(4), 468–482.

Hollander, C. N. (2019). Buenos Aires: A pszichoanalízis latin-amerikai Mekkája. *Imágó Budapest*, 8(2), 6–23.

Leuzinger-Bohleber, M. & Blass, H. (2021). Editorial Introduction: Psychoanalytical Perspectives on the COVID-19 Pandemic. In: *Wiley* (pp. 109–120). https://onlinelibrary.wiley.com/doi/10.1002/aps.1707

Levine, B. H. (2014). Psychoanalysis and Trauma. *Psychoanalytic Inquiry*, 34(3), 214–224.

Nagy, B. (ed.) (2020). *Meseország mindenkié*. Labrisz Leszbikus Egyesület, Budapest.

Nicolò, AM. (2021). The COVID-19 Pandemic and Individual and Collective Defences. *International Journal of Applied Psychoanalytic Studies*, 18, 208–213. https://doi.org/10.1002/aps.1704

Peltz, R. (2020). Living Entities that Join and Separate us: A Discussion of "Trump Cards and Klein Bottles: On the Collective of the Individual". *Psychoanalytic Dialogues*, 30, 417–423.

Volkan, V. (2021). Sixteen Analysands' and Large Groups' Reactions to the COVID-19 Pandemic. *International Journal of Applied Psychoanalytic Studies*, 18, 159–168. https://doi.org/10.1002/aps.1696

The Reality of Trauma, the Trauma of Reality

Part II

The Reality of Trauma,
the Trauma of Reality

Chapter 1

The Reality of Trauma

This chapter deals with how an unexpected powerful experience or shocking event affects the individual, and when exactly this shocking experience becomes traumatic. In various sections of the chapter, we revisit ideas that we advanced in our previous book on trauma and group-level trauma (Bakó & Zana, 2020a, 3–29; Bakó & Zana, 2021a, 21–51). We have integrated some of those insights, but in line with the topic of this book, we have shifted the focus somewhat. Perhaps the most striking change is that unlike our earlier book, we purposely do not address traumatic experiences per se, but put the emphasis on the process itself: How an unusual, intense experience, by virtue of its power or nature, affects the individual, and at what point it becomes traumatic. Taking healthy functioning as a starting point, we discuss the factors that influence the short- and long-term effects of an event, which factors help or hinder the processability of the event, and its integration into the life history. Moving on from the effects of the shocking event on the individual, we consider how different it is if the experience is at the group level, and what role the environment has on the short- and long-term effects.

Psychological Effects of a Shocking Event: Possible Outcomes

"In a traumatic situation the more-or-less whole world collapses, the defense mechanisms do not work, and we are left unprotected. So we are disappointed in ourselves," wrote Sándor Ferenczi, describing the effect of trauma on the individual in *A trauma a pszichoanalízisben* [Trauma in Psychoanalysis] (Ferenczi [1933], 2006, 112).

But what is meant by a shocking event? The definition has much in common with that of a traumatic event: by shocking event we mean an experience that is unfamiliar to the individual, which they find deeply disturbing, and against which the customary defense mechanisms do not work. The familiar world collapses – but this does not necessarily mean disappointment in ourselves.

DOI: 10.4324/9781003194064-4

The outer world, the shocking event, is not traumatizing (it does not become a traumatic reality) in every case: "we distinguish between an event, a reaction to the event, and lasting outcome of the event. If an event causes a lasting psychological impairment like nightmares, frigidity, irrational fear or the like, that event has had a traumatic effect" (Richards in Ellman et al., 2017, 200). The *me* may be able to grapple with the outer reality: the victim experiences the torment and suffering but is able to stay in contact with themselves, and eventually gets to a stage where they can integrate the experience, which enriches them and becomes a part of their personality (Bakó & Zana, 2018; Bakó & Zana, 2020a, 30–40). Whether or not a shocking event becomes traumatic or uncontainable in the long term depends on external and internal factors: a *me* with a healthy self may be sufficiently flexible, over time, to be able to process the feelings that overwhelm it. However, there are some powerful traumatic experiences that exceed the symbolization capacity of the *me*, such as any form of aggression or exclusion which a group of people commits against another group of people. Even in the case of these highly shocking, traumatic experiences, we find many individual outcomes: sometimes the survivor is crushed, and is never able to process the events. Sometimes the effect of the trauma is passed down several generations. In other cases, the experience becomes integrated later, and even enriches the survivor's personality (Hirsch, 2008; Frosh, 2019; Frankl, 2020; Erős, Foreword, in Bakó & Zana, 2020a, x–xii; Bakó & Zana, 2021a, 11–14).

There are also shocking experiences (the pandemic being a good example) whose effect on the individual are much less predictable, and they affect different people in different ways: "The drama touches everyone, but it brings out each person's fingerprints differently" (Civitarese, 2021a, 133). Some people are worn down by it, the effect on them is seriously traumatic, and they may collapse; for others it mobilizes development, and in the long term enriches their personality. In the following pages, we shall investigate the factors that influence the outcome of the shocking event.

Factors that Influence the Integrability of a Shocking Event

During normal development of the personality, the core self develops, along with the basic structures that shape identity (Stern, 1985, 2002; Pető, 2014, 51–69, 71–82). The core self ensures a sense of constancy, and through it a sense of predictability can be experienced. The core self is like the keel on a sailing ship. If the person drifts into a storm (if they find themselves experiencing frustration, stress, crisis, or trauma), then after a while, thanks to the "keel," they are able to tip back to their stable state, and incorporate the experience, which may even enrich them.

In addition to the security of the core self, another key system of reference is the formation of self-experiences and self-representations, and their quality. Through these, the person is able to react to changing circumstances (Kernberg, 2012). These reactions may be important elements in terms of basic security, because they give the experience that the individual is flexible, spontaneous, and creative. Through them s/he becomes able to react to unexpected, stressful, unpredictable situations, just as a sailing ship can react and be nimble and flexible by virtue of its sails (as well as its keel). The two systems are mutually interactive, and their continuous interaction is the basis for the development of a healthy personality.

For a healthy personality to develop and to be supported, a suitable environment is necessary. The core self, the image the individual has of himself or herself, is born in a relationship: without a safe environment that provides "good enough" early relationships able to hold and contain him or her, it will not form (Winnicott, 1953, 1960, 1971). The empathic response of the parent as a mirroring self-object is indispensable for the formation of the nuclear self. The parent as the primary self-object treats the child as if s/he had a self – and thus creates the foundation for the healthy development of a self. Later, with the internalization of the mirroring function and idealized self-objects, what is known as the bipolar self may form, which already has its own ideals and realistic ambitions, and is able to imagine the other as an autonomous independent being (Kohut, [1971], 2001; Fonagy & Target, [2003], 2005, 208–213). At the same time, although mirrored and idealized self-objects are internalized during the early development of the self, the individual needs self-objects (good enough relationships) throughout their whole life in order to maintain self-cohesion, that is, in order to be able to imagine themselves as a coherent whole. The child's ability to contain is formed during the development of the self. Initially, the infant is unable to contain the unprocessed contents that overwhelm it, and it needs the container function of another (the mother, or caregiver), or to use Kohut's expression, a mirroring self-object (Bion, 1959, 1962b; Fonagy & Target, [2003], 2005, 157–161). The mother is able to contain the experiences that the infant is as yet unable to symbolize; she is able to digest them, and to give them back to him/her in a form and dosage s/he is able to digest (Ferro & Civitarese, 2016; Lőrincz et al., 2019). The infant will now be able to internalize these jointly digested contents, and gradually s/he will acquire the ability to symbolize and transform: as a result of the development process, the individual becomes able to give a name to his feelings, to interpret them, and to narrate them in the form of a coherent story. In parallel with this develops the ability to mentalize, that is, the individual becomes capable of understanding and containing not only his own mental state, but also that of the other; he becomes able to understand their feelings, and to predict their actions (Allen et al., 2011). Based on all these processes, there forms basic trust, to use Erikson's expression (1963), which is the foundation for later relationships, and to which the individual can return after crisis or trauma.

A prerequisite for the formation of a healthy self is thus the mother's ability to contain and experience the infant's unsymbolized feelings, the beta elements, and to make them bearable (Ferro & Civitarese, 2016). If the mother is unable to contain the protoemotional feelings of the infant well enough, the capacity for symbolization (the ability to think, to shape a narrative, and to recreate) and the ability to mentalize may be damaged. Without a sufficiently safe environment, identity and the individual's inner image of themselves may become seriously fragmented and chaotic, even to the extent that they feel they are incapable of living. This can happen not only in early phases of development, but at any time during their life. The ship (the personality) depends on the sea on which it sails: it must hold itself securely, remaining stable, but it must also be able to progress – it must be flexible. A solidly built ship (with a good keel and sails) can withstand a large storm, but there are some destructive storms that would damage or destroy even the solidest of ships. Such storms may occur during life too: unprocessable personal tragedies. The outcome depends largely on the extent to which the environment, in the strict and broad sense, is able to contain the traumatic, undigestible contents that overwhelm the individual. The environment able to contain may function as the mother did in the early relationship: it takes contents that the individual cannot process, and it temporarily helps to accept and digest the contents, then to reintegrate them into the self.

Does the Shocking Experience Become Traumatic?

In the transient explosive phase that forms as a result of a shocking event, the person undergoes intense internal events: experiences, feelings, moods, fears, ideas, and memories all move into one space. Nervous, hormonal, and physiological reactions are set in motion. A whole range of processes start to interact, both conscious and unconscious, visceral and nervous, cognitive and emotional, physical and psychological. This is when it is decided how the individual will proceed (Bakó, 2017, 220). Whether or not the event becomes traumatic depends largely on the following:

1   What stage of development of the personality the individual is at (do they have inner abilities to help them protect themselves or to work through it)?

2   What psychic state they are currently in (that is, are they able to mobilize the psychological mechanisms for defense or processing)?

3   What the individual's sensitivity is to the given problem, in other words, is it an event similar in nature to one that previously led to failure, or is it an event the individual would be capable of refining in a more balanced state?

4   Is there an external relationship that might provide assistance?

5   What relationship does the individual have to spirituality, to transcendence, or religion (Bakó, 2017, 220)? In other words, is she/he able to believe in *anything*, be it God or universal human rights?

The shocking event does not necessarily become traumatic. While they are going through the experience, the traumatized person remains in contact with both themselves and the external world, with reality. In healthy processing of the experience, a development can be noted: the experience accompanying the shocking events undergoes a change, and when it becomes interiorized, it is integrated, and becomes an element of the personality. Self-coherence is restored. We can think of the self as a sum of parts in dynamic interaction (see The Dynamic Model of the Self): the arrangement of the parts of the self is disrupted, and there is chaos, but after the chaos a different arrangement sets in, a new equilibrium.

Referring back to the case of Beáta (a 36-year-old HR manager, see the *Diary January/February 2021 – The Period When the Vaccines Appear*), the family is shocked by the change brought by the lockdown ("At first it seemed impossible that the chaos caused by lockdown would bring anything normal"); but after a temporary chaotic period, the jolt out of customary lifestyle does bring a positive change, and rather than weaken the family, it strengthens it, leading to a more harmonic functioning.

Trauma

Bion (1962a, 1967) coined the term "beta elements" to designate unprocessed data of emotional experience, in contrast to "alpha elements," which have already undergone processing by "alpha function," which is Bion's term for a combination of the action of primary process and secondary process and has to do with the mind's acceptance of the sensory data of emotional experience and transforming it into elements suitable to be thought about, stored as memory, and dreamed about. "Beta elements" which are denied processing by "alpha function" – or where there is no "alpha function" left to process them – become "beta prime elements" by default and constitute thereafter the randomness and bizarreness of delusions and hallucinations.

(Grotstein, 1990, 257)

If the external experience is too intense, due to the power or nature of the shocking event, then its processing and integration may exceed the individual's capacity for symbolization, and traumatic feelings (the beta elements) remain uncontained (Bion, [1970] 2006, 14; Ferro, 2006, 1045–1046; Civitarese, 2015, 1094; Vermote, 2019, 75–76). In a psychological sense, then, we can consider something a trauma if it outstrips the psyche's capacity for representation or mentalization.

Magdi (a 58-year-old teacher), whose children recently left home and who recently got divorced, is confused, and she feels she has lost her firm footing. The feelings that overwhelm her outstrip her processing capacity. She is overwhelmed by an unidentifiable anxiety, as she puts it: some fatal, horrifying terror pulls her into the depths (see Diary, January/February 2021 – The Period When the Vaccines Appear).

Another important factor is the phase of the individual's development in which the traumatic event occurred. A childhood trauma may lead to serious damage in the alpha function, which may make it difficult or impossible to digest, tame, and integrate events in the outer world, even later on (Ferro, 2006, 1045).

In the case of trauma, when frustration is "too much," a psychotic part of the personality becomes dominant:

> [T]he absent breast will not develop into a thought but will instead become a bad object that has to be evacuated by projective identification. This results in a hypertrophy of the apparatus for projective identification in order to clear the psyche of the accumulation of bad objects.
> (Vermote, 2019, 75)

Psychic catastrophe can lead to the disintegration of the personality, to a kind of psychic death. "Failure to use the emotional experience produces a comparable disaster in the development of the personality; I include amongst these disasters degrees of psychotic deterioration that could be described as death of the personality" (Bion, 1962a, 42). The traumatized person experiences complete emotional destruction (Boulanger, 2002, 45; Grotstein, 1990, 281).

Losing its connection to Others and the external world, the *me* passes into an unstructured psychological state, a kind of black hole (Cohen, 1985, 180; Grotstein, 1990, 281–286; Gerson, 2009, 1343–1347; Bohleber, 2010, 95–96; Ellman & Goodman in Ellman et al., 2017, 11). Cohen (1985, 180) writes: "In these holes structure is absent, in that there are no representations of need-satisfying interactions that provide the basis for symbolic interaction with the world and for goal-directed behavior."

Untransformed contents do not later become a part of the personality and do not fit into the personal history: "Until they are mentalized, they remain locked within an ahistorical, repetitive process as potentials for action, somatization, and projection" (Levine, 2014, 219). Without mentalization they become timeless, and remain outside history:

> Experiences of emotional trauma become freezeframed into an eternal present in which one remains forever trapped, or to which one is condemned to be perpetually returned through the portkeys supplied by life's

slings and arrows. In the region of trauma, all duration or stretching along collapses; past becomes present, and future loses all meaning other than endless repetition.

(Stolorow, 2011, 55)

The individual finds themselves in another, traumatized reality, where the same experience is repeated unchanged for ever – "The eternal hourglass of existence turning over and over – and you with it, speck of dust!" (Stolorow, 2011, 56). The victim falls into a chaos with no sense: "endlessly recurring, with no divine goal or purpose, no preordained order or meaningfulness: 'God is dead'; 'The collective character of the world is . . . to all eternity – chaos' " (Nietzsche, 1882; quoted in Heidegger, 1954, 66–91). (Stolorow, 2011, 56)

Unable to metabolize the beta elements that overwhelm him or her, the individual becomes unable to orientate themselves either in the events of the external world or in their own feelings, and thus loses their relationship with the reality of the external world, the *here-and-now* (Bion, 1962a, 8). The inner reality becomes malleable: the victim loses his/her ability to orientate themselves not only in the sense that the external world is threatening, but also the boundary between body and psyche also becomes blurred.

Kinga is a 40-year-old engineer. Her grandparents fled to Hungary from an authoritarian regime. In the unfamiliar threat of the COVID situation, she experiences feelings similar to what her grandparents felt. She describes the psychological chaos she feels, the visceral feeling of being overwhelmed, with great accuracy. The *virus* is ubiquitous, constantly present, and holds her in constant threat, in a vulnerable state. The overwhelming sensations appear in intensive somatic reactions: "I think of this virus as something that's always present, a constant threat. . . . It's like it was lurking nearby and might strike me at any time. It gets me down. My stomach's already upset by it" (see Diary, March/April 2020 – Scapegoating).

For Kinga, the reality of the external world has become "too much." As her capacity for symbolization collapsed, Kinga is overwhelmed by irrational anxiety, a nameless dread. Her case highlights another phenomenon: when the container capacity of the *me* collapses, the boundaries of the self also weaken (see later, Trauma and Self) and a psychological field forms in which transgenerational feelings mingle with those based on one's own experience, intensifying anxiety to an unbearable pitch, making it even more difficult to distinguish what is happening, to whom, and when (Bakó & Zana, 2020a, 49–50, Bakó & Zana, 2021a, 72–73).

Trauma and Splitting

When the reality of the trauma is "too much," the victim becomes unable to contain it, and defends themselves with many primitive self-defense mechanisms, such as splitting. "Insufficient capacity of containment, recourse to various defense mechanisms, such as splitting or the lethargization of intolerable emotional states, [occurs]" (Ferro, 2006, 1046).

Splitting has two functions: "on the one hand, it acts as a protective mechanism against the onslaught of unbearable reality represented by the traumatic situation; on the other, it is (or may be) a pathological form of self-regulation" (Bohleber, 2010, xxii). However, the split-off parts represent a constant threat – "The individual has an image, sensation, or isolated thought, but does not know with what it is connected, what it means, or what to do with it" (Laub & Auerhahn, 1993, 292) – and so the mind carefully keeps these unprocessed traumatic memories locked and sealed away.

Mihály is a 50-year-old managing director. Although he experiences losses, he speaks about the pandemic without feeling, as if anesthetized, as if it had nothing to do with him (see Diary, November/December 2020 – Numbers on the Rise). Mihály communicates in bodily gestures the feelings that he cannot express verbally. By contrast, when he speaks of his work, the tasks he has to perform, he is animated by feeling. It is as if the world had split into two: in the world where the pandemic raged, feelings are split off; while in the other world, the everyday world in the old sense, feelings are retained, and perhaps are even disproportionately powerful.

Fragmented memories excluded from the symbolization process and encapsulated within the psyche as an unintegrated foreign body, uncontained, and undigested (Bohleber, 2007, 329). When traumatic contents are excluded from the symbolization process and enclosed as if in a capsule, a dazed, numbed psychological state prevails: "Psychic numbing is a form of desensitization; it refers to an incapacity to feel or to confront certain kinds of experience, due to the blocking or absence of inner forms or imagery that can connect with such experience" (Lifton, 1973, 4).

However, for the self, the split off contents represent a constant threat (Rosenfeld, 1986, 56–57; Mészáros, 1990, 34), so over and over, the self tries to free itself from the unmetabolized sequelae of trauma via splitting or projection (Bion, 1962b, 307; Levine, 2014, 219–220; Vermote, 2019, 77–78; Blass, 2021, 143). "Splitting, as we all know, causes all kinds of psychic anomalies. Because cultural hierarchies split and categorize human attributes and capacities, whatever is split off – assertion, dependence, vulnerability – continues to haunt the psyche" (Layton, 2009, 113). This attempt at liberation is, however, not entirely successful. Although the threat is temporarily externalized (projected onto events or people in the present external world), since it lives on inside untouched and shut off from other parts of the psyche, it can overwhelm the psyche again at any time (Bakó & Zana, 2020a, 21–23, 38–40, 41–43, Bakó & Zana, 2021a, 60–62, Bakó & Zana, 2022, in press-a).

Since they are shut out of the domain of symbolization, or the capacity to think, these experiences cannot be tamed or integrated later either:

When the capacity to think does not develop, there will only be continuous splitting and evacuation so that experiences do not become psychic and cannot be elaborated psychically by the alpha-function, and already existing thoughts are broken up again (like a house of lego-bricks being scattered) by an alpha-function in reverse. These split-off parts conglomerate with split-off parts of the ego to form bizarre objects that are experienced as existing outside the mind.

(Vermote, 2019, 78)

These experiences are not memories in the strict sense (that is, they are not contents that have undergone transformation). Rather, we might call them images and sensations preserved unchanged:

traumatic memories are generally preserved with great precision and permanence. This is caused by their unique manner of storage: excessive arousal presumably causes the integrative functions of memory to be overwhelmed and shut down. A dissociated state of self emerges in the process, whereby the traumatic memories are encapsulated and isolated from the remaining flow of consciousness.

(Boulanger, 2002, 130)

Shut out from the symbolic domain, the split-off parts are also shut out from temporality, and become timeless, that is, they make the traumatic moment timeless and eternal:

[T]hey refer to the memory's encapsulated quality. These memories owe their special fate, different from the manner in which the memory for events functions generally, to the difference in the manner in which they are integrated and assimilated. Because of their special nature, they remain present, unextinguished, within the personality.

(Oliner, 1996, 285)

The victim remains a captive of the undigested experience, and becomes unable to escape from the raw reality of the trauma: "they remain locked within an ahistorical, repetitive process as potentials for action, somatization, and projection" (Levine, 2014, 214).

Dia is a 40-year-old interior designer. Her social sphere is much reduced, and she is completely isolated during the pandemic. She loses her points of reference and her relationship to the outer world. She also loses contact with her own feelings. Her inner world is dominated by lack of pleasure, by boredom and monotony, and at the same time she is tormented by increasingly strong and frequent physical symptoms. Now and again she has flashes of childhood memories and sensations: as a child she was asthmatic and was often hospitalized (see Diary, November/December 2020 – Numbers on the Rise). For Dia, the current trauma calls forth unprocessed childhood memories stored in the body, and the undigested experiences of past and present merge together. Although the unsymbolized memories are Dia's, they have not become an integral part of the personality. They are preserved split off, as a foreign body, unchanged.

Unsymbolized, non-verbal memories, which are stored primarily in the implicit procedural memory, cannot be shared. These memories are not accessible later either, and cannot be used for the individual to interpret current events in the external world (Oliner, 1996, 285–287; Bohleber, 2010, xxi, 95–96, 113–117; Levine, 2014, 219–220; Bohleber in Ellman et al., 2017, 51; Bokor, 2020, 15). They are deprived of their role in interpreting current external reality: "Trauma contributes to such a restructuring of the personality, so that victims of abuse are frequently unable to use memory and external reality for the purpose of pleasure and exoneration" (Oliner, 1996, 297). Dia is overwhelmed by childhood somatic memories of unchanged intensity and content – flash experiences (see also Encapsulated Self-parts and Flash Experience) but because they are unprocessed, these memories do not help her to interpret current reality. Instead, merging with the undigested contents of the present, they overwhelm her. Raw, undigested memories and experiences cannot be integrated into the self-narrative, so they do not become coherent parts of the personality. The role of external reality in regulating and forming the personality is impaired (Oliner, 1996, 286–287). As the regulating role of external reality is reduced, so the trauma victim may become indifferent to it: "Green (1997) recently described indifferent reality as those events that cannot be altered by values or wishes, facts that are indifferent to life and death. Indifferent reality resists social construction" (Boulanger, 2002, 50).

But the drive to ascribe meaning to things is a fundamental human need. The human mind "writes" the missing parts (the parts split off from the symbolic domain); in other words, it substitutes a new narrative it can digest for the gaps in the narrative. From this new narrative (in which the undigested contents are mostly conspicuous through their absence), the listening other (for instance, in a therapy process, the therapist) later tries to reconstruct the authentic, or at least a more authentic, story (Bohleber, 2010, 95–96).

Trauma and Self

Serious early trauma hampers a sense of autonomy, of the ability to differentiate between *me* and the *other*: "the early trauma led to a deficient development of autonomy. As a consequence, self and object representations were unable to establish themselves independently of one another, but were instead agglutinated due to abandonment anxieties" (Bohleber in Ellman et al., 2017, 51).

In the case of childhood trauma, the traumatic experience is owned, and becomes a part of the self-experience, but an adult trauma that the victim is unable to process may, without help, lead to the collapse of the self:

> When a child is overwhelmed by fear, contingent selves form as a protection against fragmentation; the trauma is embodied in different self-states

–unwelcome, unfamiliar, but nonetheless part of the personality. In child-hood, trauma becomes part of self-experience; in adulthood, it causes the collapse of the self.

(Boulanger, 2002, 49)

After giving birth, Mária (see Diary, March/April 2020 – Scapegoating) passed into a psychological state similar to crisis. As a result of the temporary loosening of the boundaries of the self, the inner and outer spaces merged together. The boundary between inner and outer threat, between the self and the *other* (her and the infant), the real and the perceived threat to the infant, her negative feelings and her own anxieties, disappeared.

This leads to a collapse of the self, a state in which identity is lost, domi-nated by nothingness, a deadenedness or the death instinct: "The so-called death instinct becomes an inclination to self-disappearance. It is linked less with aggression than with nothingness. Long ago, Bion made the difference between the no thing and the nothing" (Green, 1997, 1083). Extremely seri-ous trauma, destroying the survivor's identity, in the long term damages their capacity for symbolization function or containing:

The experience of extreme destruction, for example as a result of the atomic bomb, and of violence, as in the concentration camps, can rob the victim of the basis of his identity; it can result in the loss of identity, of reality perception, and of meaning, as well as in the blocking of second-ary processes such as, for example, the working through of grief.

(Affeld-Niemeyer & Marlow, 1995, 26)

In the ensuing chaos, the consolidating ability of the self is damaged, and the self-narrative becomes fragmented. The individual is no longer able to react flexibly to events in the external world, and the body may become a carrier of experience (Boulanger, 2002, 54; Levine, 2014, 214; Ellman et al., 2017).

Péter found that during the pandemic (see Diary, May/August 2020 – Conspiracy Theories Abound), the "earthquake" caused by the lockdown called forth from the depths of his personality feelings like deep pain and vulnerability, which he had never experienced before. These feelings alarmed him, particularly because he experienced them as alien. He felt that what had been holding his personality together was falling apart, that the inner strength he had relied on all his life had gone. The effect of the crisis is to weaken the boundaries of the self, which Péter felt to be a threatening, almost psychotic experience. Trauma led to the collapse of the self (Boulanger, 2002, 49), and in this state Péter has lost contact with his former self (Bakó & Zana, 2021b, 528–529).

During the COVID period, many patients, like Márta (a 23-year-old catering worker), have recounted how the most painful thing is that they feel this state might last forever. Although they know that one day it will end, internally their experience is one of being under threat: vulnerable, constricted, an unchanging state with no perceivable beginning or end. Damage to the perception of time and the collapse of the self go hand in hand (see also Trauma and Temporality). Loss of the ability to orientate oneself in time is a signal of a serious disturbance in the functioning of the self: "When the relationship between past, present, and future disintegrates, there is 'an annihilation of connectedness' (Loewald, 1980, 142), all that is left is a 'meaningless now' (144)" (Boulanger, 2002, 62).

As a result of the trauma, the ability to give meaning is lost, the *me* is stuck in a meaningless present, where the sense of time and space is damaged, the individual is no longer able to orientate themselves, to sense their experiences in the perspective of past–present–future, or to see connections (Lifton, 1973, 7; Boulanger, 2002, 62–64). As the holding and containing capacity of the internal psychological space collapses, feelings and uncontainable anxiety stretch the boundaries of the psychological space to the breaking point, and it bursts (Bakó & Zana, 2022, in press-a).

In November 2020, when we were going through the second wave of the pandemic, much more intense than the first, uncertainty, disorientation, and helplessness permeated both everyday life and sessions.

Rita, a 32-year-old artist, went into quarantine voluntarily and the only place she went to in person was therapy. She elicited a very strong, visceral reaction in the therapist. Though Rita did not experience her dread, and could not express it verbally, the therapist embodied the deep, visceral fear instead of her and with her – or rather he depicted it, experienced it, in his own body (see Diary, November/December 2020 – Numbers on the Rise).

Perhaps we might consider this an unconscious symbolization process during which the therapist's body absorbs the sensory contents that the patient cannot digest. Then, in and with his body, the therapist *dreams* them and transforms them into a bodily reverie (Civitarese, 2016, 49, Lőrincz et al., 2019, 222–228; Levine, 2014, 217–218).

Trauma and Temporality

> Time is the substance I am made of. Time is a river that grabs me, but I am the river. It is a tiger that rends me, but I am the tiger. It is a fire that consumes me, but I am the fire. The world is, unfortunately, real. I am, unfortunately, Borges [p. 771]. Time and self and death are inexorably intertwined.
>
> (Priel, 1997, 448)

The concept of time, like that of symbolic thinking, the naming of feelings, and the ability to mentalize, is an abstract construct created by humankind, and is born within a relationship (Bion, 1962b; Ogden, 1985, 134; Priel, 1997; Civitarese, 2019). Priel summarizes it thus: "[the] concept of time can be envisaged, not as pertaining to an isolated perceiving mind, but as a mutually construed organizational principle characteristic of mother-infant interactional patterns" (435). At the individual level, the development of the ability to symbolize, to transform the events of the external world into verbally expressible feelings, also brings temporality (Civitarese, 2019), the perception of the past–present–future aspect of time, and the experience of mortality. This leads to the sense of self-continuity: "In an analytic perspective, the time category is a form of living experience in which the self maintains a sense of personal continuity extending from the past, through the present, and into the future" (Meissner, 2008, 707).

The development of the sensation of time (in other words instead of always being in the present moment, experiencing the past-present-future aspect of existence) is closely related to and develops with the genesis of the individual self-experience, with the fact that the developing *me* perceives itself as a separate person from the other – from both the parent and the larger group, the intersubjective community (Bakó & Zana, 2021b, 528). The temporal and spatial aspects of the personality thus develop and are inseparably linked: the experiences of individualization (the finiteness of the boundaries of the self) and mortality (the experience of life as finite) are inseparably bound together. They develop together, they may be damaged together, and in the case of serious trauma, their perception may be altered together (Bakó & Zana, 2021b, 528–531).

Disturbances in the early relationship, and the parent's inability to contain the emotions overwhelming the infant, have an impact on a whole range of closely related processes: the development of symbolic thinking and the ability to mentalize, the process of remembering, and the development of the concept of time, which interprets events in terms of past, present, and future, and preserves them as memories. Simultaneously, with damage to temporality, spatiality is also harmed: this is the infant's ability to differentiate itself from the *other*, primarily from the mother, and later from other members of the group: to be capable of experiencing feelings different from the other, or formulate an independent opinion. During early development, if the mother is unable to contain feelings, the development of the self, and the formation of the boundaries of the *me*, is damaged. Either the individual will be unable to perceive themselves as a separate person or they will, in stressful situations, be prone to resolve unbearable inner tension by loosening the boundaries of the self – merging with another person or group.

During the pandemic, many people had the sense of time being distorted. While some people felt everything was more predictable, and easier to plan, for others it was as if this period disappeared from their lives, as Hugó (a 30-year-old psychologist) puts it: "the virus stole a year of my life" (see Diary, November/December 2020 – Numbers on the Rise). It is as if time jolted or stopped in a frozen present, as Amarilla (a 36-year-old sociologist) says speaking of a childhood experience in hospital: "They said: 'Tomorrow,' but

I thought that tomorrow would never come" (see Diary, November/December 2020 – Numbers on the Rise)

Marcel Proust recorded a similar experience, the damage done to inner time, in his brilliant novel *In Search of Lost Time* (1974). Due to illness, from childhood Proust was shut off from the outer world and childhood peers. He was excluded from games and the life of the community, and experienced (and then described in his novel) how traumatic time may have multiple layers: it can be lost and found, killed and safe, extended and compressed, telescoped, objective, and subjective (Blum, 2012, 691).

For Amarilla (a 36-year-old sociologist), this current traumatic situation evokes familiar, early experiences, and she becomes unable to bear the uncertainty, the fact that she doesn't know what time exactly her husband will get home. She collapses completely, and gets into a state close to suicide. To use her own words, from the *Diary:* "It's as if my perception of time had disappeared. I have a feeling of infinity. I'm coming apart. I'm falling down somewhere. There are no footholds, or handgrips. I'm swallowed up by the depths, by time. I'm destroyed" (see Diary November/December 2020 – Numbers on the Rise). For Amarilla, the linearity of time is lost. Being alone is unbearable, and anything would be better, even total destruction, suicide.

In the case of serious trauma in adulthood too, the ability to symbolize is damaged, and with it, the customary, linear perception of time (Boulanger, 2002, 62; Stolorow, 2011, 55; Bokor, 2020, 15–16).

> Traumatized patients often report feeling that time is standing still, or that their internal clock stopped on the date they were traumatized. They still have a sense of objective time, but not for their own development and lifetime, especially not for their future.
>
> (Bohleber, 2010, 97)

Márta (a 23-year-old catering worker) split up from her boyfriend just before the pandemic and the lockdown. She had lost a close relative shortly beforehand, and in the first months of the lockdown, she experiences a deepening uncertainty, loneliness, and vulnerability "as if time were standing still" (see Diary May/August 2020 – Conspiracy Theories Abound). In the first months, she desperately wanted to rid herself of a deeply painful state, while she also lost her perception of time. The losses (grief, splitting up, a lack of personal encounters) and the related feelings (helplessness, loneliness, emptiness) merged together. In this almost psychotic experience, the outer and inner are compounded, and are difficult to distinguish: is the empty, "life-has-stopped" world outside, or inside? The changes in the mood of the external world (dissatisfaction and anger became prevalent feelings in the outer world too) gave Márta permission to experience her own similar feelings, including dissatisfaction and anger with me. In addition to the external world beginning to mirror that there could be a change, there could be "an end to it," this feeling started to appear within her as well: not only could the virus situation ease, but so could grief and the experience of loss. The fragmented, frozen time was repaired: death, and absence of rhythm, was replaced by life, the diversity of feelings, and rhythm – the potential for change.

Can Lost Time Be Regained?

In the case of individual trauma, a good enough supportive environment may temporarily be able to contain the feelings that overwhelm the victim, and to represent temporality for them. Although the individual is stuck in the eternal presence of the traumatic moment, the environment shows that the past exists (the memory of pre-trauma experiences) and the future exists too (the potential for experiences after the trauma). Thus, the experience of existing in time can very likely be integrated for the trauma victim too; in other words, time is "regained." In group-level trauma, the container functions are damaged at several levels (the individual and group levels); thus, either temporarily or for extended periods, the supporting holding function of the environment is impaired (see later Society's Containing Capacity and How It Can Be Damaged). In addition to damage to the symbolization and mentalization capacities, the space-time construct of the group in the broad sense is damaged, and in extreme cases it may be completely destroyed. In the fall of 2020, when we were in the second phase of the pandemic, the container function of the whole of society was seriously damaged, and the social container was no longer, or only to a limited extent, able to hold the individual (see "People Don't Respect Each Other Any More": Social Snapshots). Temporality is damaged at the group level too.

If later there is still no working through of the traumatic experience (such as in the case of serious societal traumas), the traumatic moment remains frozen and becomes a constant reference point (Boulanger, 2002, 130). The survivor perceives the current *here-and-now* through the filter of the trauma, and experiences even the present as threatening. The flow of experience is not differentiated into time zones: past, present, and future merge together. Real, linear time is replaced by traumatic, circular, endless time. The traumatic moment is frozen, and it encapsulates the traumatic event too: the frozen traumatic event cannot be located into the past and narrated (Laub & Auerhahn, 1993, 292; Levine, 2014, 220). The experience of continuity (life events follow one another and relate) is replaced by the experience of circularity (the same thing, always repeated). Meanwhile, the experiences of the past that repeatedly erupt into consciousness can be understood as repeated attempts to symbolize and process the original, unintegrated traumatic experience.

Trauma and Continuity

In the early relationship, there develops the capacity for being together, and in parallel, that of being alone. In order for someone to be able to be alone, to tolerate the frustration, they have to trust that they will not be *permanently* alone, that the lack is temporary: thinking of the early relationship, the infant can trust that the mother is caring for him, and recognizes his bodily and mental needs. If the alternation between the breast, gratification, and the "lack of the breast" is predictable, then linear times is created, and the sense of continuity (Civitarese, 2019). If the infant cannot trust that this rhythm is more or less predictable, then fragmentation, lack of continuity, and meaninglessness will dominate their internal world. Priel writes, quoting Winnicott (1958, 437):

> The maternal role at the stage of unintegration – "maternal ego coverage" – enables a continuity of going on-being, protecting the infant from unthinkable anxieties. If the environment fails in this task, the infant is pushed to react, which cuts out the continuity.

Serious trauma, particularly societal traumas, may lead to the collapse of basic trust (Bakó & Zana, 2020a, 20–21; Bakó & Zana, 2021a, 39–41; Virág, 1999, 283). We can think of the collapse of basic trust as a break in the subjective and intersubjective relationship, the *me* and the *we* which disrupts the continuity between the *me* and the *we*. The *me*'s trust in the environment is deeply damaged, and the "external world mother" (society, the intersubjective community) is unable to correct it; indeed, it may become oppressive in itself. The dynamic between the *me* and the *we*, the rhythm of the relationship, is broken. Order is replaced by disharmony, disorder, and chaos. The external world is no longer predictable. The traumatized *me* can no longer rely on it with certainty, temporarily merge into the *we*, and then find itself again with renewed strength (see also *Me* and *We*, and *Their Mutual Interaction in the Atmosphere*, and *The Dynamic Model of the Self*). This is the *spatial* or relationship aspect of the break in the experience of continuity: the experience of the *me* being part of something greater than the individual is damaged (Lifton, 1979 in Peltz, 2020, 420).

Damage to the relationship continuity causes damage to the experience of *temporal* continuity. For the trauma victim, the trauma, and the attendant frustration and loss, becomes eternal. The individual no longer trusts that this can change and they are unable (at least at an emotional level) to remember that things were any different. Because chaos, disorder, and the lack of continuity are in the long term unbearable, after a time the experience of continuity is recreated. However, if the traumatic experience remains unprocessed, continuity later comes to mean not the changing reality of the present, but the frozen reality of the past. The experiences of the past are projected onto the present, and the victim experiences the danger or threat in the past as a present reality (see also Trauma and Self and Trauma and Temporality). Due to the heightened fragility and damage to the boundaries of the self, a current trauma may cause the survivor to be overwhelmed not only by their own traumatic experiences, but also by the unprocessed traumatized world of prior generations, the Transgenerational Atmosphere. If there is an opportunity for correction, the integration of the experience may begin, and the environment and the events of the present will be increasingly able to shape the internal world of the individual. Alongside the continuity of the trauma (which is actually rather the unchanged experience of the traumatic moment), increasing emphasis is given to the continuity of the present. For survivors of serious societal traumas, if integration does not take place, the post-trauma internal world becomes permanent and dormant. The anxiety, fear, and pain originally linked to the trauma are present in the life of the survivor not as past emotions or memories, but as continually present psychic realities, preserving the experience of the trauma. However, this constant state of being under threat is unbearable, so the survivor hibernates, retreating from the threatening, indigestible internal psychic contents into a deadened existence. It is mainly this deadened, traumatized internal world that maintains continuity for him (Bakó & Zana, 2020a, 19–20; Bakó & Zana, 2021a, 39–41).

For Anna (a 32-year-old interior designer), the predominantly unconscious stream of the experiences of the past hampered a decision in the *here-and-now* (see Diary January/February 2021 – The Period When the Vaccines Appear). Consciously, she asks herself whether it is ethical, whether she has the right to play the system in order to get the vaccine she wants, but unconsciously another question appears: Can she trust the authorities, the social order? Or if she doesn't pull strings for herself, might she die? Anna's grandparents self-identified as Hungarian and were assimilated. During the Second World War, they trusted that no harm could come to them, and so they did not leave Hungary when they still had a chance. Ann was born into this legacy (the Transgenerational Atmosphere), which permeates the reality of everyday life, the *here-and-now*: for Anna, the external world is unpredictable, unsafe, and every decision (even whether her daughter should go to the day nursery) becomes an issue of life and death. And yet the survivor and descendants of the survivors have a relationship to the outer world; they are able to connect to one another and to the external world in the *here-and-now*. Faint though it may be, the present does appear, and the continuity represented by reality. Relations in the present are necessary for them as confirmation that they are alive, even if they feel that a part of themselves has died or is lost. Yet these relationship experiences are weak, fragile, and unable to maintain continuity long term. At the sign of any real or perceived threat, the survivor unconsciously retreats into the continuity of the traumatic shelter. The duality of continuity (present and past) sometimes overlaps, and sometimes alternates, but always belongs together. Simultaneously, they create the link with the present and the past.

Trauma and Imagination

"The mother's adaption to the infant's needs, when good enough, gives the infant the *illusion* that there is an external reality that corresponds to the infant's own capacity to create" (Winnicott, [1971] 1999, 12–13). There comes into being the space where symbols are born: "an intermediate area of experiencing that lies between fantasy and reality" (Ogden, 1985,129).

In early development, if the illusion–disillusionment, satisfaction and frustration, is bearable and containable in the mother–child relationship, the area of illusion takes shape, making way for the transitional object and transitional phenomena. The transitional object later helps separation, bridging the gap between *me* and *not-me*, between the internal and external realities (Winnicott, [1971] 1999, 12–13). The transitional object is then situated between the self and the external reality, in an intermediate space where symbols are created, where play and fantasy have their place throughout life (Fonagy & Target, [2003] 2005, 179). Similarly to the capacity for symbolic thinking, or the birth of the time-space construct, the ability to fantasize is an intersubjective formation embedded in a relationship able to contain the feelings of the infant. These abilities thus develop in parallel and interdependently.

Fantasy, which develops simultaneously with the ability to symbolize, later moves along the plane of past–present–future. It can be detected independently in each domain of time, but it also links them together, creating continuity between the time domains. This continuity is necessary to link up reality and fantasy, but also to differentiate them. Imagination, which hovers around the border of the real and the surreal, gives freedom, provides an area for play, and makes the individual creative. It is a transitional space where relationship situations can be played out, and fears and desires can be experienced. It is a safe, intrasubjectively lived experience. It helps to make decisions, and makes it possible to imagine future situations.

> If phantasy is, as I suggest, a set of primitive hypotheses about the nature of the object and the world, one can experiment in phantasy with, "What would happen if . . . ?" It differs from the delusional phantasy, which creates an "as-if" world, and it introduces a consideration of a "what-if?"
>
> (Segal, 1994, 400)

Kamilla (a 36-year-old teacher), when she finds the external world stressful, calls up the memory of a previous good relationship in her dreams and fantasies (see Diary, September/October 2020 – Decisions). As she fled to her grandparents in her childhood, later she created a safe inner playground where she could hide away, gather strength, and over time, experience her feelings, she becomes capable of grappling with the reality of the outside world. However, for fantasy to operate healthily, an environment able to contain is still needed: a transitional space in a broader sense is necessary. We can use fantasy healthily if we are aware that it is not identical with reality, but is merely an as-if reality. The role of fantasy is to separate extreme emotions from reality, and to handle symbols as symbols (Erős, 2017, 103). With the help of fantasy, many possible scripts can be played out again and again on the stage of the mind:

I see the mind, and now the theater, as a unitary whole, that is, where there can be full representation of internal experience, of trauma and narrative, objects and part objects, primary process and secondary process, conflict and the concrete, all co-existing, influencing, and building on each other. Trauma and narrative, the unsymbolized and symbolic representations, all appear, often simultaneously in one act, or one scene, or in the total performance.

(Goodman in Ellman et al., 2017, 23)

In healthy cases, the self draws on inner resources, including the imagination, the external reality reacts continuously and flexibly, and the experience may be able to shape and enrich the self. The prerequisite for psychic health is the harmonic cooperation of the outer and inner psychological realities. The inner reality provides the sense of continuity (in the psychological sense):

> In contrast to external reality, psychic reality enhances narcissism and omnipotence. It provides a cushion and a container in which the impact of external reality can be absorbed and reworked. Psychic reality is timeless, therefore it provides the personality with the continuity that can be lacking in external reality.
>
> (Oliner, 1996, 280)

Although the feeling of continuity is created by the internal psychic reality, in order to sustain this, feedback is required from external reality. The internal reality in a dynamic relationship with the eternal reality will thus be able, among other things, to perceive temporality. The "external reality is constantly used in the service of fantasy, modifying the self-representation according to these experiences" (Oliner, 1996, 289).

As the holiday season draws near, Mária (a 35-year-old sociologist) is increasingly overwhelmed by fears, and she loses her orientation: what she should fear, what she need not, what is happening inside, what is happening outside (see Diary November/December 2020 – Numbers on the Rise). During the therapy session (which at this point was being held on Skype), the reality of the external world was projected onto the relationship between the two of us. In Mária's fantasy, a group room appears, a space where we don't know who (or what) is present, whether it is full, or empty. In the playground of therapy, Mária was able to present the feelings she had previously not been able to verbalize as a fantasy, which, although it was threatening, now had a name. This is actually the beginning of a process of symbolization, during which extreme, overwhelming feelings are separated from reality.

In serious mass traumas, simultaneously with the container capacity of the environment, even the transitional space in the broad sense created by human society, the human community, collapses. The space for play with all abstract functions such as art, religion, abstract thinking, morality, etc., – things that make the external world comprehensible to the *me* – shrinks. The victims of a serious trauma that cannot be integrated have the experience that fantasy – fears, nightmares – may become real, that the uncanny becomes reality (Erős, 2017, 103). The boundary between *as-if* reality and reality is blurred, and giving free reign to the imagination is risky. The trauma as a surreal reality robs the individual of the *as-if* reality of fantasy. As the domains of time telescope together, the past fears experienced by the trauma victim are telescoped into the current present and become permanently valid. Traumatic unconscious fantasies convey the experience of the past, which represents a constant threat in the present:

> Traumatic unconscious phantasies give form to lived-through experiences that were initially incomprehensible or unbearable. Yet, when becoming kernels of meaning(s), these traumatic unconscious phantasies also deform other emotional experiences associated with them, resulting in a congealed and deforming way of attributing meaning to emotional experiences.
>
> (Da Rocha Barros and Da Rocha Barros in Ellman et al., 2017, 65–66)

Zsuzsa is a 41-year-old kindergarten teacher. Her grandfather was repatriated after the Second World War, and he brought home fliers, which brought calamity to the family. During the pandemic, she experiences that she might bring a problem, a danger to her family, that she might infect them. She tries to banish these fears from her mind. The planes of time, the inner and outer realities telescope together, and in this damaged, shrunken psychological space, even thoughts become dangerous. The space for fantasy has shrunk, and it no longer brings liberty or a larger space. Healthy fantasy, which reacts flexibly to the events of the outer and inner worlds, is replaced by pathological fantasy and nightmare images.

Unlike fantasy that brings freedom, nightmare images shrink the internal playground, condemning Zsuzsa almost to (physical and psychic) immobility: "I try to hide away, so that I don't harm anyone" (see Diary November/December 2020 – Numbers on the Rise).

It is no longer the trauma that maintains the traumatization, but the distorted imagination projected onto reality (Kogan in Ellman et al., 2017, 161; Bakó & Zana, 2020a, 27–28; Bakó & Zana, 2021a, 48–49). However, this traumatic imagination is not free; it is unable to imagine more alternative. When the function regulating the reality of the external world is damaged, or the outer reality is "too much," the inner psychic reality and external reality diverge from one another, and the internal psychological space is dominated by unconscious fantasies and personal meaning (Oliner, 1996, 280–281, 289). Perception of external reality is distorted: "The external events which triggered the unconscious fantasy, . . . in turn, [affect] the patient's perception of external reality" (Kogan in Ellman et al., 2017, 161).

The Societal Aspect of Trauma

In the case of massive societal traumas, regarding both the long-term psychological effect and of the opportunities for healing, one crucial factor is that the same overwhelming unprocessable traumatic experience is shared by an entire community. The processing and integration of these serious collective traumas may outstrip the processing capacity of the individual, the *me*:

> Disasters that are defined as man-made, such as holocaust, war and political and ethnic persecution, use specific means of dehumanization and personality destruction in order to annihilate the human being's historical and social existence. It is beyond the individual's capacities to integrate such traumatic experiences in a narrative context on an idiosyncratic basis; a social discourse is also required concerning the historical truth of the traumatic events, as well as their denial and defensive repudiation.
>
> (Bohleber, 2010, 343)

Serious trauma may exceed the processing capacity not only of the individual, but also of the family: "Trauma can, literally, disrupt familial relations by undoing basic trust, precipitating mutual blame, and creating barriers against intimacy" (Laub & Auerhahn, 1993, 287).

A basic prerequisite for the development of a healthy personality, the formation of a coherent self, is that there be good enough early relations, which are able to mirror and contain the child's feelings and on which later relations can be built. However, for people to sustain self-coherence throughout their lives, they need secure, functioning relationships, which also help them to process losses and traumas and integrate them into the self-narrative. The relative capacity of the environment to contain social trauma is decisive in determining the degree to which the trauma victim will be capable of integrating the traumatic experience. When, under the impact of serious trauma, the individual – or even a family, or a small group of trauma victims – finds that their containing capacity collapses, the environment in the broader sense, society as a whole, can temporarily make up for the damaged containing capacity, and can help the individual(s) to symbolize the feelings that overwhelm them, and then later to integrate them (Bakó & Zana, 2020a, 3–4; Bakó & Zana, 2021a, 21–23; Bakó & Zana, in press-a). In other words, when the reality of the trauma is "too much" for the individual, though not necessarily for society as a whole, the individual or group of individuals can temporarily borrow the containing capacity of society, of the Intersubjective in the broad sense, the social or cultural third (Benjamin, 2004, 13; Gerson, 2009, 1342–1343).

Belonging to a larger whole, to a community, provides the experience of continuity going beyond the life of the individual (Peltz, 2020, 420), which in the case of serious trauma may be able to hold the *me*, and to bear the pain. "We all need to belong to and feel a part of something larger than ourselves, some form of 'collective life-continuity'," writes Peltz (2020, 420), quoting

Lifton (1979). Thus, the traumatic event can become integrated at both the personal and group levels.

Society's Containing Capacity and How It Can Be Damaged

Society, as a community of people, fosters security, and holds the individual in several ways. (Bakó & Zana, in press-a). It has holding and containing functions that derive from institutional systems, discourse, language, history, and culture (González, 2020b, 424). When social order works well enough, in the long term it is able to represent and convey general human values and norms, the experience of continuity, to the individual (the subject) as a member of the social community. Alongside this more rigid, slowly changing "visible" layer to the social container, the human community as a whole, the "intersubjective ensemble" has a far more dynamic, unconscious layer, which transmits unconscious relationship knowledge and unconscious alliances in the group (Kaës, 2007, 6, cited by González, 2020a, 392). Similarly to how holding and containing functions operate in early childhood, there arises a potential space that enables the regulation of emotions, learning, relatedness, and shared giving of meaning (Winnicott, 1953; Ogden, 1985), or in the therapy process the third (Ogden, 1994; Green, 1997). The group, now the *we*, also creates its own social, cultural, or moral "Third" (Benjamin, 2004, 13; Gerson, 2009; 1342–43, Benjamin, 2011, 35). According to Gerson,

> concept of the "cultural third" designates the existence and impact of all the non-personal contexts and process within which each individual lives and that shapes the nature of their development; included here are linguistic forms that exert a powerful influence on the structures of thought and affect. It should, of course, be borne in mind that these usages of the concept of the third exist both in external and psychic realities, are configured both objectively and subjectively, and are registered and maintained in both conscious and unconscious configurations.
>
> (1342–1343)

In early development the infant has access to the *we*, to the Intersubjective in the broader sense, or to the intersubjective Third, through the parent. Initially through the parent, then later in his own right, the infant settles into society and joins the Social, the space of shared ascribing of meaning (Bakó & Zana, 2022, in press). By accepting belonging to the group, the *me* accepts the group's rules, the unconscious contract offered by the *we*:

> One gains belonging in an intergenerational chain of subjects only by accepting dependence on and constraint by the unconscious pacts and covenants which bind the group. This occurs in all intersubjective

formations – from primary ensembles like the family, to small and large groups and institutions.

(González, 2020a, 393)

The individual forgoes their autonomy, the *me* becomes part of the *we*, as a result of which the subject can henceforth only be understood and interpreted as part of the group (González, 2020a, 393).

In exchange for this sacrifice of independence, the *me* can experience the feeling of belonging to a whole greater than the individual, the "collective life-continuity" (Lifton, 1979 in Peltz, 2020, 420); in other words, he joins the community of humans not only in the present, but becomes part of the past and future of humanity. Peltz (2020, 420) writes:

> Even as we have decentered the individual subject as a threshold of "I's are Us" – or *we*-s are *me* – we have yet to theoretically legitimate the powerful longing to believe in and belong to groupings larger than two or three at best, and to depend on one's relationship to those groups and the larger notion of collective.

Linked into the human community, the individual has access not only to shared knowledge, but also to protection (Bohleber, 2010, 171), the experience of being contained. In this volume, when we consider the containing and transforming or symbolizing functions of the *we*, we place the emphasis on this unconscious function of the human community, the "intersubject ensemble," on the unconscious social processes (Lawrence, 2005, 68–69; Bermudez, 2018, 544–547), on the function of a "supra-human plane of the group" (Layton, 2006, 239–240; González, 2020a, 390–393; González, 2020b, 430; Peltz, 2020, 418–420).

The Healthy Social Container

As we saw in the early development of personality, it is basically the parent who mirrors and contains the baby's feelings, validating them, giving them credence. However, a person needs to receive mirroring not just in the early stages of development, but throughout his or her life. Individuals need not merely functioning relationships, but a milieu in a broader sense, which is able to reflect and contain them: "Psychic structure depends on an evolving social context, and trauma makes us aware of the potential for destruction inherent in this lifelong context dependency" (Cohen, 1985, 185). The role of society's "mother-mirror" should be to reflect the traumas of the individual, and to interpret them according to the external world.

A healthy group is able to contain and mirror multiple extremely varied experiences, while the sense of belonging to a community, unity, is also maintained.

> In a healthy group – internal or external – multiplicity is in creative tension with coherence. A group is at its most generative when it contains the greatest diversity among its members while sharing the most unity of purpose.
>
> (González, 2020a, 393)

Insofar as the healthy container function of society, the moral, social, or cultural third (Benjamin, 2004, 13; Gerson, 2009, 1342–1343; Benjamin, 2011, 34) and its symbolizing capacity (Bakó & Zana, 2020a, 10–11) is maintained, society will have mature solutions for threatening, shocking events: it will be able to reinforce the feeling of solidarity, and spur the individual or groups to supportive action. The individual remains part of the *we*, the Third in the broad sense, and remains in contact with "the magnetic chain of humanity" (Benjamin, 2011, 208). The traumatic experience becomes a shareable, joint, common experience:

> A new form of human solidarity would also become possible, rooted not in shared ideological illusion but in shared recognition and understanding of our common human finitude. If we can help one another bear the darkness rather than evade it, perhaps one day we will be able to see the light – as individualized, finite human beings, finitely bonded to one another.
>
> (Stolorow, 2011, 78)

Thus, for many in Hungary, during the first phase of the COVID period (the period from March 2020 to the end of summer 2020), the public message "Let's take care of each other" became a common experience binding us together.

Samu (40 years old, T) is extremely cautious, avoids meeting people in person, but comes in person to therapy (see Diary, September/October 2020 – Decisions). He trusts that he and the therapist will take care of each other. Samu is able to take on the feelings transmitted by the outside world (mutuality, trust, solidarity) and make them his own, because previously his trust in a relationship had been established. Trust in the other (in a therapist, or another important person close to him) reinforced the patient's general trust in the world: he was able to believe that as he takes care of others, so others take care of him. At the same time, he maintains his relationship to reality, he knows that the world harbors dangers (the risk of infection remains) and he is able to change his behavior accordingly to suit the situation: to voluntarily withdraw into quarantine, if necessary (Bakó & Zana, in press).

Perversion of the Social Container

Depending on the maturity of a given society, its problem-solving abilities, its culture, its past experience, and current state, it may be able to react and contain, to varying degrees, the experiences that overwhelm the individual or the whole of society; or even rely on the containing capacity of humankind as a whole, on universal human values and norms.

The social container that serves as a safety net should not, however, be thought of as one singular homogeneous container. Much rather it is a varied matrix of dynamically changing "containers," the sum of which forms the container capacity of society as a whole.

The individual has multiple, constantly shifting alliances and identifications, according to which she includes and excludes others, or is accepted and excluded herself. If the container matrix works well enough, the individual can use the container function of many smaller groups and communities. These can complement and if necessary compensate one another dynamically.

However, social containers can only function optimally if the social institutions "support" them: if they support them, and create an external framework for the functioning of the containers, for instance, by meeting exclusion with corrective measures. This "framework" lays down clearly what is "acceptable" and "unacceptable" in the given society. Although the individual or group suffers the trauma of exclusion or stigmatization, it can rely on this having a consequence at societal level: not only in the legal sense, but in "general judgment," which is reflected in the social narrative (Bakó & Zana, in press).

If the trauma prompts sympathy and solidarity, if the environment is empathic, and reflects that this trauma is indeed a trauma, then this aids the healing process. If, however the social mother-mirror is blind, insensitive, or if society itself is the perpetrator, then the traumatized individual or group is left alone with the experience. "If defensive impulses predominate in society, or rules of silence prevail, traumatized survivors are left alone with their experiences" (Bohleber, 2010, 121). The most serious perversion is the collapse of the intersubjective Third, the collapse of humanness: "It is the erosion of confidence in being a human in this world" (Togashi, 2014, 266).

In the case of societal traumas, by the lack of empathy we mean the collapse of the holding, containing capacity of the intersubjective community (Peltz, 2005, 352–358), or to use Laub and Auerhahn's words, the "interpersonal environment," which is thus no longer able to transmit values between the individual (*me*) and the group (*we*): "By the failure of empathy, we mean a massive failure of the interpersonal environment to mediate needs" (Laub & Auerhahn, 1989, 379). In the case of serious societal trauma, when the whole of society is affected by the trauma and deeply involved, the containing and transforming function of society as a whole may be seriously damaged, and society may be dominated by a *lack* of empathy. We experienced a drop in the role of empathy in Hungary in November–December 2020, when as the pandemic situation deteriorated, the collective mood also changed rapidly (see Diary November/December 2020 Numbers on the Rise). As one patient put it: "The magic of the situation disappeared." There was less solidarity, conspiracy theories spread, and increasing space was given over to scapegoating, exclusion, and aggression, signaling serious injury to society's containing and transforming, empathic capacities.

When the intersubjective Third (Benjamin, 2004, 16) or the "social container" (Peltz, 2020, 421) function crumbles, society is unable, or able only to a limited extent, to temporarily contain the undigested sensations of the trauma victim(s), to help them to work through and integrate the experience. Dominance is given to more primitive functions working against integration – such as splitting, projection, and pathological projective identification (Boulanger, 2002, 45–46; Bohleber, 2010, 95–96, 153–179; Levine, 2014, 220; Bakó & Zana, 2020a, 10–11; Bakó & Zana, 2021a, 29–31). The role of more mature solutions, such as solidarity, is reduced. The experience is no longer a joint one, it cannot be shared. Benjamin (2004, 16) writes that "The perversion of the moral third accompanies the kill-or-be-killed complementarity and marks the absence of recognition of the other's separateness, the space that permits desire, the acceptance of loss." The *me* is left alone, and the sense of loneliness and vulnerability increases. The weakened *me* steadily loses its ability to contain the feelings that overwhelm it: being under threat, anxiety, vulnerability (Bakó & Zana, in press).

Pál (33 years old, an executive) makes a good living. In April 2021, he started to grow increasingly fearsome of becoming poor, and started taking extreme measures to save (see Diary, Late April/Early May 2021 – A New Reopening Begins). Pál's father came from a very poor family, and had built himself up out of "nothing." In the family, there was a constant fear of growing poor, a fear they might lose everything, that dire poverty and starvation might again become a reality. The external world, the current *we* reality (wartime rhetoric, that we are in battle with the virus, with virus-deniers, etc.) rather than ameliorating or refining Pál's inner reality, served instead to justify and reinforce it.

A serious trauma may have the effect of loosening the boundaries of the self, so they temporarily become more porous than usual (Bohleber, 2010, 119). The *me* becomes increasingly receptive to the external world, the *we* (see Me and We, and Their Mutual Interaction in the Atmosphere). The group may be supportive, if the social container, the containing capacity of the *we*, is functioning properly. But if the containing and symbolic functions are damaged, it may also be destructive: the destructive fantasies and nightmares dominating the *we* may also overwhelm the *me* (Bakó & Zana, in press). As Gerson (2009) put it:

> So imagine life when the third is dead, when the container cracks and there is no presence beyond our own subjectivity to represent continuity. . . . [the] inner deadness and . . . nihilism that has taken root in that empty and meaningless space.
>
> (1343)

Tamás is a 40-year-old managing director. When my consulting room shut for the second time in October 2020 and we returned to online therapy, he gave expression to strong, almost uncontrollable emotions, anger, envy, and disappointment (see Diary, November/December 2020 – Numbers on the Rise). He felt it unjust that while some people (such as the accountant) could work safely from home, for him this was not possible, because of his job. He felt he had been abandoned. In the case of the patient, the change of setting, and the entrance of the accountant onto the scene brought to the surface feelings of transference (anger, humiliation, envy) that were present in his life, but which he tried to keep distant from the therapy relationship – and he was able to verbalize these feelings. This was a significant step forward in the therapy, and we could begin to deal with these overwhelming, difficult feelings. At the same time, Tamás's feelings are not independent from the emotions that overwhelmed society, the then-and-there Atmosphere (see The Atmosphere). But Tamás is engaged in therapy, where we have a jointly declared goal of containing these feelings; society, on the other hand, the *we*, in this period is no longer, or only to a limited extent, able to fulfill its containing and transforming functions. At this point, multiple individual and group realities exist in parallel, not communicating with one another.

To use the highly pertinent metaphor of contamination to picture this phenomenon, we can say that when the "immunity" – the container capacity – of the intersubjective community, the *we*, is damaged, it no longer provides protection to the individual with weakened individual immunity, who is more vulnerable to the effects of the external world due to the loosened boundaries of the self. On the contrary, through contamination in the psychological sense (Le Bon, 1913, 2014, 22; Volkan, 2009, 207–209), overwhelming the individual with toxic, destructive contents, the *we* threatens, in extreme cases, to completely destroy (in the psychological sense) identity, individual will, to dissolve the *me*. In this damaged, vulnerable state, when the boundaries of both the *me* and the *we* are weakened, the shared intersubjective field is more easily overwhelmed, contaminated by the traumatic experience of previous generations (the Transgenerational Atmosphere). The unsymbolized, unmentalized traumas of the past may overwhelm not only the individual, but the intersubjective community, the *we* as a whole. The experience of time is distorted, past and present are no longer differentiated, and the traumatic societal memories of the past overwhelm the individual and certain social groups as present experiences (Bokor, 2020, 24–26).

The social snapshots of November 2020, the attacks or shows of aggression on the bus, on the tram, at the gas station (see Diary, "People Don't Respect Each Other Any More": Social Snapshots) well illustrate the prevalent "collective mood" in the *there-and-then*: the containing capacity of the social community had crumbled, and was no longer able to regulate the emotions overwhelming the individual and the community. The undigested emotions deriving from a chronic sense of threat sought, and found, a target, and were projected onto a social group, a minority. In this way (and Hungary was not alone in this), during COVID, the elderly became a target group (Søraa et al.,

2020; Volkan, 2021, 160), homophobia gathered traction (Ellman, 2021, 189–120), and racist statements directed at ethnic minorities, such as the insults directed at Roma (or Gypsies) in one of the social vignettes.[1]

These social vignettes reflect not only a lowering of the individual's (the *me*'s) capacity to tolerate frustration; they also point to damage in the unconscious containing and transforming function of the *we*. The community is no longer able to tame and regulate the feelings that overwhelm the individual, or even to protect the individual from attacks: in the best scenario, they are passive and mute (the silent witnesses on the bus or tram, who by extension become victims of the aggression themselves), or in a worse case, the undigested feelings conveyed by the *we* over the loosened boundaries of the self may become generalized and overwhelm and contaminate a group of individuals.

Through the trauma-weakened boundaries of the self, there may come not only undigested contents, but also contents symbolized or "pre-digested" by others (such as those constructed by an authoritarian regime), uniform narratives, and these may overwhelm and contaminate the individual, a group of individuals, or in extreme cases most of society (Bakó & Zana, in press).

The Collapse of Humanness

The deepest level of transgenerational traumatization can be caused by social processes that affect a large part of the community of humans, such as world wars, or traumatizing generalized social processes that affect many countries, or even continents. Aggression, attacks, and exclusion perpetrated by groups of people against other groups of people can be particularly traumatic: at such times, trauma victims experience as a group that the environment is indifferent, that it does not want to hear about the injury they have experienced, and in fact in extreme cases it supports the injury and genocide (Cohen, 1985; Laub & Auerhahn, 1989; Bohleber, 2010; Togashi, 2014). The partial or complete exclusion from a human community is an unprocessed trauma which follows and haunts later generations. As Laub and Auerhahn (1989) write in regard to the trauma of the Holocaust:

> The essence of Holocaust trauma is the breakdown of the communicative dyad in the internal, representational world of the victim. This generic survivor experience is linked to the sense of living under a death sentence put into effect by the policy of genocide.
>
> (380)

Such processes can be approached as a collapse of the container function of the whole of humanity: the human community is no longer able to contain and transform the archaic anxieties and destructive processes gathering strength in the individual and in communities, anxieties and processes that damage the self-integration not only of the individuals necessarily drawn into the process (blurring the boundary between the *self* and the *other*), but also destroying the already damaged container, the *we* in the very broad sense, thus questioning what it means to "be human." This degree of collapse of the container function can exert an effect on many coming generations (Cohen, 1985; Laub & Auerhahn, 1989; Bohleber, 2010; Togashi, 2014). The trauma cannot "unhappen," it cannot be undone; we can only make the psychological space around the patient safe and acceptable (Bakó, 2017, 223). The purpose in therapy is for the traumatized person to be able to restore his own self-integrity, to integrate the event, and to order it into a coherent self-narrative. A prerequisite for this is acceptance and safety, not only in the immediate environment but also in the broad one. However, silence at societal level, turning the trauma into a taboo, and shame associated with the trauma may at the societal level hamper the normal mourning process, and reinforce the difficulty of processing the trauma at the individual level, thus foreshadowing a morphing of the trauma into a transgenerational one. If the social processing of the trauma, the mourning process, fails to happen later too, there is a high chance the trauma will become transgenerational, and affect not only the victims, but the whole of society, for generations (Volkan, 2009, 211–212). Serious trauma, when the boundary between the internal worlds of the *self* and the *other* become blurred, may cause the *me* to perceive the experience as generalized, universal, so the *me*-experience may become a group-level *we*-experience (Bakó & Zana, 2020a, 10–11; Bakó & Zana, 2021a, 29–31). A shared internal world may provide a kind of security, so those sharing trauma validate and conserve it, and are then more likely to transmit the experience.

> Since the human being quite generally cannot live without explanations, he tries to give the trauma an individual meaning and historicize it with this in mind. These historicizations after the fact are usually screen memories. It is the task of the analytic process to recognize these screen memories as such and reconstruct the authentic story, whereby the historicization is open-ended, basically endless. Baranger, Baranger, and Mom warn against the vast no-man's land of this 'nameless trauma,' which the analyst does not enter without risk. One of the dangers, they say, lies in hasty and erroneous historicizations, which can bring the analysis to a standstill, allowing the transformation of the trauma to slip back into a repetitive circular pattern again.
>
> (Bohleber, 2010, 95–96)

The Witness Role and Its Perversion

The Silent Eyewitness

The survivors of serious societal traumas are all also eyewitnesses: the victims, the multitude who observe events passively, the families of the perpetrators, and even the perpetrators themselves. "Traumatized individuals are not only victims of a destructive political reality, but are also its witnesses"

(Bohleber, 2007, 343). But in terms of the long-term outcome, it matters a great deal whether the passive eyewitnesses of the trauma later become witnesses: whether they are able to bear witness to the traumatic experience in words, pictures, music, or in any symbolic form, or whether they become what are known as *silent eyewitnesses*, storing the traumatic experience in their viscera, undigested, carrying the traumatic experience unchanged even for generations, and passing on as a legacy.

Zalán (a 49-year-old doctor) experiences an insoluble moral dilemma over what to do about people with fake vaccination certificates. As a "private individual," he believes everyone has a right to think differently about vaccination, but as a "leader" he feels responsibility for the community (*End of May-End of July 2021: "The COVID Balloon Has Burst"*). In the end, the "private individual" wins out. He turns a blind eye to the irregularities, but inside, *silently*, he continues to harbor this unresolved inner tension and conflict.

The Role of the Third

In order for the eyewitness to become a witness, it is important for there to be a listening other, a witness who listens to what happened from the perspective of a third: while empathizing with the eyewitness, they are also able to keep a distance, and represent this external perspective to the eyewitness who experienced the trauma:

> That which earns the designation trauma is that which outstrips and disrupts the psyche's capacity for representation or mentalization. That which cannot be represented or mentalized – thought about or contained within the mind – cannot enter into one's subjectivity or the reflective view of one's personal history. Absent the potential for mental representation, these events and phenomena are historical only from an external, third-person perspective. Until they are mentalized, they remain locked within an ahistorical, repetitive process as potentials for action, somatization, and projection.
>
> (Levine, 2014, 219)

By listening to and hearing the confession, the witness validates the experience, which is thus set free from the captivity of the intrasubjective space and becomes intersubjective, transformable, and reality (Horváth, 2005, 7–15).

Mór (a 40-year-old coach) and his wife validate the experience for each other that the risk has not disappeared even though at this point (summer 2021) the environment is transmitting a different message (see Diary, End July 2021 – Uncertainty).

The listening other, the witness, can be a family member, a friend, or an interviewer (Horváth & Zana, 2017, 84–90) or a therapist (Mészáros, 2003, 73). In the therapeutic relationship, the hitherto unshareable experience becomes shareable, hence intersubjective: "The intersubjective analytic third is now seen as an unconscious emotional field where the patient can come to life by 'becoming increasingly able to dream one's experience, which is to dream oneself into existence'" (Ogden, 2004, 862, cited by Vermote, 2019, 85). By sharing the experience, the traumatized individual finds a partner in suffering, loss, unpredictability, isolation, and fear. The role of witness can even be played by a work of art: the one bearing witness can express events in narrative, images, or music, and the potential space of words, images, or music will represent the intersubjective space, implying an unknown but receptive other. For us, the writing of this book was also a form of witnessing: while we recorded events, the subjective snapshots, we also bore witness to the period we had lived through together. The book met our own experience in a potential space, the intersubjective space of therapy, and the intersubjective reality in the broad sense. In our approach, the *we*, the intersubjective community, and the social Third fulfil the role of witness, if they hear about and mirror events to the individual or group of individuals, thus validating the experience, which becomes a part of humanity's shared, partly unconscious, history. The legend of the Flood or Atlantis can thus bear witness to the shocking experiences of people from ancient times, even the experiences of many ethnic groups. We do not know exactly what happened, to whom, and when, but these stories are to this day a part of the collective memory of our culture. The whole of humanity bears witness, and, written or unwritten, the memory is preserved and passed on, through the collective unconscious. In other words, it has been contained.

Postmemory

In the case of serious societal traumas, bearing witness continues in the following generation. One special form of this is retrospective witnessing by adoption, which Marianne Hirsch (2008) terms postmemory. Postmemory is a form of memory when the descendants of the survivors experience the traumatic events of others, or previous generations, as if they were their own. They later embed these memories and experiences into their life histories. As Ferenc Erős wrote in the foreword to our previous book:

> Thus the relationship with the oppressed and persecuted Other is a tool, and can be used as a model: just as I "remember" my parents' memories, so I can "remember" anyone else's sufferings. Postmemory is a "personal interpretation of history": witness by one who is absent, in the sense that the witness is absent not only spatially, but also temporally, from the location where the event happened. Postmemory makes it possible to symbolically transform traumatic experiences, to communicate them, and can become a source of creativity. Today we are witnessing the birth of a transgenerational culture. Postmemory, which has given birth to great

works of art such as László Nemes's film *Son of Saul*, represents and bears witness to the present about the traumas which proved to be unprocessable for preceding generations. Postmemory is also the "memory of the present," because it makes relevant, and thus susceptible to debate, issues such as culpability, victimhood, the relationship between perpetrator and victim, collaboration, identification with the aggressor, and problems of dehumanization.

(Foreword by Erős in Bakó & Zana, 2020a, xii;
Bakó & Zana, 2020b, 13–14;
Bakó & Zana, 2021a, 11–14)

In general we can say that the more traumatic the environmental effects, the greater the chance that they will become traumatic, and the greater the chance they will be passed onto the following generations. At the same time, the individual's reaction to trauma is (fortunately) not predictable. Even among the survivors of severe societal traumas, there are many who are unbroken by the trauma; indeed, they are strengthened: the *me* is not weaker, but stronger because of it. In their case, often the milieu of creative work (artistic creation, science, helping professions) creates the psychological space in which they can resolve and also preserve, or even build their individual identity, which creates an opportunity for witnessing (Frankl, 2020). The creative process can be viewed as a *we*-experience, but a healthy, nourishing form thereof, which reinforces not the merging of the individual, but his independence. Artistic creation and the creative process itself are a shared psychological space in which the sufferer of trauma shares the experience in an abstract, creative way with an imaginary, receptive good object, and through creation the experience is both digested and shared.

Verbalizing my grief over the loss of Zsuzsa, and sharing it, helped me to process this difficult experience (see Diary, March/April 2020 – Scapegoating). The experience I have is that our relationship is ongoing, and because I have shared it in this book, it lives on in others too, not only in me (Tihamér, December 2021).

Note

1 www.ndi.org/publications/impact-COVID-19-hungarys-roma-communities

References

Affeld-Niemeyer, P. & Marlow, V., Translated by: Barbara Wharton, B. (1995). Trauma and Symbol: Instinct and Reality Perception in Therapeutic Work with Victims of Incest. *Journal of Analytical Psychology*, 40(1), 23–39.

Allan, G. J., Fonagy, P. & Bateman, W. A. ([2008] 2011). *Mentalizáció a klinikai gyakorlatban* [Mentalazing in clinical practice] (Fordította: Bulath, M. Lektorálta: Sarkadi, B. és Schmelowszky, Á. Lélekben Otthon Könyvek). Oriold és Társai Kiadó, Budapest.

Bakó T. (2017). Intraszubjektivitás a traumafeldolgozásban. In: Gerlinger L. & Kovács P. (szerk.) *Egy hajóban . . . Tisztelgő tanulmánykötet Riskó Ágnes születésnapjára* (pp. 219–229). Medicina, Budapest.

Bakó, T. & Zana, K. (2018). The Vehicle of Transgenerational Trauma: The Transgenerational Atmosphere. *American Imago*, 75(2), 273–287.

Bakó, T. & Zana, K. (2020a). *Transgenerational Trauma and Therapy. The Transgenerational Atmosphere*. Routledge, London and New York.

Bakó, T. & Zana, K. (2020b). A Transzgenerációs Atmoszféra: Az Emlékezés Folyamata Kollektív Társadalmi Traumákban. *Lélekelemzés*, 2, 63–80.

Bakó, T. & Zana, K. (2021a). *A transzgenerációs trauma és terápiája. A transzgenerációs atmoszféra*. Medicina kiadó, Budapest.

Bakó, T. & Zana, K. (2021b). COVID and Mass Trauma: The Atmosphere as a Vehicle for Group Experience. *American Imago*, 78(3), 515–538. www.muse.jhu.edu/article/837107.

Bakó, T. & Zana, K. (2022). A trauma realitása – a realitás traumája. *Lélekelemzés*, 2, 13–37.

Bakó, T. & Zana, K. (in press). The Reality of Trauma; The Trauma of Reality (Translated by Robinson, R). *Psychoanalytic Dialogues*.

Benjamin, J. (2004). Beyond Doer and Done to: An Intersubjective View of Thirdness. *Psychoanalytic Quarterly*, 73(1), 5–46.

Benjamin, J. (2011). Facing Reality Together Discussion: With Culture in Mind: The Social Third. *Studies in Gender and Sexuality*, 12(1), 27–36.

Bermudez, G. (2018). The Social Dreaming Matrix as a Container for the Processing of Implicit Racial Bias and Collective Racial Trauma. *International Journal of Group Psychotherapy*, 68(4), 538–560.

Bion, W. R. (1959). Attacks on Linking. *International Journal of Psycho-Analysis*, 40, 308–315.

Bion, W. R. (1962a). *Learning from Experience* (pp. 1–116). Tavistock, London.

Bion, W. R. (1962b). The Psycho-Analytic Study of Thinking. *International Journal of Psychoanalysis*, 43, 306–310.

Bion, W. R. ([1970] 2006). *Figyelem és értelmezés*. [Attention and interpretation] Translated by Schmelowsky, Á). Lélekben Otthon Kiadó, Budapest.

Blass, H. (2021). A new Civilization and Its Discontents in Times of COVID-19? *International Journal of Applied Psychoanalytic Studies*, 18, 139–148.

Blum, H. P. (2012). The Creative Transformation of Trauma: Marcal Prost's In Search of Lost Time. *Psychoanalytic Review*, 99(5), 677–696.

Bohleber, W. (2007). Remembrance, Trauma and Collective Memory: The Battle for Memory in Psychoanalysis. *International Journal of Psychoanalysis*, 88(2), 329–352.

Bohleber, W. (2010). *Destructiveness, Intersubjectivity and Trauma. The Identity Crisis of Modern Psychoanalysis*. Routledge, London and New York.

Bokor, L. (2020). A jövő, mint az emlékek tükre, avagy az emlékezés dinamikája a terápiás folyamatban és a kulturális narratívák kialakításában. *Lélekelemzés*, 2, 12–20.

Boulanger, G. (2002). Wounded by Reality: The Collapse of the Self in Adult Onset Trauma. *Contemporary Psychoanalysis*, 38(1), 45–76.

Civitarese, G. (2015). Transformations in Hallucinosis and the Receptivity of the Analyst. *International Journal of Psychoanalysis*, 96(4), 1091–1116.

Civitarese, G. (2016). Embodied Field and Somatic Reverie. In: *Truth and the Unconscious in Psychoanalysis* (pp. 40–52). Routledge, London and New York.

Civitarese, G. (2019). The Concept of Time in Bion's "A Theory of Thinking". *International Journal of Psychoanalysis*, 100(2), 182–205.

Civitarese, G. (2021a). Heart of Darkness in the Courtyard, or Dreaming the COVID-19 Pandemic. *Psychoanalytic Psychology*, 38(2), 133–135.

Cohen, J. (1985). Trauma and Repression. *Psychoanalytic Inquiry*, 5(1), 163–189.

Ellman, L. P., Nancy R. & Goodman, R. N. (eds.) (2017). *Finding Unconscious Fantasy in Narrative, Trauma, and Body Pain: A Clinical Guide*. Routledge, London and New York.

Ellman, P. L. (2021). Safe Spaces, Unsafe Spaces, and Gendered Spaces: Psychoanalysis during the Pandemic. *International Journal of Applied Psychoanalytic Studies*, 18, 188–196.

Ericson, E. A. (1963). *Childhood and Society*. Norton, New York.

Erős, F. (2017). Kísértő érzelmek: a történelem fantomjai. *Imágó Budapest*, 3, 101–110.

Ferenczi, S. ([1933], 2006). A trauma a pszichoanalízisben. [Trauma in Psychoanalysis] In: *Technikai írások* (pp. 112–120). Animula Kiadó, Budapest.

Ferro, A. (2006). Trauma, Reverie, and The Field. *Psychoanalytic Quarterly*, 75(4), 1045–1056.

Ferro, A. & Civitarese, G. (2016). Psychoanalysis and the analytic field. In: Elliott, A. & Prager, G.(eds.) *The Routledge Handbook of Psychoanalysis in the Social Sciences and Humanities* (pp. 132–148). London, Routledge.

Fonagy, P. & Target, M. ([2003] 2005). Pszichoanalitikus elméletek a fejlődési pszichopatológia tükrében. [Psychoanalytical Theories. Perspective from Developmental Psychopathology] (Szerk.: Bókay, A. és Erős, F. Fordította: Milák, P., Pető, K., Ratkóczi, É., Unoka, Zs), Gondolat, Budapest.

Frankl, E. V. (2020). *Az élet értelméről*. [Über den Sinn des Lebens] (Translated by Kalocsai-Varga), É. Libri, Budapest.

Frosh, S. (2019). Postmemory. *American Journal of Psychoanalysis*, 79(2), 156–173.

Gerson, S. (2009). When the Third is Dead: Memory, Mourning, and Witnessing in the Aftermath of the Holocaust. *International Journal of Psychoanalysis*, 90(6), 1341–1357.

González, F. J. (2020a). Trump Cards and Klein Bottles: On the Collective of the Individual. *Psychoanalytic Dialogues*, 30(4), 383–398.

González, F. J. (2020b). With Fellow Travelers to Nodal Places: Reply to Dajani, Doñas, and Peltz. *Psychoanalytic Dialogues*, 30, 424–431.

Green, A. (1997). The Intuition of the Negative in Playing and Reality. *International Journal of Psychoanalysis*, 78, 1071–1084.

Grotstein, J. S. (1990). Nothingness, Meaninglessness, Chaos, and the "Black Hole" I – The Importance of Nothingness, Meaninglessness, and Chaos in Psychoanalysis. *Contemporary Psychoanalysis*, 26, 257–290.

Hirsch, M. (2008). The Generation of Postmemory. *Poetics Today*, 29(1), 103–128.

Horváth, R. (2005). *A tanú szerepe: A magyar Holokauszt-irodalom a világirodalomban*. In: Maamakim. *Holokauszt-tanulmányok. Holokauszt a világirodalomban* (vol. 1, pp. 7–15). ELTE BTK, Holokauszt-tanulmányok Program, Budapest.

Horváth, R. & Zana, K. (2017). "Valuable and Also Difficult": At the Meeting Point of Historical and Psychological Interviews. In: Kangisser Cohen, S., Fogelman, E. & Ofer, D. (eds.) *Children in the Holocaust and its Aftermath*. Historical and Psychological Studies of the Kestenberg Archive, Berghahnbooks.

Kernberg, O. F. (2012). Some Observations on the Process of Mourning. In: Kernberg, O. E. (ed.) *The Inseparable Nature of Love and Aggression* (pp. 243–266). American Psychiatric Publishing, Washington, DC.

Kohut, H. ([1971] 2001). *A szelf analízise. Animula Kiadó, Budapest* [The Analysis of the Self]. International Universtities Press, New York.

Laub, D. & Auerhahn, C. N. (1989). Failed Empathy – A Central Theme in the Survivor's Holocaust Experience. *Psychoanalytic Psychology*, 6(4), 377–400.

Laub, D. & Auerhahn, C. A. (1993). Knowing and Not Knowing Massive Psychic Trauma: Forms of Traumatic Memory. *International Journal of Psychoanalysis*, 74, 287–302.

Lawrence, W. (2005). Thinking of the Unconscious, and the Infinite, of Society during Dark Times. *Organisational and Social Dynamics*, 5(1), 57–72.

Layton, L. (2006). Racial Identities, Racial Enactments, and Normative Unconscious Processes. *Psychoanalytic Quarterly*, 75(1), 237–269.

Layton, L. (2009). Who's Responsible? Our Mutual Implication in Each Other's Suffering. *Psychoanalytic Dialogues*, 19(2):105–120.

Le Bon, G. ([1913], 2014). *A tömegek lélektana* [Psychologie les foules]. (Translated by Balla, A). Belső EGÉSZ-ség kiadó, Budapest. [English source: Le Bon, G. (2009 [1895]). The Psychology of Crowds, ed. by Cuffaro, A. & Kauders, D., Sparkling Books.]

Levine, B. H. (2014). Psychoanalysis and Trauma. *Psychoanalytic Inquiry*, 34(3), 214–224.

Lifton, J. R. (1973). The Sense of Immortality: On Death and the Continuity of Life. *American Journal of Psychoanalysis*, 33(1), 3–15.

Lőrincz, Z., Gyomlai, É., Szajcz, Á., Zana, K. & Sinkovics, A. (2019). A bioni mezőelmélet. Egy kortárs interszubjektív megközelítés bemutatása. [The Bionian field-theory. Introduction to a contemporary intersubjective approach] *Lélekelemzés*, 2, 197–231.

Meissner, W. W. (2008). Self and Time. *Journal of American Academy of Psychoanalysis*, 36(4), 707–736.

Mészáros, J. (1990). Társadalmi elfojtások megjelenése a pszichoanalízisben. *Thalassa*, 1(1), 31–38.

Mészáros J. (2003). A modern traumaelmélet építőkövei. Ferenczi paradigmaváltása a traumaelméletben. In: Juhász A. (ed.) *A gyöngéd analitikus és a kemény tudományok* (pp. 66–74). Animula Kiadó, Budapest.

Ogden, H. T. (1985). On Post-Traumatic Space. *International Journal of Psychoanalysis*, 66, 129–141.

Ogden, H. T. (1994). The Analytic Third: Working with Intersubjective Clinical Facts. *International Journal of Psychoanalysis*, 75, 3–19.

Ogden, T. H. (2004). This Art of Psychoanalysis: Dreaming Undreamt Dreams and Interrupted Cries. *International Journal of Psycho-Analysis*, 85, 857–877.

Oliner, M. M. (1996). External Reality: The Elusive Dimension of Psychoanalysis. *Psychoanalytic Quarterly*, 65, 267–300.

Peltz, R. (2005). The manic society. *Psychoanalytic Dialogues*, 15(3), 347–366.

Peltz, R. (2020). Living Entities that Join and Separate us: A Discussion of "Trump Cards and Klein Bottles: On the Collective of the Individual". *Psychoanalytic Dialogues*, 30, 417–423.

Pető, K. (2014): *A csodálatos csecsemő. Pszichoanalízis és határterületei*. Oriold és társai kiadó, Budapest.

Priel, B. (1997). Time and Self: On the Intersubjective Construction of Time. *Psychoanalytic Dialogues*, 7, 431–450.

Proust, M. (1974). *Az eltűnt idő nyomában* [In Search of Lost Time]. Kriterion Könyvkiadó, Budapest.

Rosenfeld, D. (1986). Identification and Its Vicissitudes in Relation to the Nazi Phenomenon. *International Journal of Psychoanalysis*, 67(1), 53.

Segal, H. (1994). Phantasy and Reality. *International Journal of Psychoanalysis*, 75, 395–401.

Søraa, R. A., Manzi, F, Kharas, W. M., Marchetti, Massaro, D., Riva, G. & Serranoa, J. A. (2020). Othering and Deprioritizing Older Adults' Lives: Ageist Discourses during the COVID-19 Pandemic. *European Journal of Psychoanalysis*, 16(4), 532–541.

Stern, D. N (1985). *The Interpersonal Word of the Infant: A View from Psychoanalysis and Developmental Psychology*. Basic Books, New York.

Stern, D. N. (2002). A csecsemő személyközi világa a pszichoanalízis és a fejlődéslélektan tükrében. Animula Kiadó, Budapest.

Stolorow, D. R. (2011). *World, Affectivity, Trauma: Heidegger and Post-Cartesian Psychoanalysis*. Routledge, London and New York.

Togashi, K. (2014). Sense of "Being Human" and Twinship Experience. *International Journal of Psychoanalytic Self Psychology*, 9(4), 265–281.

Vermote, R. (2019). *Reading Bion* (Series Editor: Birksted-Breen, D.). Routledge, London and New York.

Virág T. (1999). Soá és ősbizalom. In: Hamp, G., Horányi, Ö. & Rábai, L. (szerk.) *Magyar megfontolások a Soáról. Balassi Kiadó – Magyar Pax Romana Fórum – Pannonhalmi Főapátság* (pp. 281–284). Pannonhalma, Budapest.

Volkan, V. D. (2009). Large-Group Identity, International Relations and Psychoanalysis. *International Forum of Psychoanalysis*, 18, 206–213.

Volkan, V. D. (2021). Sixteen Analysands' and Large Groups' Reactions to the COVID-19 Pandemic. *International Journal of Applied Psychoanalytic Studies*, 18, 159–168. https://doi.org/10.1002/aps.1696

Winnicott, D. W. (1953). Transitional Objects and Transitional Phenomena – A Study of the First Not-Me Possession. *International Journal of Psychoanalysis*, 34, 89–97.

Winnicott, D. W. (1960). The Theory of the Parent-Infant Relationship. *International Journal of Psycho-Analysis*, 41, 585–595.

Winnicott, D. W. (1971, 1999). *Playing and Reality* (pp. 1–156). Tavistock Publications, London.

Chapter 2

The Atmosphere

In this part we consider the mutual interaction of the *me* (the individual or subject) and the *we* (the group, the intersubjective community). Setting out from our earlier model of the Transgenerational Atmosphere and extending it, we introduce the concept of the Atmosphere: as in the case of the Transgenerational Atmosphere, we conceive of the Atmosphere as an intersubjective field which is born through the interaction of *me* and *we* in the *here-and-now*, and which makes non-verbal sharing of feelings and experiences possible. The main difference to the previous model is that by the Atmosphere we mean not a damaged psychological field, but a constant presence, a psychological milieu simultaneously embracing and penetrating the *me* within. Moving on from healthy functioning of the Atmosphere, we examine how group-level trauma changes the complex, delicate relationship between the *me* and the *we*. We consider how a trauma experienced at the group level may lead to a dysfunctional function (a traumatization) of the Atmosphere, and how this manifests itself.

The Transgenerational Atmosphere

Originally, we developed the model of the Transgenerational Atmosphere to help us understand mass societal traumas, or, in other words, cases when (1) the experience is traumatic; (2) it affects a large group of people (i.e., it is a mass experience); and (3) when it is a crime of human origin (a man-made disaster), that is, the trauma victims feel as a group that their environment is indifferent to them and is not interested in the injury they have suffered; indeed, in extreme cases, it supports the violence or genocide (Bakó & Zana, 2021b, 528–531). In our previous work (Bakó & Zana, 2018, 2020a, 2020b, 2021a), setting out from the direct deep psychological effects of individual trauma, and progressing toward the effect over generations of collective trauma, we deal particularly with the role of the social environment in the success or failure of processing trauma, and the hereditary transmission of trauma. The Transgenerational Atmosphere, in addition to providing a new perspective from which to view the psychological effects of trauma in the first

DOI: 10.4324/9781003194064-5

and subsequent generations, and the special attention it requires in therapy, also offers a model for the non-verbal transmission of experiences. In this chapter, we shall briefly summarize the parts on which the current model, the Atmosphere, builds. In our earlier model, we set out from the idea that in societal trauma, the boundary between the *self* and the *other*, between the internal worlds of the subject and the other members of the experience community, becomes blurred and permeable (Bakó & Zana, 2020a, 21–23; Bakó & Zana, 2021a, 41–43). This loosening of the boundaries of the self leads to the development of a shared psychological field. We called space-time field, which maintains this frozen shared traumatic moment, the Transgenerational Atmosphere. The Transgenerational Atmosphere as a psychological space (a field) creates an opportunity not only to share the unsymbolized traumatic experience, but also for the self to extend, or in the case of serious trauma for the transposition of self-deposits split off from other parts of the self (Volkan, 2013, 233; Bakó & Zana, 2020a, 30–45; Bakó & Zana, 2021a, 51–67). Taboo memories that are swept out of the narrative are transmitted to children, though often in an unsymbolized form, which in more distant generations cannot be linked to the original trauma, or only very indirectly. As the trauma recedes in time, so it becomes more difficult to identify the legacy. The original event is lost in the past, but its effect may be gathering in strength. The memory of it is marked not by words, but by less symbolized contents: deep anxiety, psychosomatic symptoms, or even archaic, generalized feelings such as fear of strangers and/or xenophobia.

Post-trauma Intrasubjective Experiencing and Processing of the Event

In the case of survivors of serious societal trauma, the integration of the trauma may exceed the individual's processing capacity (such as was the case for the first generation of Holocaust survivors). As a defense, the trauma survivor distances herself from an incomprehensible reality and from her own feelings, creating for herself a strange, intrasubjective psychological space, from which she shuts out, and splits off, unintegrated contents. As a consequence of her dissociating internal and external contents, the traumatized individual is, psychologically speaking, left alone: she loses her relation both with external reality (she is unable to form relationships, or accept help) and with her own reality (her own feelings). In order to survive, then, the *me* sacrifices itself: distancing itself from the external world, from incomprehensible reality and even its own uncontainable feelings, it retreats and creates an intrapsychic reality, but this comes at a price: the sensation of trauma, and being under threat, is fixed, and becomes dormant, living on as a psychic reality. The survivor perceives the current *here-and-now* through the filter of the trauma, and experiences even the present as threatening. The traumatized individual thus falls into a distorted space-time trap, where the feeling of vulnerability becomes constant.

Encapsulated Self-parts and Flash Experience

By splitting off overwhelming emotions, the survivor also splits off a part of the personality, from parts of the self. From these traumatized parts of the self, there forms an inner deposit, isolated from other parts of the personality. This inner self-locket (which almost completely corresponds to Abraham and Torok's concept of the crypt [Abraham & Torok, 1984] but also rhymes with Volkan's concept of self-deposit [Volkan, 2013, 233]) guards both the traumatic experience and the feelings related to trauma and loss. The feelings stored in the split-off parts of the self, isolated from the external world, from the *here-and-now*, can no longer be accessed: they cannot be evoked, or dynamically transformed. Since they are shut away, their intensity remains unchanged. They remain untamed and unprocessed. When the traumatized individual is affected by a trigger experience (this may be an external or internal stimulus), it may evoke the original experience, which then bursts into consciousness. We have termed this experience a "flash experience": the flash experience is the undigested memory of the traumatic event. The reaction and feeling in the given situation are not only disproportionately intense and destructive, but may also contain feelings such as shame, guilt, or aggression, which are incomprehensible purely in the light of the given event or the personal life history. These feelings, which may have been related to the original trauma, now as a result of being shut up and hibernated, adhere, undifferentiated, to other feelings.

Encapsulated Self-parts in the Following Generation

The expanded intrasubjective field created by the trauma victim, the Transgenerational Atmosphere, also makes it possible for these split parts of the self to be shared directly with the next generation, bypassing the process of symbolization. For the next generation, these deposits (Volkan, 2013) are alien parts of the self, which contain undigested contents (images, experiences, sensations, and events) (Kogan, 2021, 171–172). Because the child's self is involved in the *we*-self (see The *We*-self), these parts of the self, although alien, become parts of his own self. When this shut-off part of the self, which has been taken in an undigested form, and the experiences (images) encapsulated in it burst through, it is particularly threatening and incomprehensible for a child. Because he has no relationship to it in his own right, he perceives it not as a part of his own inner self, but as a threatening external attack, locating (or projecting) the feeling in his narrower or broader environment. In this state of being under threat, the familiar world of the Transgenerational Atmosphere provides security – at least, this is the experience of the heir. Like the parent, he finds refuge in the hibernated *we*-state, which keeps the perceived threat of the external world at a distance. The heir is utterly defenseless against the parent's attack. The Transgenerational Atmosphere, which he has so often experienced as a protection, can become a severely traumatizing milieu. The child is the guarantee of the parent's "happiness": not a separate person, but an auxiliary part of the self, whose function is to keep the parent "alive." Incorporated into the Transgenerational Atmosphere, the child feels loved and accepted. The parent, however, who is occasionally overwhelmed by the traumatic contents (in a flash experience), tries to locate them outside herself, to project them: into the external world, or into the child who functions as a part of her own self, ascribing to the child the unbearably difficult feelings.

The We-self

The Healthy We

In a healthy parent–child relationship, the parent is present in the child's life as a self-object. She is a model, a point of reference, a safe milieu, the primary satisfier of needs, also in the psychological sense. The parent allows and indeed assists and inspires the child to form of his own personality, to change. This process takes place in an experiential milieu created jointly by the parent and child, while each possesses his/her own internal psychological space, separated from the other. A healthy union takes shape, a healthy mother–child *we*-experience, which is capable of changing flexibly, of following the developmental needs of the child. In the jointly created experiential field, they interact with one another, through which both of their personalities develop. This shared experience makes it possible for the child to develop a stable, independent self (*me*-identity) and for the self to be integrated. A good enough early relationship, and healthy development of the self, creates room for the function of normal projective identification mechanisms, which later serve as the basis for normal empathy and understanding (Bion, 1962b; Fonagy & Target, [2003] 2005, 158).

The Pathological We

In a family with transgenerational trauma, the development of the child's self and the parent's self takes place very differently. The healthy mother–child relationship enables the birth of the child's *me* as a separate self, but in the Transgenerational Atmosphere, this is not possible, the parental self is seriously damaged, and "unviable." The fragmented, vulnerable, traumatized self attempts correction, but because of the splitting of inner and outer contents, the self-correction mechanism is also damaged. The damaged self makes an attempt at correction by extending the boundaries of the self in such a way as to draw others into the individual's own intrasubjective space as parts of the self. The Transgenerational Atmosphere as a psychological field gives space for the extension of boundaries of the self: the survivor expands not only her own intersubjective internal world (in other words, she shares experiences), but also her self. There forms a divided self-state which we have termed the "*we*-self." The survivor is able to relate to others, to share experiences and memories, and even to exist, only by making the partner, the child, a part of her self: she interprets them as a part of her own self. The *we*-self is thus inflexible, and does not allow the child's self to grow up, become independent, or to separate. For the survivor, separation is incomprehensible and equivalent to death. The child remains a part of the transgenerational *we*-self, as a supportive part of the parent's self. The Transgenerational Atmosphere, as a damaged psychological space, is not able to contain or transform either the mother's or the child's undigested sensations into something digestible; thus, it is not able to operate as a healthy container. The dominant psychological mechanisms are pathological rather than mature, and they include projection, pathological projective identification, and splitting. Not only is the mother unable to contain the undigested sensations of the infant, but she tries to use him as an auxiliary part of the self, to contain her own undigested sensations, projecting into the child the split-off, pathological, inner contents. This mechanism prevents the development of the normal regulation of feeling, the self-soothing ability: like the mother, the child will be compelled to evacuate the contents that overwhelm him into the external world, into an other, or into a sealed internal space.

When the child is born, the parent does not meet it, or mirror it. What is created is not an intersubjective self-other relationship, but an expanded self-state. Laub and Auerhahn (1989) write:

> Frequently, survivors will try to reestablish a sense of connectedness through their families and children, asking them to share in an illusion of togetherness and make a world that is complete again – a world that is familiar and known. Survivors often expect their children to be exquisitely sensitive to their needs, to know their minds, and to be a part of their selves, and children of survivors often are very sensitive to their parents' feelings, especially to their fears and sorrows.
>
> (389)

The child has a mission: to make the "deadened" parent alive again, to "give meaning" to her life: the child as a part of the parent's self may represent split-off experiences and feelings such as happiness, hope, or success. Children not born for their own sake – who see reflected in their mother's eyes something other than themselves – with a lack of intersubjective relatedness are not able to build their own core self or integrated self, which gives security. Their own self and the parental self do not separate from one another. Every attempt at separation is mortally threatening to both the parent and the child. For the parent, the risk is that with the separation from the child, she will lose a part of her own self;, moreover, the very part of herself keeps her alive. The child's experience is that it kills the mother – not in a symbolic, but a real sense, so the thought of separation brings unbearable guilt. After all, leaving the relationship would endanger not only the mother, but the child too. Without the *we*, which to him represents continuity and security, self-integrity, he feels unable to live. If the child wanted to separate, he would lose the *we*-self that functions as a core self, a part of the self that ought to be viable. The *we*-identity simultaneously provides a familiar, secure experience, while due to the permeability of the self boundaries, the fears and sense of being threatened flow from the traumatized victim to the heir.

Traumatic Space-Time, the Damage to the Boundaries of the Self in the Transgenerational Atmosphere

A similar traumatized psychological space, sealed off from the external world, may be created as an effect of any serious trauma that the individual is unable to process. In the case of individual trauma or family trauma, the environment mirrors back to the traumatized individual(s) that this internal world, though reality for them, is not so for his environment, for everyone else. Thus, with time, there is space for correction, and over the generations the effect of the trauma is lessened. But in the case of societal traumas, a whole community shares an overwhelming, unprocessed, traumatic experience. The individual senses that the experience is generalized, universal, and the *me*-experience becomes a group-level *we*-experience. The boundary between the internal world of the *me* and the other becomes blurred; it blurs into the internal world of the other members of the traumatized generation. We call this the cross-sectional extension of the Transgenerational Atmosphere. In the case of transgenerational traumas, the *we*-experience is reinforced by the distorted mirroring of the environment, thus validating and preserving this frozen (deadened) state. Those who shared the trauma validate the experience, and the shared internal world provides a kind of safety. If this is coupled with societal silence or denial, this reinforces the living out of the group experiences as reality (the threat is experienced as constant, not only in the past) and the defense (taking refuge in the intrasubjective reality, the "numb state") is justified. The unreal world of the trauma thus becomes the *we*-experience of an entire social group, and considerably increases the chances that the traumatized generation will draw the subsequent generations into this atmosphere. We call this the longitudinal extension of the Transgenerational Atmosphere. In transgenerational trauma, the damage to psychological space (the boundary between *me* and the other) is inextricably linked to the perversion of the temporal dimension. Spatial damage, the blurring of self boundaries, creates an opening for the expansion of the traumatic time, within a generation and across generations: the perception of the trauma as frozen in time, timeless, makes it possible for *me*-experiences to blur together. Past, present, and future are not successive, but simultaneously present realities, in which the internal worlds of generations do not succeed one another, but are simultaneously present (Bakó & Zana, 2018, 2020a, 2020b, 2021a). In the psychological space of the Transgenerational Atmosphere, boundaries disappear or become unclear: between the past–present and future temporalities; between inner and outer realities; between self and the other; and between generations.

Born into the Transgenerational Atmosphere: The Next Generation

The child is born into the Transgenerational Atmosphere. For him, the Transgenerational Atmosphere is both a traumatic milieu and a defense. However, the defense mechanisms that protect him (such as splitting) react not to his own life experiences, but are inherited defenses he has been given.

Without a stable core self of his own, the child needs the parental self that keeps him alive, and the associated self-experiences. Without an independent experience of self, he will not be able to experience genuine intimacy or closeness, and this will for him be substituted by the experience of symbiosis located within the Transgenerational Atmosphere. Thus, he has a need to maintain the Transgenerational Atmosphere. It is very difficult to exit from the atmosphere, although not impossible. Family members drawn into the Transgenerational Atmosphere (members of both the traumatized first generation and the following generation) experience the exiting of any family member, of any endeavor to separate, as if they had to relinquish a vital organ. Every person drawn in feels unable to live without the other, and experiences separation as unsurvivable – so maintaining the Transgenerational Atmosphere, the whole symbiosis, is a question of survival for the family. The "benefit" for the first generation is that through the Transgenerational Atmosphere, the experience of trauma becomes sharable, the trauma victim is not left alone, and they can share their loneliness. Maintaining the Transgenerational Atmosphere is in the interest of the next generation too, because only in the atmosphere can they experience intimacy and closeness with their otherwise lonely parent, who retreats into their own intrasubjective world: the atmosphere is often the only way to relate in families with transgenerational trauma. The price of the relationship, or closeness, is being drawn in, being stuck in the deadened, hibernated feelings of the Transgenerational Atmosphere, where the child has very little scope for action. However, the impact of the Transgenerational Atmosphere formed in societal traumas does not lessen; indeed, it can gather strength from one generation to the next. The broader environment plays a role in sustaining it and its long-term destructive influence, when it is unable to contain the trauma, and either fails to mirror or mirrors distortedly: either by denying the trauma, or by offering a community of shared experience (for instance, a shared victim role). If the social environment reinforces the unreal world of the atmosphere through silence or exclusion, then the internal world of the atmosphere is confirmed, validated, and its transmission may affect many generations to come.

What Is the Atmosphere?

In this section, we address the question of the function of the individual psyche: How does the subject, the *me*, become receptive to the reality represented by the intersubjective community, the *we*, and what triggers this? How are the many *me*-experiences, themselves in continual flux, able to shape the intersubjective reality? How are the *me*-experience and the *we*-experience able to affect each other so rapidly, and so deeply? What does the individual make of the external world as it changes extremely rapidly in mass traumatization? To what extent is it adaptive or dysfunctional when the relationship of the *me* to the external world changes, or fails to change, as a result of the reality represented in the group?

During the pandemic, both we and our patients experienced the sometimes rapid shifts in collective mood, which deeply affected all of us, and also appeared in therapy. In March 2020, the collective mood changed almost in a matter of days. In the period immediately before the lockdown, most people were very uncertain about how great the danger was; indeed, whether there was any danger at all.

Alíz, a 35-year-old doctor, was cautious, and wore a mask in shops even before the rules prescribed this. She found that people looked at her suspiciously, which prompted her to say: "I'm not ill, I'm just cautious" (Bakó & Zana, 2021b, 515). Eszter (38 years old, a financial specialist) recounted a similar experience from this period: she was uncertain whether to wear a mask to go to the shop, and only in therapy was she able to say that she was less afraid of infection than of the judgment of others (see Diary, March/April 2020 – Scapegoating). The experience they both had signaled that in this period, when a threat had appeared in the external world, at the same time as uncertainty in the *me*, the effect of the *we* had also gained power. In this turbulent world, the *me* tries to orientate itself: How does the majority behave? It also tries to feel the pressure of the *we*: it is now more difficult to think and behave as an individual, and the space of individual considerations shrinks. For Eszter, a third-generation Holocaust survivor, the real threat was not the virus, but that she doesn't blend in, that they notice her. The desire to merge, not to stand out, partly reflects the relationship of *me* and the *we* in the pandemic *here-and-now*: in the critical situation affecting the whole of society, the effect of the *we* grows stronger. But it also signals a growth of the power of the past, of the Transgenerational Atmosphere: a decision to be made in the current situation (should I wear a mask or not) projects the grandparents' mostly untold dilemma, the experience of the Holocaust, onto the present. Through this, the weight of the current decision becomes disproportionate: for Eszter, making the right decision is almost a question of life and death.

We created the concept of Atmosphere as a development of the notion of Transgenerational Atmosphere. The Atmosphere describes far more generally the relationship between the self and the other, subject (*me*) and intersubject (*we*), the non-verbal (non-symbolic, or rather pre-symbolic) transmission of emotions. We envisage the genesis of the Atmosphere as a psychological space to be similar to that of the Transgenerational Atmosphere, inasmuch as it is based on a loosening of the boundaries of the self. This thinning of the boundary between the self and the other is what enables a shared intersubjective field, the Atmosphere, to come into being. However, one essential difference in comparison to the Transgenerational Atmosphere is that we see the Atmosphere as a damaged psychological field arising not only as the result of trauma. Indeed, we posit that the Atmosphere is a constantly present psychological vehicle, both surrounding and simultaneously penetrating the self, an intersubjective "container" full of emotions and thought contents. In this sense, the Atmosphere is the intersubjective community, the psychological field of the *we*, which carries the past of the *we* (memories, values, collective fantasies), and also it is generated over and again in the *here-and-now* through the constant changing interaction of the *me* and the *we*. In this reading, the Atmosphere has healthy vital functions for the individual: it helps to translate the reality of the external world for the *me*, by dreaming a mass experience in the Bionian sense (see also Transformation in the Atmosphere and The *We* Reality), the *we* reality, or it helps to temporarily contain and transform traumatic experiences that exceed the individual's capacity for symbolization and overwhelm them (Bakó & Zana, 2021b, 518). When we think of the Atmosphere as a field, we base this on many broadly familiar concepts and theories, such as Bion's concept of the protomental matrix (Bion, 1962a, 62–63, 87; Vermote, 2019, 65), the idea of field from post-Bionian field theory (Baranger & Barager, 2008, 796–799; Ferro, 2006; Vermote, 2019, 112–113), and the concept of transitional space or the analytical third (Winnicott, 1953, 1971; Ogden, 1985, 1994; Green, 1997, 1072–1073; Vermote, 2019, 85–87). Green (1997, 1073) writes:

> Let us remember, the transitional space is not just "in between"; it is a space where the future subject is in transit, a transit in which he takes possession of a created object in the vicinity of a real external one, before he has reached it.

Similarly to Green's approach, the Atmosphere is not merely an in-between space, but a psychological space with its own character (Ferro, 1992; Ferro & Foresti, 2008; Civitarese, 2013), the reality of which is essentially different from the psychological reality of the individuals who create it. It is an unconscious (or rather pre-symbolic) emotional field filled with feelings and sensations, which is capable of dreaming, and in which new (psychological) contents are being formed. In a Bionian approach, the field or matrix (1962a, 62–63, 87) is filled mainly with unconscious or undifferentiated contents: "To Bion this field, which he also called 'the protomental matrix,' is a zone where soma and psyche are not yet differentiated, but where there are constellations of undifferentiated thoughts and feelings that coexist and shift" (Vermote, 2019, 56). The bipersonal field has similar characteristics: "The concept of the field represents a notable expansion of that of the relationship in that many facts can be considered free-floating, unsaturated, waiting to be identified and not yet conveyable within the relation" (Ferro, 1992, 56).

The Atmosphere resembles the matrix and the field inasmuch as it contains the undifferentiated, free-floating, unidentified contents of the group (the *we*) (Vermote, 2019, 56; Ferro, 1992, 56), but as we shall later see, it also has a transforming function (see Transformation in the Atmosphere). The most essential difference between the concepts is perhaps that while in the preceding theories the field was created mainly to designate bipersonal situations (the analytical situation), the Atmosphere is an attempt to describe the psychological space of a much broader group, the intersubjective community, and the particularities of its workings, and relationship with the individual (with the individual's psychological space).

Me *and* We, *and Their Mutual Interaction in the Atmosphere*

While in this current book and our other published articles (Bakó & Zana, 2021b, 519–520) by *me*, we intend the subject; for the group, the intersubjective community, we usually use the expression *we*. This indicates our desire to emphasize collective processes, and processes of the collective or social unconscious (Lawrence, 2005, 68–69). Baranger and Baranger (2008) write that the group is not the sum of its members:

> Up to now, we have simply affirmed that a melody is not the sum of the notes or that a group is not the sum of its members; in other words, we are emphasizing the existence of a "gestalt" in the analytic situation and we define this gestalt as our specific field of work.
>
> (2008, 807)

Similarly to the way Civitarese uses the concepts of the intersubjective or the transcendental intersubjective community (in press), we envisage the group in the broad sense, the *we*, not simply as the origin of *me* experiences, but as a functional unity independent of these experiences (Tubert-Oklander, 2007, 115; Baranger & Baranger, 2008, 807; González, 2020a, 383–389; Civitarese, 2021b, 8; Bakó & Zana, 2021b, 519–520). *Me* and *we*, subject and intersubject, entities inconceivable the one without the other, are in constant interaction, shaping one another: "*I* that is *we* and *we* that is *I*" (Hegel, 1807, 108, quoted by Civitarese, 2021b, 11). González (2020a) writes:

> Subjectivity is inter-subjectivity in a radical way that extends beyond a singular one and singular other to pluralities of differences. We are both

particles and waves; our subjectivity has a double provenance. This makes subjectivity inherently dynamic, inherently unstable, inherently dependent on groups of others, just as groups of others depend on the individuals that comprise them.

(383)

Neither of them came first. They develop simultaneously, building on one another. They are two sides of the same coin (Fonagy & Target, 2007, 919; Civitarese, 2021b, 9).

One human mind cannot be understood independent of another: "The human mind is, then, no longer considered independent and isolated. . . . Instead, we find ourselves constantly in dialogue with other subjects and their consciousnesses, and our mental life is 'co-created'" (Bohleber, 2010, 7). In an even broader context, the personal history and past of the *me* cannot be separated from the processes underway in the present and past in the community of humans, the *we*, from social processes or from History with a capital H:

> The collective implies n-dimensionality, a relationship of one-to-many, where many can extend even to the plane of history. . . . distinction between the capital-H History of mass forces versus the small-h history of the individual is a heuristic contrivance, since individuals are necessarily embedded in groups whose histories are Histories.
>
> (González, 2020a, 397)

Going even further, even individual unconscious processes cannot be understood independent of collective unconscious processes. The personal and the collective unconscious are inseparable (González, 2020a, 390–391).

When interpreting individual psychological process, we cannot ignore the collective aspect of the *me*, the subject:

> A description of individual psychic life must include its collective aspect, the one-to-many object relation. This collective thread within the individual has a dual nature: both promoting a sense of coherence, perdurability, or consistency within the subject (who I tend "to be" when I am in any group) as well as a sense of multiplicity, instability, and inconsistency (how I am a "different person" in different groups).
>
> (González, 2020a, 393)

This approach has an important consequence for therapy: traditionally, the psychoanalytic process emphasizes the patient's important relationships, particularly early relationships, and focusing on the therapy relationship seeks manifestations of this in transference and countertransference, or in the function of the jointly created intersubjective Third.

Our theory of the Atmosphere expands the concept of intersubjectivity in the therapy context too, assuming that within the field created by two individuals, or in the Third, in every case the intersubjective community in the broad sense is also represented.

Our theory considers the individual as part of the group, the *we*, and when interpreting individual unconscious processes, takes into consideration (1) the events of the past – history with a capital H, in which we see condensed and manifest in unique patters the history of humanity, the history of a given ethnic group, and the history of the patient's family; (2) the events of the present, that is, the social context; and (3) the collective or social unconscious processes characteristic of the *here-and-now* (Benjamin, 2004, 13; Gerson, 2009, 1342–1343; Benjamin, 2011, 35; González, 2020a, 397; González, 2020b, 430; Peltz, 2020, 420).

The *me* and the *we*, the individual and the collective community in the broad sense, form an inseparable unit which are continually interacting (Peltz, 2020, 420): the *we* is always present in the *me*, and the *me* in the *we*. The collective or intersubjective dimension of the subject, the "groupal dimension of individual subjectivity" (Peltz, 2020, 422) is an aspect of human existence which cannot, or only to a limited extent, be understood with a human (i.e., subjective) mind, and is rather a question of experience: it can be felt in a deeply defining, transcendental experience that in some form touches almost every human (such as the experience of God, the oceanic feeling, or existential anxiety, which also haunts every person). " 'Who are we' and 'if this is us, then who am I' (385–386), are large questions, generating large anxieties at the level of what Durban (2017) calls 'anxieties of being,' " writes Peltz (2020, 421).

"Who am I?" is a question to which only God, as a metaphor for the collective consciousness or collective self, has an answer: "I am who I am" (ehyeh-asher-ehyeh, Exodus 3:14). For the subject, the *me* existing in the *we*, this question is impossible to answer, since it is unable to define itself independent of the *we*, the continuously varying "eternal" and "infinite" intersubjective community, beyond the scale of human comprehensibility, a *we* whose presence it senses (experiences) but to which, like the God of the Old Testament, it is unable to give a name. It cannot, because from the subject's perspective it has no word for it, that is, at least on the individual level, it remains unsymbolized content. Since the *me* is an entity which does not exist and cannot be understood *per se*, it is unable (at least as an independent being) to live the experience of existing, of "I am": this is represented for it by the *we*, the transcendental community, "God."

How the Atmosphere Works

In our approach, *me* (subject) and *we* (intersubject), the individual psychological space created by the *me* and the shared psychological field created by the *we* (the Atmosphere), are constructs that interact with one another in a mutual dialectic relationship. The constantly changing psychological realities of the multiple selves are continually shaping the psychological reality of the *we*, and the fluctuating *we* – through the shared psychological field of the Atmosphere – constantly affects the *me* as the individual experiences and perceives the external world in the *here-and-now*.

For a mature personality, a *me* with stable self-boundaries, it usually takes a long time, a process of symbolization, for their opinion of something to change radically. The *we* (as we all experience in the *here-and-now*) can change both more rapidly and more radically, particularly in stress situations, for instance, under the effect of mass trauma. Sometimes the radical change of the *we* may seem incomprehensible and unpredictable, either seen from the perspective of historical processes or observing events in the *here-and-now*: for example, when a social attitude toward refugees changes relatively quickly from acceptance and solidarity to a very different, excluding, aggressive collective mood – so the Atmosphere, the climate of the shared psychological field changes: but why and how (Bakó & Zana, 2021b, 520)? The new, sometimes radically new, reality transmitted by the external world, the "collective mood," affects the individual, often placing great pressure on them. The individual's attitude (in the case of a mature personality) changes more slowly and thoughtfully. What does the individual do with a collective mood, or, to use a Bionian expression, a group mentality, different to their own? In Bion's interpretation, the group mentality can be considered a form of intercommunication between the individual and the group whose purpose is for members of the group to live according to basic assumptions; in other words, the individual submits to the will of the group: "Group mentality [. . . is . . .] defined as 'a machinery of intercommunication that is designed to ensure that group life is in accordance with basic assumptions" (Bion, 1961, 65, cited in Vermote, 2019, 55). The basic assumption also has a considerable protective, supportive role: "If anything, once the group has also created a structure of rationality, the two can work as a pair and thus respond flexibly to stimuli" (Civitarese, 2021b, 11). The group mentality, which deeply influences and determines the group's emotional and mental state, leaves little room for individual opinions and emotional states that are out of line (Vermote, 2019, 51).

Although the collective mood always affects everybody, in "peacetime" (when the *me* is strong enough and when the *we* is tolerant and accepting), the healthy *me* has enough space to experience individual feelings and develop its own ideas (Volkan, 2009, 206). However, when the individual is overburdened (for instance, in the case of crisis or trauma), s/he is unable alone to give meaning to events in the outer world and s/he turns to the intersubjective community:

> [W]hen the capacity of the internal group is overwhelmed, then it is necessary to get in touch with another mind (or several minds) to be able to perform the same task of giving personal meaning to experience.

Since each person "wears" a public identity or "mask" (in Latin, "persona" is "mask"), which is constantly negotiated within the social sphere, this meaning will always be not only personal, but also "impersonal," i.e. always political by nature (Esposito, 2015).

(Civitarese, 2021b, 9)

Many thinkers, artists, and scholars have made and still are making attempts to understand how destructive ideologies, such as fascism, extreme nationalism, or racism, managed and manage to become so successful, influencing the emotions of masses, and mobilizing them so rapidly. Currently, we are collectively experiencing how extreme views and dispositions are overwhelming many people: a profusion of collective fantasies is attached to the Virus and the Vaccine, and extreme emotions activate masses of people, giving rise to uncontrolled fear and aggression (Bakó & Zana, 2021b, 520).

But what do we mean by *masses*, and how does this notion differ from the *we*? Le Bon (1913, 2014) writes:

From the psychological point of view the expression "crowd" assumes quite a different signification. Under certain given circumstances, and only under those circumstances, an agglomeration of men presents new characteristics very different from those of the individuals composing it. The sentiments and ideas of all the persons in the gathering take one and the same direction, and their conscious personality vanishes. A collective mind is formed.

(17)

Thus, in the crowd, the *me*, individual identity, is utterly lost. The individual merges into a shared identity of the large group (Volkan, 2009). Her intentions and considerations no longer reflect her own beliefs, but rather a shared conviction. Another important characteristic of the crowd as a construct is that it is born of the moment, of the *here-and-now*:

The psychological crowd is a provisional being formed of heterogeneous elements, which for a moment are combined, exactly as the cells which constitute a living body form by their reunion a new being which displays characteristics very different from those possessed by each of the cells singly.

(Le Bon, 1913, 2014, 20)

Similar to the *we*, or more precisely its psychological space, the Atmosphere, like Le Bon's definition of the crowd, partly (but only partly) has a transient, *here-and-now* aspect. This transience, the *here-and-now* aspect of the intersubjective construct, is expressed by Bohleber as follows:

The basic unit of this "intersubjective matrix," formed by an intersubjective consciousness, is the "present moment," which stages the intrapsychic event in which two subjects encounter each other . . ., both subjects simultaneously assimilate an experience, creating a temporal connection that makes them part of one and the same structure.

(2010, 7–8)

In our reading, Le Bon's crowd is a *we* that operates undifferentiatedly, whose psychological space is uncontrollably overwhelmed by destructive impulses.

But the feelings that overwhelm a crowd are not necessarily destructive. Merging into the crowd, into the *we*, can also be a positive, uplifting, euphoric experience, which the individual has in special moments, for instance, when merging into a crowd celebrating with joy, or mourning together, or having religious or spiritual experience. What the two experiences have in common is the *me*'s brief, temporary (thus highly ephemeral) but practically total merging into the *we*.

Perhaps it is worth drawing a distinction here between the contents conveyed by the psychological Atmosphere born of the crowd in the *here-and-now* and the intersubjective community (a *we* with the capacity to contain). While the Atmosphere created by the crowd is ephemeral, the *we*, the intersubjective community (or the transcendental intersubjective community, the Social) conveys fundamental assumptions, eternal and changing basic values, that support the *me* involved in the *we*: for instance, he can rely on aggression and destruction not being acceptable to the *we*, or in times of trouble or crisis that the environment will be empathic, supporting him, and not abandoning him. Of course, it also conveys the "approach" of the given era, the consensus of the age, which impinges upon everybody.

The *me*, the subject, is always dependent on the current *we*: the sensibilities and basic assumptions of a given age affect all of us. We suckle on it as on our mothers' milk: in other words, in the early relationship, through the mother we gain access to the intersubjective community, and its basic assumptions are incorporated into the *me*. These may later alter or be refined, but very few people are able to feel and think radically differently from the Atmosphere of a given historical era. Thus, while the Atmosphere of the crowd is ephemeral, the Atmosphere of the intersubjective community, the *we*, conveys values that are the foundation of human culture. In this approach, the crowd is a *we* that functions at a low level at a given historical moment. Serious crises of human society, wars and genocide, can be seen as times when universal human culture, the Atmosphere of the *we* conveying values, is overridden for a shorter or longer period by the tumultuous Atmosphere of a given historical moment.

Although this book focuses primarily on the relationship between the individual and the *we* in the broad sense, the intersubjective community, it is important to point out that the individual, the *me* is always part of multiple smaller groups, smaller *we*-s. There are groups that affect the *me* constantly, throughout life, such as the nation, an ethnic group, the family, or a religious community. Others become dominant in a certain phase of life, such as belonging to a group of fans in the teenage years, or later to a professional or political community. Yet other groups form for a very short time, and affect the individual temporarily and superficially (in terms of individual identity), such as a group that forms to go on holiday together. Other groups form temporarily, and affect the individual for a short time but in a deep and decisive manner, even changing the personality for a brief time, such as groups that demonstrate for a common cause, go on strike, help, fighters, comrades-in-arms.

Over a lifetime, the *me* is immersed sometimes superficially, sometimes deeply, and for varying lengths of time, in the identity of smaller groups that define him/her. The multiple *me*-s continually interacting dynamically and the small-group *we* together form the intersubjective *we* in the broad sense, which also continually influences them in turn. Their relationship is mutual and dynamic.

Ideology, Nation, and Leader

In common with many other author-psychoanalysts, we too are deeply concerned by the psychology of masses, how ideologies leading to serious exclusion or genocide (such as Nazism or terrorism) spread like wildfire and gain ground on a historical scale; and the question of how the leader emerges from the masses to direct them, even manipulating them to the extreme. Integrating the ideas of previous authors into our model, we have tried to address these age-old questions from a slightly different perspective.

As a theoretical framework, the Atmosphere and the perverted Atmosphere may go some way toward explaining the dilemma that so many have tried to understand with varying degrees of success: how extreme ideologies such as fascism are able to mobilize masses of people with lightning speed, to draw them in and prompt them to action, as Wilhelm Reich poses a question in his book *The Mass Psychology of Fascism* (1980):

> In social psychology, the question is exactly the reverse: What is to be explained is not why the starving individual steals or why the exploited individual strikes, but why the majority of starving individuals do not steal and the majority of exploited individuals do not strike.
> (Reich, 1980, 15)

However, he fails to find a clear explanation: "For the irrational thinking and behavior of the masses which contradicts the existing socio-economic situation is itself the result of an earlier socio-economic situation. It has been customary to explain the inhibition of social consciousness by so-called tradition" (Reich, 1980, 16). Neither social nor economic reasons, nor even the personality of the leader, explain how the "mood, the psychic world" of the masses is able to change so quickly, apparently irrationally, and as a result the mass is able to mobilize. Like the psychoanalytic authors already referred to, and thinkers from allied disciplines, we view ideologies as intersubjective constructs. In the approach of many authors on the subject, ideologies are predominantly based on unconscious collective fantasies (Reich, 1980; Bohleber, 2010; Kogan, 2017; Ellman et al., 2017). Bohleber describes them as follows:

> The first of these fantasies is that of being the only one entitled to maternal care and affection; all rivals are eliminated. The second is the fantasy of participating in a state of ideal purity not disrupted by any form of otherness. The third is the fantasy of being part of an imagined organic whole, envisioned as the restoration of union with the maternal primary object, a fantasy whose purpose is to overcome a form of existence that is cut off and alienated.
>
> (Bohleber, 2010, xxii)

One important element of unconscious collective fantasies, and one on which extremist nationalism builds upon, is that the individual becomes part of an imaginary integral unit: "At the core of national identification lies spuriously omnipotent elation at being part of a greater whole" (Bohleber, 2010, 171). In our reading, this greater whole is the *we*, into which in extreme cases the *me* merges without discrimination, even at the price of forsaking its own values, or interests. In this approach, the concept of nation is likewise a collective construct, based on real and fictive elements but predominantly on unconscious collective fantasies:

> Modern research on nationalism provides significant support for this argument, describing nations as collective constructions strongly marked by phantasmal elements (Anderson, 1983). The idea of the nation is a compound of fact and fiction, thus providing rich scope for unconscious collective fantasies to intermingle with rational notions.
>
> (Bohleber, 2010, 157)

But how are these collective fantasies able to reach the *me*, involve it deeply, and mobilize it? In our approach it is the Atmosphere, the shared psychological field created by the *we*, that transmits these contents.

When this functions healthily, we can imagine the boundary between the *me* and the *we* as a semiporous membrane: the *me* appropriates features of the external reality, but filters out the crude contents alien to the self. In other words, the *we* does not override the values held by the *me*. And conversely, the *we* also allows itself to be formed by many diverse *me* experiences. The relationship between the two is flexible and dynamic. If the pathological functions become dominant (if both the *me* and the *we* are damaged), then the fantasies transmitted by the Atmosphere and the basic assumptions over-whelm the *me*, out-maneuvering its conscious control. This may explain the individual's subsequent astonishment and perplexity at their own behavior, which in many cases does not follow on from their previous life history or experience: "How could I possibly have believed that, or become a part of that?" Additionally, it may explain the psychology of self-sacrifice in revolutions, when the individual, in a manner that surprises even themselves, is capable of endangering or sacrificing their own life for the sake of a "greater cause."

> In a crowd every sentiment and act is contagious, and contagious to such a degree that an individual readily sacrifices his personal interest to the collective interest. This is an aptitude very contrary to his nature, and of which a man is scarcely capable, except when he makes part of a crowd.
> (Le Bon, 1913, 2014, 22)

How is it to be explained that some individuals are able to resist the pressure of the *we* even in particularly difficult cases, to safeguard their boundaries (their own opinions and convictions), and there are others who attune to the collective mood with almost startling rapidity?

For an immature personality (when the *me* is by definition weak, and the boundaries of the self are unstable), the *me* is more receptive to the feelings conveyed by the outer world, the current Atmosphere of the *we*, and more easily identifies with them. In the case of social traumas, when even a stable *me* is weakened, and in addition the containing and transforming functions of the *we* are damaged (see also Traumatic Space-Time, the Damage to the Boundaries of the Self in the Transgenerational Atmosphere), there is a particularly high chance that the Atmosphere, and a *me* immersed in the Atmosphere, will be overwhelmed by destructive contents. Through damage to the space-time construct, the undigested experience of the past, the Transgenerational Atmosphere, becomes more dominant and hampers or completely obstructs the individual in their attempts to orient themselves in sensations and values.

But what is the leader's role in this process? The selection of the leader is the result of a collective unconscious process:

> Leaders are chosen because they accord with the basic assumption of the group. According to Bion, the characteristic of a leader that accords with the basic assumptions is that he should possess "magical" qualities, which inspire awe, rather than proposing scientific solutions. In a basic assumption group "hatred of learning by experience" (Bion, 1961, 86) prevails.
> (Vermote, 2019, 58)

Often, it seems that in these critical historical situations, the individual becomes prone to identify with a leader of strong character. Many writers believe that even in this case we should speak of identification not with another individual, but rather with a collective fantasy that is embodied by the given individual: "It is not the leader himself but the group fantasy that replaces the individual ideal ego by a collective ideal ego, thus generating manic elation" (Bohleber, 2010, 172). In our approach, the *me*, the subject, comes under the effect not of another *me*, but (through the loosened boundaries of the self) of a striking character who stands out from the Atmosphere (the Leader), becomes dominant, and overwhelms the psychological space of the individual(s).

By virtue of its dual origins (González, 2020a, 393), the *me* (the subject) has impulses which are difficult to reconcile. On the one hand, it strives for independence, to be distinct from the other, from others ("who am I as a different person"), in other words, to create and support an independent mature self. However, the price of independence is to confront mortality – the individual's finiteness, temporality, and loss. When the capacity for bearing this exceeds the *me*'s processing ability (for instance, after an unprocessed personal or societal trauma or crisis), the other, the collective aspect of the *me*, may grow ("the collective thread within the individual" González, 2020a, 393): the desire to merge into a "greater whole," be it God, an idea, or a collective fantasy.

> Perhaps . . . the basic assumption ensures the individual's reimmersion in the "God," which, according to Husserl (Zahavi, 2001), is the community or transcendental intersubjective, which is not only intellectual or linguistic (spirit or "verb"), but also instinctual and carnal.
>
> (Civitarese, 2021b, 11)

In our model, we thus interpret mass processes, and identification with the leader, as the *me*'s need or impulse to immerse in and merge with the *we*. However, this process (the *me*'s immersion in the *we*) is far from being a feature only of pathological processes; as we shall see, it is the foundation of all development (at the individual and group levels) which makes humans human, a part of the human community, and possessors of human knowledge.

The Intersubjective Background to Sharing of Experience

But how is the *me* able to merge into the *we*? What is the role of this mechanism in personality development (Bakó & Zana, 2021b, 521–522)?

In order for the self to be able to merge, the boundaries of the *me*, or the self, need to be loosened.

> To make use of the other as an extension of self-experience, the other has to enter a dialectic as originally pointed out by Hegel (1979 [1807]) and emphasized by Winnicott (1956) and Fairbairn (1952), by temporarily abolishing the boundaries of the self in order for the other to find himself within.
>
> (Fonagy & Target, 2007, 923)

This process of loosening the boundaries of the self, the mind's ability to open up to another mind, is far from being pathological: in the light of modern intersubjective approaches, this process is the basis for all learning, related-ness, and the sharing of information: "[t]here is an interlocking of subjectivi-ties that is followed by an opening of the mind to gathering information and seeing something new" (Fonagy & Target, 2007, 920). The opening of the mind allows space not just for the sharing of information, but it is also the basis for regulating emotions: "We believe that the extension of consciousness beyond the child's body perhaps reflects the way infants come to be able to regulate their emotions (Gergely & Watson, 1996, 1999)." (Fonagy & Target, 2007, 923). Following up this idea, Trevarthen (2015) concludes that some-thing else is at work: connectedness in the intersubjective space has as its goal the shared giving of meaning:

> The function of interpersonal connectedness is, from infancy, more than brains being co-conscious of an external world, and more than emotional regulation of interpersonal states. It is actively aesthetic and moral in the internal purpose and feeling of each moving human body, and the infant is a wise, sensitive, and proud contributor to this sensibility and the meanings it gives to a shared reality.
>
> (Trevarthen, 2009, Trevarthen, 2015, 396)

Similarly to the way in which, thanks to the mind's ability to open up, in an early relationship potential space is generated, enabling the regulation of emotions, learning, connectedness, and shared giving of meaning (Winni-cott, 1953; Ogden, 1985), or in later therapeutic processes the third (Ogden, 1994; Green, 1997), so in the intersubjective space created by the group, the *we*, again, thanks simply to the mind's ability to open up, creates its own "third": the Atmosphere (Bakó & Zana, 2021b, 521–522).

Being with the other, as an ability and experience, is a basic human need, and it forms the foundation of all relationships, learning, regulation of emo-tions, and temporal continuity:

> [A] sense of being human can be organized through sharing with the other about how the person was born, and how he has been with the other, through an authentic and honest relationship with others, or through a hope of passing on something significant to the next genera-tion. I argue that these human processes serve to connect a person's sub-jective experience from the past with the present, from the present to the future, and to the experience of others in the present.
>
> (Togashi, 2014, 265)

It is while being together with connected minds that the infant learns how to regulate its emotions, and thus later to be able to fit into a community not just with and through its mother, but in its own right, thus joining the Social, the space of shared giving of meaning. Belonging to the Social, the intersubjective community, brings the promise not only of shared knowledge, but also that of protection: "Societies construct or propagate the relationship between Self and Other in various ways. In this, social agencies may draw upon notions of ideal states revolving around care, unity, and purity" (Bohleber, 2010, 177). The *me* receives and accepts the knowledge, the relationship to the world, offered by the intersubjective community, the *we*, and together with this, it lets in the collective fantasies and basic assumptions generated by the current *here-and-now*. It constantly adjusts and tunes its own *me*-experience in the light of changes in the "collective mood" transmitted by the *we*, the Atmosphere. As to when and to what extent the *me* is capable of maintaining and regaining its own boundaries, this, as we shall see in later chapters, is dependent on many factors.

The Dynamic Model of the Self

In this book, mainly inspired by our personal experience and our therapeutic practice during the time of COVID, we have developed the structure and function of earlier models (see Trauma and Self), and advance a model for the functioning of the self that departs slightly from the customary view. We consider the self to be a system, and we place the emphasis on the movement of this system, on its energetic components, the constant changes in the ordering ability, balance, and equilibrium of the self. We propose to view the *me* self as a field in which parts in dynamic interaction (the parts of the self) are constantly influencing one another, and which is constantly interacting with the intersubjective field, the *we*-self, which permeates it without and within.

Healthy Functioning of the Self

In our understanding of the function of both the healthy and the pathological self, we emphasize movement and interaction. Rather than the core self, we posit one or two dominant parts of the self. The dominant part(s) of the self form in a relatively early phase of development, and through life become decisive parts of the personality and identity. They continually influence the function of other parts of the self, and the dynamic between them. In normal cases, this influence is mutual, and the dominant parts of the self are also capable of change, of moving flexibly together with the other parts. The parts of the self have characters which are typical of them, and these become prevalent or weaker depending on whether the given part of the self is given greater or lesser emphasis. The more the characters have a role on the stage of the self, the more varied is the play (the character's scene and space for movement is larger), and the greater the chance that the self can react flexibly to an unexpected event (Ferro, 1992; Ferro & Foresti, 2008; Ferro,

2009; Civitarese, 2013). In this approach, by a healthy functioning of the self, we mean that there is contact between the various parts of the self, that they affect one another. There may be a difference in emphasis between them (depending on the phase of life or the life situation), but all parts of the self can have a role. After a shocking event, the inner equilibrium of the self is naturally upset, yet if it is functioning healthily, the self is able to regain its former equilibrium, and perhaps a new structure can be created that works better than the previous one.

If the self's functioning is pathological, it allows little room for maneuver to the individual parts of the self. The structure of the self becomes rigid and inflexible, and inhibiting processes are dominant within it. This may be the result of pathological development, but it can also be caused by a shocking event that is overwhelming. In our model, the traumatic effect can be seen as a disorder in the function of the field, a disorder in the movement of the interrelated parts of the self. It is damage to the ability to generate from the chaos a new flexible equilibrium based on mutuality, giving space to all the parts of the self. Chaos (in the psychological sense) cannot be endured for long. If it persists for an extended period, it may lead to complete collapse and even suicide, as in the case of Etelka (a 33-year-old teacher), whose defense mechanisms, which previously worked well, collapsed in the uncertainty of the pandemic, the previous rigid, but functional, equilibrium was upset. She saw no way out of the psychological chaos other than suicide (see Diary, January/February 2021 – The Vaccines Appear).

In every case the self strives to return to some order, but this does not necessarily mean inner, psychological freedom: a new state of equilibrium may be created, but at the price of some rigidity, or at the price of some parts of the self no longer having room for maneuver, and being excluded from the game (being split off). Maintaining a pathological equilibrium places a great burden on the *me*: it continually has to ensure that the split-off parts of the self remain split off, since this is the foundation of the delicate equilibrium. The motion of the parts of the self cannot adapt flexibly to the *here-and-now*. The focus is on maintaining the inner, rigid equilibrium, such as in the case of Mária (a 35-year-old sociologist) who stayed cooped up with her family for almost a year and a half (see Diary, January/February 2021 – The Vaccines Appear). The external world, the *here-and-now* reality, changes, but in vain: Mária is incapable of flexible change, and remains stuck in a previous safe place.

INTERACTION BETWEEN THE *ME*-SELF AND THE *WE*-SELF

As we saw earlier, the identity of the individual, the subject, cannot be understood independent of the social and historical context. The given culture, social order, ideological influences into which the individual is born and in which she lives, unconsciously define and pass on the way that the *me* relates to basic social issues, situations, and hierarchies; in other words, they influence and shape her identity to the end of her life. As Layton puts it:

> To better understand the regressive and foreclosing use of identity categories, I have elaborated a concept I refer to as normative unconscious processes (Layton, 2002, 2004a, 2004b, 2005, 2006). With this term, I refer to the psychological consequences of living in a culture in which many norms serve the dominant ideological purpose of maintaining a power status quo. More particularly, I have investigated the consequences of living within particular class, race, sex, and gender hierarchies. My assumption is that these hierarchies, which confer power and exist for the benefit of those with power, tend not only to idealize certain subject positions and devalue others, but tend to do so by splitting human capacities and attributes and giving them class or race or gender assignations.
>
> (Layton, 2006, 239–240)

Thus, the workings of the individual or *me*-self cannot be understood or interpreted independent of the function of the *we*-self to which it is linked. The healthy *me*-self is in harmony with its environment (in the psychological sense), with the *we*-self.

It allows in experiences and the *we*-self, but they are filtered through the personality as through a semiporous membrane. At the same time, it emits contents – sensations, ideas, opinions, judgments, which influence the working of the *we*-self. In this approach, the (*me*-)self is always a function of the *we*-self. The individual, the *me*-self, may be capable of integrating self-parts from the *we*-self (self-deposits, to use Volkan's expression, Volkan, 2013, 233), and with them feelings, images, collective fantasies, temporarily with "discriminations," though in extreme cases just as they are, and integrating them as its own. In the case of extreme shock or trauma, due to the increased permeability of the boundaries of the self, there is a greater chance of this "borrowing": many individuals may go through a similar experience or feeling previously alien to the *me*: this may be destructive or constructive. At the same time, the unpredictable mutual influence of the individual self-experiences, which are in dynamic interaction, continuously changes the *we*-self: certain parts of the self, certain characters, may grow stronger in the intersubjective field (the Atmosphere) and may come to dominate it.

Although this book focuses primarily on the relationship between the individual and the *we* in the broad sense (the intersubjective community), it is important to emphasize that the individual, the *me*, is always part of multiple smaller groups, smaller *we*-s. Over a lifetime, the *me* is immersed sometimes superficially, sometimes deeply, and for varying lengths of time, in the identity of smaller groups that define him/her. The individual is part of multiple *we*-s; many realities exist for him/her. Ideally, these are compatible, or at least there is no long-lasting irresolvable conflict of interest between them.

The multiple *me*-s continually interacting dynamically and the small-group *me*-s together form the intersubjective *we* in the broad sense, which also continually influences them in turn. Their relationship is mutual and dynamic (Bakó & Zana, 2022, in press).

The Atmosphere and the Collective Unconscious

The concept of the so-called collective unconscious (also known as the transindividual, the social, or the family unconscious), collective memory, and collective fantasies has from the outset fascinated psychoanalysts, and many models have been put forward to help understand the phenomenon (to mention just a few: Freud, 1913; Jung, 1915; Szondi, [1937], 1992, 1996; Abraham & Torok, 1984; Layton, 2006; Tubert-Oklander, 2006; Gerson, 2009; Bohleber, 2010; Benjamin, 2011; Ellman et al., 2017; González, 2020a).

How can we understand the collective unconscious within the theoretical framework of the Atmosphere? In our approach, the Atmosphere is capable of unconscious transformation (see later Transformation in the Atmosphere), that is, it is capable in the Bionian sense of dreaming and containing the experiences of the present and past, thus including collective memories and fantasies of the collective unconscious. We can thus define the collective unconscious as origin of the unconscious transforming function of the collective (the *we*). When we consider the unconscious function of the Atmosphere, we use the definition of the unconscious from Bionian Field Theory; in other words, we consider the unconscious not in the classic sense as repressed contents, but as the origin of the intersubjective transformation process (Ferro, 2011, 91). In this approach, we consider the collective unconscious as an intersubjective field, as a dream of the Atmosphere (Ferro, 2011, 91; Vermote, 2019, 112–113).

Márta (a 23-year-old catering industry worker) was very uncertain about what would be safe at Christmas. The change of setting called forth uncertainty: the room she fantasized about, which at first was large and empty, had by the next session become full of furniture, with darkness and gloom, and on the wall, as on a screen, an old film begins to play out (perhaps from deep in the unconscious). It is frightening, because it is not the *here-and-now* reality; it reflects a distorted, alien reality. The other (the therapist) becomes alien, and she herself is alien (see Diary November/December 2020 – Numbers on the Rise). In therapy, Márta's uncanny experience, beyond its personal link to her, also reflects the *here-and-now* experience of the *we*: Christmas draws near, but there is a shadow of fear and uncertainty over the festivities, and the shared unconscious projects images onto the present which are both familiar and unfamiliar: the uncanny. Another important aspect of the "collective unconscious" is the remembering function. In this sense, the collective unconscious is the sum of the non-verbal experiences and memories of the past. However, in our approach, we are dealing not primarily with unconscious contents in the classical sense, but rather with the sum of unsymbolized and pre-symbolic memories. In this approach, the Atmosphere helps us to understand remembrance and transmission: the Atmosphere is the intersubjective field that creates the opportunities for collective unconscious (or rather pre-symbolic) memories to be preserved and passed on to heirs (Bakó & Zana, 2021b, 523–524).

The Healthy Functioning of the Atmosphere

The function of the *we* and of the psychological space it creates, the Atmosphere, harbors not only danger for the *me*. The only way to understand the *me*, the subject, is as embedded in the *we*, even in the case of a healthily functioning *me*. The psychic processes in the individual cannot be understood independent of this psychological vehicle, the Atmosphere of the *here-and-now*, in which they are embedded and operate. In this way, the Atmosphere can be seen as a vehicle for transmission of universal knowledge: it can convey not only knowledge of the *here-and-now*, but also universal knowledge created in the past (by knowledge we mean here not knowledge acquired by learning, but the non-verbal experiential matter conveyed by humanity, implicit knowledge). Extending this idea, the Atmosphere can convey not only the knowledge of many generations, but even the prehistoric experiences of humanity (pre-verbality, pre-symbolic domains). These deep visceral experiences are conveyed in the deeper strata of the Atmosphere: in ordinary situations, the Atmosphere is shaped by the *here-and-now*, but in serious mass trauma it may invoke the experiences and reactions not only of past historical eras, but even of prehistorical times (Bakó & Zana, 2021b, 522–523).

In times of trauma, the role of the Atmosphere is greater. As we wrote in detail in the section *Trauma*, when an experience is too powerful, overwhelming, there is damage to the *me*'s ability to contain the overwhelming feelings, and to transform the outer reality into an integrated inner psychological reality. Serious trauma may lead to the disintegration of the personality, as the *me* plunges into an unstructured psychological state. Twenty-three-year-old Márta (see Diary, May/August 2020 – Conspiracy Theories Abound, and Trauma and Temporality), who in the first phase of the pandemic was overwhelmed and paralyzed by a series of losses (mourning, splitting up from a partner, being cooped up, a lack of personal contact) and the related feelings (helplessness, loneliness, emptiness), desperately tried to free herself from this state of deep suffering, while she also lost her ability to perceive time. When Márta says, "As if life had stood still everywhere," she expresses not only the disintegration of temporality, but another related deeply upsetting experience, which is difficult to put into words: the disintegration of the self, the personality (Bakó & Zana, 2021b, 524). In this uncontained, structureless existence, in which even the experience of time is damaged (Priel, 1997, 439), the *me* tries to rely on the Atmosphere, temporarily borrowing its function of regulating emotions, its containing capacity, or even its transforming function, in a similar manner to the infant who initially uses the containing and transforming functions of the mother. The above process of giving greater access to the *we*, the Atmosphere, is made possible by an intrinsically traumatic experience: even in the case of a mature personality, the effect of serious trauma may be to weaken the boundaries of the self, making them temporarily porous: "In the traumatic situation, the person affected can often no longer maintain the boundaries between himself and the other" (Bohleber, 2010, 119). With greater porosity of the boundaries of the self, the individual shows much less discrimination in allowing experiences from the external world to enter, or to put it another way, the *me* is less able to distinguish itself from the Other, from the psychic contents transmitted by the Atmosphere. In this approach, the trauma takes the *me* back to a psychological state similar to the early relationship: because the boundaries of the self are weaker, the mind is once more inclined to open up, to allow in the Other (Bakó & Zana, 2021b, 524–525). This mechanism explains not only the harmful consequences of trauma, but the growth that takes place through trauma: with a more open state of mind than usual, there may be an opportunity to reevaluate ordinary things.

In the first lockdown, Sára (a 36-year-old chemist) is surprised to notice that for her, social life is a burden, and she feels good keeping to the compulsory social distancing (see Diary, March/April 2021 – The Third Wave). Ottó (45 year old, a chemist) tells of a similar experience: during the lockdown, he realized with a shock that he is basically introverted, and the pandemic helped him to "find the way back to the real me" (see Diary, September/October 2020 – Decisions). Anna (a 32-year old interior designer) is bringing up a small child alone. In the first lockdown period, she was very careful. In the second, when the actual threat is much greater, she is less cautious (see Diary, September/October 2020 – Decisions). Having lost her ability to orientate and interpret events in the outer world ("how big a problem is it really?"), she relies more than usual on the role of the *we* in reflecting the outer world.

In healthy cases, the relationship between *me* and *we* is flexible: a weakened *me* is able to temporarily rely on the *we* and merge with it (in other words, to rely on the supporting strength of the community), and then, having gained strength, it regains its own ability for containment and processing, and restores its boundaries. In a well-functioning milieu, a good enough *we* can allow the *me* to become distant, and it is also flexible in the sense of being able to contain many differing *me*-experiences, even with extreme individual emotions and moods. The *me* and the *we* are thus in a mutual, dynamically changing relationship, sometimes clearly distinct (the *me* as a sovereign being), and sometimes intermerging (*me* as a part of the Other, the community). In the case of mass trauma, when not just the individual or a small group of trauma victims are affected, but also the vast majority of those individuals forming the *we*, the Atmosphere can be life-saving: it helps to contain experiences that are too powerful for the individual, and also, when the symbolizing function is temporarily damaged by the trauma, it can help in transforming the experience.

Transformation in the Atmosphere

A peculiar feature of the human mind is the desire to interpret events in the external and internal worlds, through which events in the outer and inner worlds gain meaning. The *me* translates and transforms the facts of the external world, outer events (the so-called beta elements) into an inner, psychological reality. For this, it uses its transforming (Ferro & Civitarese) ability or its dreaming (Ogden, Grotstein, Cassorla) ability (Lőrincz et al., 2019, 205). "Dream thinking is the predominantly unconscious psychological work that we do in the course of dreaming." "In dream thinking, we view our lived experience from a multiplicity of vantage points simultaneously, which allows us to enter into a rich, nonlinear set of unconscious conversations with ourselves about our lived experience" (Ogden, 2010, 328). The external reality can become an integrable internal psychic reality if it goes through the process of symbolization. In the early relationship, it is the parent who first lends the containing and transforming capacity to the infant, but as life goes on, later the child will also need an *Other* (be it a family member, friend, or therapist) who helps to make digestible what was for the individual "too much," having exceeded his/her processing capacity – such as a traumatic experience (Bakó & Zana, in press). In this model of the Atmosphere, we assume that a properly functioning *we* has at its disposal an unconscious transforming, dreaming capacity. In other words, the *we* is constantly translating and interpreting the events of the outer world in the *here-and-now*; to use a Bionian expression, it "dreams" the intersubjective community, the psychological reality of the *we*. The constantly fluctuating *we* reality affects the individual's inner reality – in the best-case scenario, fine-tuning it rather than overriding it. In the case of trauma, the *we* can have a function similar to the parent in an early relationship: the Atmosphere (as a psychological field) is able to transmit, to lend containing symbolic capacity to the damaged, weakened *me*. Just as in therapy, the jointly created field or third dreams a reality to which the patient is receptive (Ferro & Civitarese, 2016; Ferro, 2009, 219; Ferro, 2015, 522; Lőrincz et al., 2019, 217; Vermote, 2019, 82–85); thus, the Atmosphere, the intersubjective field created by the *we*, is able to "dream" a reality that is for the large majority of individuals an integrated psychic reality – in other words, it allows space for many different individual realities (see later The Trauma of Reality). However, in the case of serious trauma, the magic thinking may become dominant, and the *me*, losing its relationship to the reality of the outer world, starts to operate and act according to its own inner logic:

"Such 'thinking' has no traction in the real world that exists outside of one's mind" (Ogden, 2010, 322).

In winter 2020, in the period before the Christmas holiday season, Hungary is in the second wave of the pandemic. The number of those falling ill is on the increase, but fears and caution are overridden by the pre-Christmas mood. Klára (a 45-year-old photographer) is basically cautious, and in retrospect she doesn't understand how she can have been so irresponsible as to go to a series of department stores when they are so crowded. The familiar caution, anxiety, and fears have temporarily disappeared, and she and her partner relaxed together in the pre-Christmas shopping fever (see Diary, November/December 2020 – Numbers on the Rise). The weakened *me* temporarily loses its ability to orientate itself, including its ability to transform the events of the external world into a coherent internal reality. In the vignette provided herein, a couple exhausted by constant anxiety, readiness, and the monitoring of the external world, temporarily allow in the *we* reality and, unconsciously forgetting their own anxieties, they dissolve in the present Atmosphere (Bakó & Zana, 2021b, 525–528).

The Dream of the Atmosphere

One form of transformation, of dreaming, is the nocturnal dream. But who is the dreamer, and whose dream are they dreaming? Or as Civitarese puts it: "[b]ut when the noise of concrete reality is deafening, who is the author of the dream and what is the dream about?" (Civitarese, 2021a, 134).

In the first phase of the pandemic, a startlingly similar image appears in the dream of two patients: the relatively calm and peaceful everyday world (a gathering in a garden or a stroll in the hills) is interrupted by a threat coming unexpectedly from the sky, the image of a nose-diving aircraft (see Diary, March/April 2020 – Scapegoating). Particularly interesting in these two dreams is that two patients with different individual and family backgrounds portray the horror with a similar symbol: aircraft plummeting from the sky. Since 9/11, aircraft have become a shared unconscious symbol of unpredictable, senseless, and incomprehensible terror. The two dreams have in common not only the symbol that portrays the danger, the unexpected terror, but there is also another shared feeling dominating the dream: that of being left alone. The two vignettes are good examples of how in group trauma, individual experience, the reality of the *me* and the reality of the community, the *we*, the reality of the present and of the past, are deeply interwoven. Both dreams characterize the dreamer, mirroring his/her own individual subjective present and past inner reality, but these dreams also reflect the *here-and-now* reality of the Atmosphere, the "group-as-a-whole," and open a window to the social unconscious (Lawrence, 2005, 67–69; Bermudez, 2018, 538, 647–648). These dreams can also be seen as a form of social or "moral witnessing" (Bermudez, 2018, 551–553). They also provide an example of the dreaming, transforming function of the *we*, as a previous shared collective trauma becomes a shared metaphor in a subsequent traumatic situation, helping to contain and transform the traumatic experience (embodying it in images and words). Both dreams have the terror of an unavoidable threat and the feeling of experiencing the trauma alone. However, this is no longer a crude sensation, but a more symbolized, narratable terror that can be shared. In the two nocturnal dreams, there also appears the dreaming function of the intersubjective field: the dreams unconsciously use shared images, metaphors, which symbolize for the intersubjective community in the broad sense the deepest level of horror and human terror, similar to the Holocaust, for instance, when the unthinkable has happened (Goodman & Meyers, 2012; Peltz, 2020, 421).

Mária (a 35-year-old sociologist) had a dream (see Diary, January/February 2021 – The Vaccines Appear) in which the reality of the external world (lockdown restrictions) appeared as a space journey lasting many long years. Although space travel was not a prison (something that had appeared in a previous dream) and there were things to make alleviate the hardship (such as Wi-Fi), it meant relinquishing a great many things, and much loss: while she was shut away, the child "grows up" and valuable years were "lost." The dream is highly illustrative not only of Mária's inner reality, but also of the current reality of the external world, of the *we*: the sense of hopelessness, loneliness, being shut away, and timelessness. "I can't stand it that long," she said, expressing the *then-and-there* feeling shared by many. While the opportunities are limitless (many vaccines have appeared in the external world, in the dream she can travel to the Sun, and there is Wi-Fi en route), yet these represent not opportunities, but deep, timeless loneliness, and being restricted. The fireworks image from a much later dream of Mária's, from December 2021, is a particularly good example of how the dream of the *me* and the *we* are interwoven (see Diary, Closing Image – How Will the Fireworks End?) Mária's experience (the fireworks were set off, and people looked on, either as adults or changing into small children from one moment to the next, to see how things would end) encapsulates the deepest questions and fears of every individual and of the totality of humanity. It depicts uncertainty about the future: What does the future hold for me, and for humanity? It contains the personal experience of the past: the experiences of birth, separation, and merging. But there is also the history, the past of the *we*, of humanity: vulnerability to natural and non-natural disasters, and the desire to merge into something greater that gives security. And finally, it contains the *we*'s dream about the present, the *here-and-now*: we sense that the world changes, but we do not know what this change brings for us. Sometimes we watch the fireworks as adults, sometimes we tremble like children. As Mária crouches down in her dream, she becomes smaller in terms of years too, and finally she is reassured in her father's arms. This depicts not only the regression of the individual, but also how during mass traumas the whole of humanity is overwhelmed by archaic experiences: uncontrollable fear of ultimate destruction, and also a desire to merge together, the *me*'s desire to unify with the *we*, which helps it to bear the unbearable.

In Eszter's dream (a 38-year-old financial specialist), a dog undergoes a transformation. From afar, the dog is friendly, but close up it is frightening and threatening: it has been infected and is now infectious (see Diary, March/April 2020 – Scapegoating). The dream also includes the Holocaust story of Eszter's family, the Transgenerational Atmosphere, but this is also the dream of the *we*: the invisible, ubiquitous virus, the sense that we cannot believe our eyes, or trust our senses: an Other who seems full of life might actually carry a threat, a mortal danger.

In one of Eszter's later dreams (see Diary, March/April 2021 – The Third Wave), she fights a fearsome, invisible power in a dictatorship. She tries to save somebody, but she too is lost. In addition to the personal threads, this dream too has an intimation of the reality of the present, the *then-and-there* world, the dream of the *we*: exclusion and the fear of being excluded, self-sacrifice, and the fear of self-sacrifice. A little later, at the end of April 2021, in Eszter's dream (see Diary, Late April/Early May 2021 – A New Reopening Begins), the dilemma of saving versus fear that appears in Eszter's dictatorship dream recurs: if I help the other, I might put myself in danger. The character of the dog, similar to the dog in Eszter's earlier dream, threatens to change: if I set it free (if it breaks free), the small dog may change into a monster. The monster, which might escape from the bottle at any time, conveys not only Eszter's own feelings (aggression), but is present in the dream of the *we*, the Atmosphere of the present: the uncontrollable tension and aggression is increasingly overwhelming and gives less and less space to fears or to empathy (the yelping of the little dog is drowned out by the howling of the monster) (Bakó & Zana, 2022).

Attila's (36-year-old photoreporter) dream conjures up the mood and internal world of Eszter's dictatorship dream, and was generated in the same period. It portrays a post-apocalyptical world, in which humanity has experienced war, the invasion of the "aliens," and something has changed irrevocably (see Diary, Late April/Early May 2021 – A New Reopening Begins). In addition to his own helplessness and clumsiness, Attila dreams the dream of the *we*: it is increasingly difficult to contain the prolonged uncertainty and threat, the *we*'s symbolizing, transforming ability is reduced, and the floundering *me* is threatened with immersion in feelings transmitted by the mass, the crowd, by the loss of *self*: "I'm not a photographer any more, but a civilian, just one in a helpless crowd."

In early development, the infant enters the domain of the symbolic order aided by the "third" (the symbolic father), language, and the intersubjective community. But this entails loss: it loses its relationship with the (symbolic) mother, who for it represents being-at-oneness, infinity, and timelessness.

A third is needed to get the baby out of this functioning and inscribe him in a symbolic register so that thinking and communicating with others becomes possible. This symbolic register is a language which is already there and consists of signifiers. . . . Entrance to the symbolic order introduces a lack. This lack opens the closed dual world with the mother. . . . Once in the register of the symbolic order, the child loses his immediate contact with the mother. This lack is translated into a desire, a moving force between human beings.

(Vermote, 2019, 26)

When, for instance in the case of serious trauma, the *me* is immersed in the *we*, only the reverse process takes place: it experiences oneness with the symbolic mother (with the *we*), it experiences timelessness and infiniteness – and in exchange it loses its relationship to the symbolic domain, to its own identity separate from others.

The Pre-symbolic Aspect of How the Atmosphere Works

We work on the assumption that operating in the Atmosphere, there are not only dreaming functions, but also early transforming functions, which are pre-symbolic, pre-verbal, or pre-representational. The two kinds of transforming function (symbolic and pre-symbolic) probably work in parallel, albeit one or the other may be prevalent at any one time. We assume that the world of the Atmosphere best resembles a kind of "unknowable emotional experience" similar to Bion's O (Vermote, 2019, 118).

[T]ransformations that happen at a level where there are no representations yet. These transformations occur in a formless, undifferentiated, a-sensuous zone which he calls O. In O there are already some constellations but they are not yet experienced in a sensuous form, like a figure that is already present in a block of marble which a sculptor still has to reveal.

(Vermote, 2019, 17)

In this approach, we define the Atmosphere as a predominantly pre-symbolic or pre-representational emotional field whose inner dynamic is characterized mainly by its falling outside the symbolic order, and outside the domain of temporality (it is unknowable and infinite): "I shall use the sign O to denote that which is the ultimate reality represented by terms such as ultimate reality, absolute truth, the godhead, the infinite, the thing-in-itself" (Bion, 1970, 26; Vermote, 2019, 144). The O cannot be known, it can only be felt, or one can be at one with it (Vermote, 2019, 123). We all experienced this during the pandemic: we felt that often we became one with the mood of our environment, while often we did not understand what was happening, including our own reactions. In mass trauma, the equilibrium between the transformative function in the Atmosphere may be upset. The functions at the more symbolic level, those of containing and transforming, may be damaged and retreat, and the transformation present in the O may grow in strength and become dominant. Indeed, in the case of serious trauma, unsymbolic functions also become strong, flooding the Atmosphere with undigested and uncontained contents – aggression, paranoid fantasies, and psychotic anxiety (Bakó & Zana, 2021b, 527–528).

Temporality and Continuity in the Atmosphere

As we saw earlier (see Trauma and Temporality), the capacity to symbolize develops concomitantly with the acquisition of temporality which is predicated upon a sense of the continuity of the self. However, the experience of self-continuity is most fragile indeed.

> The only reality of self-experience is contained within the present moment; everything else is unreal – as related to the past which is embedded in memory but no longer exists, and to the future which can be anticipated but has not yet become real.
>
> (Meissner, 2008, 730)

In order for the *me* to be able to experience self-continuity, to experience both the past and the future as comprehensible inner realities related to the present reality, it relies on memory. This helps it to give meaning to its own personal experiences, to be able to structure them into a recountable narrative, and for the future to be predictable, imaginable. This is only possible if the *me* is able to experience continuity within the broader human community; in other words, if it perceives itself as part of the human community, the *we*. Two important conditions are associated with this: the first is that the *me* be able to perceive itself as a being with a separate identity (i.e., it should not merge totally with the *we*, the integrity of its own self should be preserved), and second, that it should be able to sense itself as part of the *we*. If the *me* experiences that it is part of a large whole, the *we* is able to represent to it the continuity of the collective, of humanity as a whole; in other words, a collective *here-and-now* reality that fits with the experiences and values of the past (the past of humanity) and in which the future of humanity can be envisaged. If the *we*-self functions well enough, it provides to the vast majority of individuals the psychological milieu in which during early development the personal self-experience can be born, and in which the *me* is later able to experience continuity. Just as memory is a requisite for self-continuity at the individual level, so in order for the *we*-self to maintain continuity, a collective memory is indispensable, and this is conveyed by the Atmosphere. The Atmosphere as a psychological space is in our approach primarily a non-verbal, pre-symbolic space of remembrance.

Péter (a 20-year-old student), experienced previously unknown uncontrollable emotions, emptiness, and disintegration, and he lost contact with his previous self (*May/August 2020 – Conspiracy Theories Abound*). He also lost contact with his biographical memory that he had of himself, and he experienced himself as alien. As a result of the loosening of boundaries, which not just he but everyone experienced, including the external world in the broader sense, he could no longer identify who these overwhelming feelings (anxiety, anger, vulnerability) belonged to, nor what belonged to either the present or the past. Perhaps the most shocking thing for him in this state was the distortion of the sense of time: he experienced this state as timeless, and he felt it would go on forever. Time had collapsed (Volkan, 2009, 211). When during therapy the sense of the continuity of time returned (past, present, and future became distinguishable entities), he regained his internal equilibrium, that is, his relationship with himself (see also Trauma and Self and Trauma and Temporality).

In the case of trauma, as we have seen, the experience of time is damaged, the *me* is temporarily unable to see itself in terms of past–present–future, and the awareness of mortality seems unbearable. The damaged *me* can at such times turn to the Atmosphere, which temporarily lends it time: it represents time stretching beyond individual (subjective) time, it represents the *we* time (the multi-generational family time, or that of a larger group, a nation, a people, or even humanity). Through the Atmosphere we can imagine what happened before we were born, and feel it to be our own, and we can imagine that we "live on" after our death: "The earlier phases of the story of our life are lost to memory and its very beginnings are not our, but our parents', history. And the end, death, will be recounted only in the stories of those who survive us" (Ricoeur, 1992; Priel, 1997, 448). For this, however, we need the remembering other: we need the collective memory that points beyond subjective memory, the memory function of the Atmosphere. Paradoxically, one condition of intersubjective meeting (forming relations) is that the *me* accept loss – including its own mortality: "loss is accepted so that an intersubjective encounter can be formulated" (Hartman, 2011, 472). The birth of the independent me, the self, entails the experience of mortality:

> The "use" of time is related to the renunciation of the illusion of immortality, that is, to the acceptance of the irreversibility of time. . . . It implies the recognition that the beginnings, as well as the end, of life are not under the aegis of the self but belong to others.
>
> (Priel, 1997, 448)

The *me* thus wavers continuously between separation (its own, separate self-experience) and a merging into the Atmosphere, the intersubjective community. The Atmosphere offers the individual access to what it lost with the ability to think, and to symbolize: access to the memories stored in the collective unconscious, to timelessness and the infinite – to the godhead, and the Ultimate Truth (Grotstein, 2007, 59, cited by Vermote, 2019, 167). This non-verbal knowledge is the pre-symbolic aspect of the Atmosphere. The O carries and transmits it to the *me* (Bion, 1965; Vermote, 2019, 122, Civitarese, 2019). "O describes both the unnameable unrepresentable external reality Grotstein describes as 'the world as it is, the universe without representations' (2011, private conversation) and the individual's primal internal preconception of that natural world" (Reiner, 2012, 6; Vermote, 2019, 144) (see also The Pre-symbolic Aspect of How the Atmosphere Works).

This is of great assistance when the *me* collapses, for instance, as a result of crisis or trauma: alongside the unique validity of finiteness, there appears the promise of merging into a greater whole, of immortality. Despite the *me* losing the ability to interpret world events for itself, surrendering its independent self-experience and thus its relationship with temporality, by dissolving in the *we* it gains access to the alarming, yet seductive timelessness conveyed by the Atmosphere, the experience of belonging to a greater whole (Bakó & Zana, 2021b, 528–531).

In the first lockdown period, the 77-year old Manyi (a retired teacher) assures his family that he keeps to the rules, but he often leaves his home. "I'm not scared of dying," he says (see Diary, March/April 2020 – Scapegoating). More than life (more than risking his personal safety), Manyi is afraid that he might not be *allowed to live*, live in the fuller, human sense. Though he does not lose contact with reality and maintains his self-integrity, unconsciously he undergoes a different experience that points beyond his own personal life: universal human existence, the *I am* experience.

The Trauma Victim and the Traumatizing Atmosphere

In 2021, when vaccines became available, the so-called eastern vaccines that did not have a European license prompted strong feelings of ambivalence throughout society. Titusz (a 35-year-old businessman) had decided to hold out for the "American" vaccine. But when vaccination became available, he suddenly decided on the "Eastern" vaccines (see Diary, March/April 2021 – The Third Wave). Titusz followed events in the external world, partly consciously, and partly unconsciously. The reality transmitted by the *we* constantly affected his mood and feelings. In January 2021, it was the eastern vaccines that were a risk, and this was the main source of his anxiety. Then, as he put it, "most unexpectedly" something in him changed: his anxiety rose to an unbearable pitch, and fear of becoming infected pervaded everything. Now the eastern vaccine was the lesser of two evils. In the example above, the *we* is no longer able to contain either the anxiety that overwhelms individuals or the paranoid fantasies. Overwhelming feelings lead to extremely rapid changes in the Atmosphere, which is burdensome in itself (Bakó & Zana, 2022, in press).

When the *me* is paralyzed, it is unable to act, but the *we* may still be capable of action. The *me*, deeply involved in the Atmosphere, can thus rely on the *we* for its action too, whether it be to reject or to accept, to flee or to attack. Sidestepping the symbolic function of the *me*, the Atmosphere is able to react extremely rapidly, even to change radically, and thus draw the *me* involved in the Atmosphere into rapid action. Shared, extremely rapid action can be life-saving when the *me* becomes helpless – not only and not primarily in terms of the individual, but also in terms of the survival of the group. This also conceals a trap: the *me*, submerged in the security offered by the *we*, in the promise of merging, sacrifices itself and its own boundaries. Due to the relaxing of the boundaries of the self, fantasies and basic assumptions conveyed by the Atmosphere sidestep the conscious control of the subject and overwhelm the *me*, which is no longer able to differentiate whether it or the other feels something; whether it thinks this, or the other thinks it. The other aspect of the trap is that in the case of mass trauma, the *we* and the function of the field it creates may also be damaged. It loses flexibility and gives less space for individual feelings and opinions. Even the *we* can be overwhelmed by experiences that it cannot process: its containing and transforming capacities can be damaged, and its more archaic function may become dominant.

The reality of trauma actually becomes traumatic for the *me* if the containing capacity of the *we* is also damaged. This is more likely to happen if the trauma affects a large proportion of a community or people. The boundaries of the self may become permanently loosened due to prolonged group-level trauma, and the *me* is permeated by the Atmosphere not only temporarily and with "discriminations," it merges with the timeless whole not only provisionally, but allows the Atmosphere, the now distorted reality of the *we*, to also enter for a prolonged period, without discriminations (see also The Reality of Trauma). The *we* is no longer supportive and accepting, but itself is traumatized and traumatizes: it is no longer able to contain the diversity and variety transmitted by the *me*, the time transmitted by the individual (finiteness, mortality). Instead, it tries to hold the *me* in an omnipotent state of timelessness, unity, and uniformity.

The issue here is not simply a damaged *me* and a damaged *we*; much rather, it is a relationship crisis between the *me* (subject) and the *we* (the Intersubjective).

> We cannot say that the subjectivity of the subject emerges from the "intersubjective" or transpersonal layer of being, nor the other way round. We must necessarily think that there are always two poles in dialectical relation with each other. Therefore, the group is the necessary and sufficient condition for there being a subject and vice versa. Psychic illness does not arise from the dialectical relationship per se but from the crisis of this relationship.
>
> (Civitarese, 2021b, 9)

The damaged Atmosphere is no longer capable of transformation at a more mature level, of dreaming. Rather, it conveys increasingly concrete feelings, be they paranoid fantasies, aggression, or archaic anxiety (see Diary, Events in Society: Vaccines and Projections, and The Period before Christmas). Due to the loosened boundaries of the self, these undigested contents become shared experiences and overwhelm the *me* that has already been weakened by the trauma: *me* and the *other*, the past and the present worlds, telescope together. As a consequence of the loosened boundaries and the damage to the symbolic capacity within the shared psychological space, in the traumatized Atmosphere, feelings and contents are rapidly shared and, unchecked, become common currency. The social equivalent of this psychological process is the spread of intolerant, destructive tendencies and dictatorial ideologies. For instance, related to the pandemic, the feelings projected onto the elderly (Søraa et al., 2020), then shortly afterward intolerance and aggression projected onto minorities defined by ethnicity or sexual orientation (see Case Vignettes from Society, November/December 2020), or to mention a historical example, the rise of fascism (see Diary, Events in Society – Vaccines and Projections, and The Period before Christmas).

> The idealization of purity, free from otherness, and an unconscious fantasy of fusion with a maternal primary object, drives nationalism and racist ideology that is, tragically, as much part of our current cultural concerns as it was in the 1930s and 1940s.
>
> (Foreword by Fónagy in Bohleber, 2010, xiii)

As we saw earlier (see Temporality and Continuity in the Atmosphere), one effect of serious social trauma is damage to both the ability for symbolization and to the customary linear perception of time (Stolorow, 2011, 55). Linearity and continuity are replaced by discontinuity, fragmentation, and an "endless repetition."

In healthy functioning, the *me*-experiences representing temporality are markedly present, and complement the timelessness and infinity in the Atmosphere, but in the case of mass trauma, with the weakening of the *me* and its symbolization, the timelessness of the Atmosphere becomes dominant. One consequence of this is the feeling that the situation one is in will always be so. Additionally, because of the porousness of the boundaries of the self, the Atmosphere is pervaded by experiences of not only the present, but also the fragments of the past, the Atmosphere, the result being that the present and past flow together. This is the damage to the sense of continuity at the collective level: the *we*, incapable of containing and transformation, is overwhelmed by the Transgenerational Atmosphere, which carries undigested collective unconscious fantasies (see also Transgenerational Atmosphere within the Atmosphere).

The timelessness and uniformity of the damaged Atmosphere is not identical to the "godhead" carried by the healthy *we*, which transmits to the individual a time pointing beyond the individual's life, the "eternal," and the continuity of belonging to a greater whole. The timelessness of the traumatic *we* is comparable to the frozen time of trauma, a present moment stretched to infinity, which is characterized by fragmentation and "endless repetition." To merge with this brings not containing but a sacrifice of individuality, of the *me*.

In the damaged Atmosphere, the *me* not only experiences a sense of being lost in space and time (disintegration of one's own self), but it also loses its relationship to the *infinite and timeless* in the healthy sense, a relationship with the greater whole, and it undergoes the Nietzschean experience of "God is dead." In this context, the experience of the death of God can be interpreted to mean a grave disintegration of the continuity of the *we*-self, a meaninglessness that points beyond the individual life, and the infinite loneliness of an individual detached from the *we*: there is no one to turn to, nothing to immerse oneself in (Bakó & Zana, 2021b, 531–535). The metaphor of "God is dead" is a painfully accurate reflection of the deep and prolonged crisis of the relationship between the *me* and the *we*: the hopeless loneliness and sense of being lost of a *me* that has lost trust in the *we*.

Transgenerational Atmosphere within the Atmosphere

The Atmosphere, the reality of the present, is always transformed and pervaded by the reality of the past. In healthy cases, however, the past and the present can be distinguished from one another: the *we* learns from the experiences of the past and is able to use them, without the past and past experience intermingling and mixing with the present (Bakó & Zana, 2021b, 535–536).

Zsuzsa (a 41-year-old kindergarten teacher) experiences disproportionately great fear, and is constantly concerned about infecting her family and endangering them (see Diary, November/December 2020 – Numbers on the Rise). Her grandfather's story, the past, the forced labor, the sense of constant fear (the reality of the past) are projected indelibly onto the present. Zsuzsa is no longer able to distinguish which feeling comes from the past, and which is linked to the present. She experiences an overwhelming, visceral anxiety.

> At that point, traumatic affect is no longer known, experienced, or remembered, but re-enacted and relived, because trauma is neither thought nor felt but experienced as present and immediate. Action and not imagination become the mode of its transmission, intimate interaction the locus of its occurrence.
>
> (Laub and Auerhahn in Ellman et al., 2017, 168)

The current trauma has the effect of activating in the present the experiences of earlier generations, which are unprocessed and have been excluded from narrative, made secret, and taboo (Bokor, 2020, 23–25). The present reality of the Atmosphere (the intersubjective field created by the *we* in the *here-and-now*) is increasingly permeated by the unthought residue of the past, the Transgenerational Atmosphere.

Due to the damage to the transforming and containing functions, those in the Atmosphere lose the ability to differentiate. The effect of the Transgenerational Atmosphere can be strong enough to telescope the planes of time: the *we* no longer learns from the experiences of the past, it is unable to integrate them, but perceives the past as a present reality; it loses its ability to orientate, and reacts to the events of the past instead of those of the present (Bakó & Zana, 2018; Bakó & Zana, 2020a, 30–40; Bakó & Zana, 2021a, 51–63). It receives the experiences and reactions of the past unreflectingly. Thus, it may react to a current trauma, for instance, the pandemic, with disproportionate anxiety, then aggression, exclusion, and violence. The acute crisis of the pandemic has invoked and intensified the still living, largely unprocessed recent horrors of the human community, such as the Holocaust. Anna (32 years old, an interior designer) is a third-generation Holocaust survivor. When she tries to understand the background to the upsetting feelings and deep dilemmas regarding vaccination, she says "I'd like to make the right decision *now*" (see Diary, March/April 2021: The Third Wave), not like her parents, who during the Second World War did not apply for a Swiss visa, trusting that no harm would come to them in Hungary. The internal world of the present (should I fight to get vaccinated) is deeply permeated by the internal world of the past, the Transgenerational Atmosphere. When she decides for a vaccine that she feels will give her protection in the *here-and-now*, Anna is actually deciding to get a Swiss visa for her parents, which will give them security in the past. *Their* psyche and *mine* telescope together: Anna wants to make the right decision. Her feeling is that the earlier decision was her own too, and she got it wrong (Bakó & Zana, 2021b, 535–536).

In my own dream (see Diary, The Transgenerational Atmosphere in a Dream: The Therapist's Own Experience, and November/December 2020 – Numbers on the Rise), in addition to the pandemic, the inner and outer realities of the *here-and-now* (increased risk to the elderly, fear of the other and closeness), the present reality is colored by the reality of the past, the Transgenerational Atmosphere, and this gains intensity as the dream progresses. While the character of Klári is closely linked to the world of the here-and-now (the elderly are the most endangered in the pandemic), the reality of the past, of the Holocaust, shows through: the elderly are "left behind." Later the world of the Transgenerational Atmosphere grows prevalent in the dream: I am left alone. Increasingly squeezed out of the safe place that is my due. Eventually, the children are left to themselves too: not only the unknown children, but those who are close to me as well. And so am I. Perhaps the most shocking moment is that before waking up: the deep guilt, in which lies the guilt of many internal worlds, perhaps of several generations. In addition to survivors' guilt (through omitting to remember, they have deserted those who have died), the guilt of observers, of participants, is also present: we who were part of it and allowed it to happen.

István (a 33-year-old electrical engineer) comes from the third generation of a family forcibly repatriated (see Diary January/February 2021 – The Period When the Vaccines Appear) and in January 2021, he is increasingly overwhelmed by tiredness and exhaustion. In his dream, he rushes into the basement of an extremely dilapidated building, and falls into a trap, but he dares not ask for help. His experience is that people can be dangerous, *they can infect*: not just with the virus, but also with "mental illness" – in other words, the alien and dangerous feelings transmitted by the *we*.

Győző (a 52-year-old agronomist) comes from a family that lost everything in the Communist period because of their aristocratic origins. He has a recurrent dream that he cannot make connections with other people: they don't hear what he says, they don't see him – he is excluded. These dreams become more and more frequent during the lockdown period (see Diary, January/February 2021 – The Period When the Vaccines Appear). The pandemic situation, lockdown, and social distancing make exclusion, isolation, and loneliness very common experiences for many. The reality of the *here-and-now we* echoed and amplified Győző's childhood experience.

Tímea (a 25-year-old student) is a third-generation Holocaust survivor. She came to therapy with issues of sexual identity. Due to the threat of the pandemic, increasing social tension, and threatening social processes (see Diary, A Fairytale but Not for Everyone), her anxiety rose to an almost psychotic pitch, and she experienced as real the danger that because of her sexual identity not only she, but also the whole family would be shot and left to fall into the River Danube. For her, this threat was real and genuine in the *here-and-now* (see Diary, November/December 2020 – Numbers on the Rise).

To this is related another of my personal experiences (The Therapists' Own Experiences: Where Is the Wolf?), which I had during the debate on *A Fairytale for Everyone* (see Diary, November/December 2020 – Numbers on the Rise). In my dilemmas, which found expression in the letter I wrote at the time, is to be found my own story, the past of the family as Holocaust survivors: partly the weight of making the right decision this time, or recognizing the true danger (unlike my family, for example, who then-and-there did not recognize the significance of the anti-Jewish laws, like Anna's family). On the other hand, there is another fear related more to the world of the past than to the reality of the present: that when I sign a petition (for instance), I make myself vulnerable to those in power, I draw attention to myself. Although these feelings were faint and mainly unconscious, in the emotionally saturated situation, they made it difficult for me to judge what was the right course of action. My own example, and the discussion that took place in the Hungarian Psychoanalytical Society (see Diary, November/December 2020 – Numbers on the Rise), again showed that neither as private individuals nor as a small group are we independent of the mood of the environment that surrounds us, the Atmosphere, the feelings transmitted by the intersubjective field, which embraces and permeates us. The polarization of the signatories versus non-signatories reflected what was happening in the *we* in this period: society was unable to tame the tensions that the pandemic caused, to converge opinions, to contain opposing feelings, and dilemmas that inside were uncontainable we then projected onto the external world: opposing, irreconcilable camps of maskers and non-maskers, those waiting for the vaccine and virus-deniers, the right wing and the left wing. The *we* was no longer able to coherently process the outer reality. Instead, it transmitted fragmented, non-communicating part-realities to the *me* (see later The Trauma of Reality). The weakened *me*, which is no longer able to rely on the security provided by the *we*, may lose its orienting ability, so the question arises: Am I reacting to the *here-and-now*, or to a past experience? In the weakened state caused by the crisis, the memories and shadows of the past (the Transgenerational Atmosphere) are more likely to be projected onto the present, greatly hampering our ability to judge what is right when we react to the present. What relates to the *here-and-now* situation, and what relates to the then-and-there? In many people (in us too), there appeared the image of "those who stay silent are guilty," or the aspect of the attitude of watching and waiting that is fatally dangerous. The shredding of the book (see Diary November/December 2020 – Numbers on the Rise) called forth the memory of book-burning, the transgenerational memory of previous historical times. "Where books are burned, they will eventually also burn people." Many wondered: "what could be the reality today?" As Nancy R. Goodman said in relation to 9/11: "How did people know when to leave?" (Goodman & Meyers, 2012). In the *there-and-then* reality, this danger was not an issue. However, these days, the current reality of a nation cannot be separated from the international reality in a broader sense. In this broad reality, it might now happen, that for instance someone be beheaded for their convictions (see Diary, November/December – Numbers on the Rise), and this reality thus becomes a shared psychological reality.

Here-and-now or There-and-then

The appearance of these horrific images and fantasies (e.g., that people are burned, shot, and left to fall into the Danube) show the steadily more pathological function of the Atmosphere: traumatic experiences from generations ago in the past and of other groups (nations) interweave the present *here-and-now* reality of the deeply traumatic events we are experiencing now, they color the internal reality perception of the social groups and the *me* deeply involved in the Atmosphere, they make it difficult to orient oneself, to judge what one should be wary of, and how much. These fears from the distant past and faraway places contribute to the difficulties in fighting the true threats (the pandemic, and the social/political processes which are far from disconnected from it). So much so, that the genuine threat fades: it seems that the pandemic is no longer the real danger.

To Act or Not to Act?

Indeed, although the pandemic brought a new situation, the social effects that the pandemic induced are familiar not only at the individual level, but at group level too. One is thus justified in posing the difficult question familiar of old: At what point does non-action become a sin? In retrospect, of course, it is easier to see clearly than in any given historical moment. In the field of the Atmosphere, in which the experiences of the *me* and the *other*, the present and the past, flow together, it is very difficult to orient oneself: often in a given moment, it is impossible to decide whether we are reacting to the genuine present reality, or to a past reality. The processes underway in the community of psychoanalysts show how difficult it is to make a "good enough" decision in this historical situations (see Diary, November/December 2020). The group in question has deeper self-knowledge than average, and understanding their own feelings and others' is everyday work for them. And yet nobody, not even we, can pretend to be immune to the effects of the external world, and we too are capable of losing our way for shorter or longer periods, when the effects of the external world are too strong, and overwhelming. In the case of a societal crisis, we are all involved.

> The analyst is, in certain traumatic situations of present-day reality, affected by a phenomenon one of us has called the phenomenon of "overlapping worlds" [4]. This is a phenomenon in which dates, facts, or incidents related by the patient directly affect the analyst in their manifest content because they belong to his or her own day-to-day, current, and traumatic language. It produces in the therapist a traumatic effect and reinforces a narcissistic manner of functioning that can, at any moment, divert him or her from his or her role, thus leaving the patient without an analyst. By recognizing the implications of the phenomenon of overlapping worlds, we have been able to pursue our analytic dialogue without having recourse to the two possible defenses: either isolation, or hyperprofessionalism.
>
> (Braun de Dunayevich & Puget, 2019, 28)

In crisis situations, the issue of neutrality is problematic at several levels. It appears at the group level, and crystallizes in therapy too. Hollander (2019) writes of the issue of neutrality:

> If we recall, from the 1960s politically active analysts believed that it was impossible for an analyst to be neutral, especially in the midst of broad military and paramilitary attacks on civil society. By the mid-1970s this view had gained more weight, and an increasing number of mental hygiene experts found themselves facing clients who were traumatized by state oppression. Whether they worked with Las Madres de Plaza de Mayo in Argentina, or with organizations helping fleeing refugees, analysts realized that an open identification with the human rights movement encouraged their clients to trust them, and promoted the formation of a working alliance, which helped their struggle with the difficult process of psychic healing. Extreme political oppression makes it obvious that neutrality is an impossibility, both in the political and professional spheres. In the radical words of the Afro-American movement: either we are a part of the problem, or we are a part of the solution. Many analysts realized that when they were working with European Holocaust victims, it had a positive effect on the therapy if the client found out that the therapist was also a Holocaust survivor.
>
> (Hollander, 2019, 22)

Very similar thoughts and questions also arose after the 9/11 attacks: Should I share something about myself? Should I give advice? Does an analyst do that? Can they? "I began wondering if I would ever be telling patients I was leaving Washington, or telling them they should. (Do psychoanalysts say such things?)" (Goodman & Meyers, 2012).

In crisis situations, the dilemma of neutrality inevitably crops up at the group level too. The dialogue conducted in the community of Hungarian psychoanalysts reflects not only our own social environment. A similar dialogue was underway in other IPA associations: for instance, the British and Polish associations were occupied by similar questions (though on different topics, reflecting the current then-and-there questions), and several associations decided on action, on expressing an opinion. The analyst's approach, which gives preference to reflection over action, faces a serious challenge in situations when an attitude is not sufficient, when action is really needed. The Argentinian authors Braun de Dunayevich & Puget, 2019) question the hypothesis of psychoanalysis in the case of regime-level terror, dictatorship, and oppression, drawing a parallel between the Holocaust and the state terrorism experienced in (Peronist) Argentina between 1976 and 1983. In times of crisis, those who question the professional security of "peacetime," the place of neutrality that gives a point of reference, say:

Politically active analysts published critical articles about the current crisis and the trends in psychoanalysis that they believed represented cooperation with the status quo. One of the central questions that arose over and over again in the debate was neutrality, which activists again criticized as an impossible professional ideal. They considered the position of the APA as an upholder of neutrality as hypocritical.

(Hollander, 2019, 15–16)

A bad decision made in a key historical moment may discredit a society of psychoanalysts, and lead to its disintegration:

The analysts who left believed it was important to react to clients' anxieties and fears and to accompany them in their struggles, so that they could handle a confrontation with the dramatic crisis which had beset the country. A particularly important topic was the loss which both clients and analysts experienced in many areas of life, due to the erosion of civil society as a result of attacks by military and paramilitary forces.

(Hollander, 2019, 16, paraphrase)

Psychoanalysts and societies facing the challenges of the present are haunted by the shadows of the past, while the issue is also genuinely pertinent in the *here-and-now*: Is "business as usual" sustainable, at the individual and group level, or is there a place for a more active attitude?

References

Abraham, N. & Torok, M. (1984). "The Lost Object-me": Notes on Identification within the Crypt. *Psychoanalytic Inquiry*, 4, 221–242.

Anderson, B. (1983). *Imagined Communities: Reflections on the Origin and Spread of Nationalism.* Verso, London. https://is.muni.cz/el/1423/podzim2013/SOC571E/um/Anderson_B_-_Imagined_Communities.pdf (downloaded at 08 January 2023).

Bakó, T. & Zana, K. (2018). The Vehicle of Transgenerational Trauma: The Transgenerational Atmosphere. *American Imago*, 75(2), 273–287.

Bakó T. & Zana K. (2020a). *Transgenerational Trauma and Therapy. The Transgenerational Atmosphere.* Routledge, London and New York.

Bakó, T. & Zana, K. (2020b). A transzgenerációs atmoszféra: az emlékezés folyamata kollektív társadalmi traumákban. *Lélekelemzés*, 2, 63–80.

Bakó, T. & Zana, K. (2021a). *A transzgenerációs trauma és terápiája. A transzgenerációs atmoszféra.* Medicina kiadó, Budapest.

Bakó, T. & Zana, K. (2021b). COVID and Mass Trauma: The Atmosphere as a Vehicle for Group Experience. *American Imago*, 78(3), 515–538. www.muse.jhu.edu/article/837107.

Bakó, T. & Zana, K. (2022). A trauma realitása – a realitás traumája. *Lélekelemzés*, 2, 13–37.

Bakó, T. & Zana, K. (in press). *The Reality of Trauma; the Trauma of Reality.* Translated by Robinson, R. Psychoanalytic Dialogues.

Baranger, M. & Baranger, W. (2008): The Analytic Situation as a Dynamic Field. *The International Journal of Psychoanalysis*, 89(4), 795–826.

Benjamin, J. (2004). Beyond Doer and Done to: An Intersubjective View of Thirdness. *Psychoanalytic Quarterly*, 73(1), 5–46.

Benjamin, J. (2011). Facing Reality Together Discussion: With Culture in Mind: The Social Third. *Studies in Gender and Sexuality*, 12(1), 27–36.

Bermudez, G. (2018). The Social Dreaming Matrix as a Container for the Processing of Implicit Racial Bias and Collective Racial Trauma. *International Journal of Group Psychotherapy*, 68(4), 538–560.

Bion, W. R. (1961). Experiences in Groups and Other Papers. *Experiences in Groups and Other Papers*, 6, 1–6.

Bion, W. R. (1962a). *Learning from Experience* (pp. 1–116). London, Tavistock.

Bion, W. R. (1962b). The Psycho-Analytic Study of Thinking. *International Journal of Psychoanalysis*, 43, 306–310.

Bion, W. R. (1965). *Transformations: Change from Learning to Growth* (pp. 1–172). London: Tavistock.

Bion, W. R. ([1970] 2006). *Figyelem és értelmezés*. [Attention and interpretation] (Translated by Schmelowsky, Á.). Lélekben Otthon Kiadó, Budapest.

Bohleber, W. (2010). *Destructiveness, Intersubjectivity and Trauma. The Identity Crisis of Modern Psychoanalysis*. Routledge, London and New York.

Bokor, L. (2020). A jövő, mint az emlékek tükre, avagy az emlékezés dinamikája a terápiás folyamatban és a kulturális narratívák kialakításában. *Lélekelemzés*, 2, 12–20.

Braun de Dunayevich, J. & Puget, J. (2019). Állami terror és pszichoanalízis. *Imágó Budapest*, 8(2), 24–35. [English source: "State Terrorism and Psychoanalysis," *International Journal of Mental Health*, 18/2 (Summer 1989) 98–112.]

Civitarese, G. (2013). The Cat's Eyes: Internal Focalization and Casting in the Psychoanalytic Dialogue. In: *The Violence of Emotions, Bion and Post-bionian Psychoanalysis* (pp. 74–110). Routledge, London.

Civitarese, G. (2019). The Concept of Time in Bion's "A Theory of Thinking". *International Journal of Psychoanalysis*, 100(2), 182–205.

Civitarese, G. (2021a). Heart of Darkness in the Courtyard, or Dreaming the COVID-19 Pandemic. *Psychoanalytic Psychology*, 38(2), 133–135.

Civitarese, G. (2021b). Experiences in Groups as a Key to "Late" Bion. *International Journal of Psychoanalysis*, 1–27.

Durban, J. (2017). Home, Homelessness, and "Nowhere-ness" in Early Infancy. *Journal of Child Psychotherapy*, 43(2), 175–191. https://doi.org/10.1080/0075417X.2017.1327550

Ellman, L. P., Nancy, R. & Goodman, R. N. (eds.) (2017). *Finding Unconscious Fantasy in Narrative, Trauma, and Body Pain: A Clinical Guide*. Routledge, London and New York.

Esposito, R. (2015). *Persons and Things: From the Body's Point of View*. Polity Press, Cambridge, UK.

Fairbairn, W. D. (1952). Chapter I. Schizoid Factors in the Personality (1940). *Psychoanalytic Studies of the Personality*, 7, 1–27.

Ferro, A. (1992): Two Authors in Search of Characters: The Relationship, the Field, the Story. *Rivista di Psicoanalisi*, 38(1), 44–90.

Ferro, A. (2006). Trauma, Reverie, and The Field. *Psychoanalytic Quarterly*, 75(4), 1045–1056.

Ferro, A. (2009). Transformations in Dreaming and Characters in the Psychoanalytic Field. *International Journal of Psychoanalysis*, 90, 209–230.

Ferro, A. (2011): Shuttles to and from the Unconscious: Reveries, Transformations in Dreaming and Dreams. *Italian Psychoanalytic Annual*, 5, 89–106.

Ferro, A. (2015). A Response That Raises Many Questions. *Psychoanalytic Inquiry*, 35(5), 512–525.

Ferro, A. & Civitarese, G. (2016). Psychoanalysis and the Analytic Field. In: Elliott, A. & Prager, G.(eds.) *The Routledge Handbook of Psychoanalysis in the Social Sciences and Humanities* (pp. 132–148). Routledge, London.

Ferro, A. & Foresti, G (2008). "Objects" and "Characters" in Psychoanalytical Texts/Dialogues. *International Forum of Psychoanalysis*, 17(2), 71–81.

Fonagy, P. & Target, M. ([2003] 2005). *Pszichoanalitikus elméletek a fejlődési pszichopatológia tükrében [Psychoanalytical Theories. Perspective from Developmental Psychopathology]* (Szerk.: Bókay, A. és Erős, F. Fordította: Milák, P., Pető, K., Ratkóczi, É., Unoka, Zs). Gondolat, Budapest.

Fonagy, P. & Target, M. (2007). Playing with Reality: IV. A Theory of External Reality Rooted in Intersubjectivity. *International Journal of Psychoanalysis*, 88(4), 917–937.

Freud, S. (1913). *Totem and Taboo. The Standard Edition of the Complete Psychological Works of Sigmud Freud, Volume XIII (1913–1914): Totem and Taboo and Other Works* (pp. vii–162). W. W. Norton & Company, New York and London.

Gergely, G. & Watson, J. S. (1996). The Social Biofeedback Theory of Parental Affect-Mirroring: The Development of Emotional Self-Awareness and Self-Control in Infancy. *International Journal of Psychoanalysis*, 77, 1181–1212.

Gergely, G. & Watson, J. (1999). Early Social-emotional Development: Contingency Perception and the Social Biofeedback Model. In: Rochat, P. (ed.) *Early Social Cognition: Understanding Others in the First Months of Life* (pp. 101–137). Erlbaum, Mahwah, NJ.

Gerson, S. (2009). When the Third is Dead: Memory, Mourning, and Witnessing in the Aftermath of the Holocaust. *International Journal of Psychoanalysis*, 90(6), 1341–1357.

González, F. J. (2020a). Trump Cards and Klein Bottles: On the Collective of the Individual. *Psychoanalytic Dialogues*, 30(4), 383–398.

González, F. J. (2020b). With Fellow Travelers to Nodal Places: Reply to Dajani, Doñas, and Peltz. *Psychoanalytic Dialogues*, 30, 424–431.

Goodman, N. R. & Meyers, M. B. (2012). *The Power of Witnessing: Reflections, Reverberations, and Traces of the Holocaust—Trauma, Psychoanalysis, and the Living Mind* (Chapter 24, pp. 301–318). Routledge Press, London.

Green, A. (1997). The Intuition of the Negative in Playing and Reality. *International Journal of Psychoanalysis*, 78, 1071–1084.

Grotstein, J. S. (2007). *A Beam of Intense Darkness*. Karnac, London.

Hartman, S. (2011). Reality 2.0: When Loss Is Lost. *Psychoanalytic Dialogues*, 21(4), 468–482.

Hollander, C. N. (2019). Buenos Aires: A pszichoanalízis latin-amerikai Mekkája. *Imágó Budapest*, 8(2), 6–23.

Jung, C. G. (1915). The Theory of Psychoanalysis. *Psychoanalytic Review*, 2(1), 29–51.

Kogan, I. (2017). Anti-Semitism and Xenophobia. *American Journal of Psychoanalysis*, 77(4), 378–391.

Kogan, I. (2021). The Impact of the Coronavirus Pandemic on the Analyses of Holocaust Survivors' Offspring. *International Journal of Applied Psychoanalytic Studies*, 18, 169–176.

Laub, D. & Auerhahn, C. N. (1989). Failed Empathy – A Central Theme in the Survivor's Holocaust Experience. *Psychoanalytic Psychology*, 6(4), 377–400.

Lawrence, W. (2005). Thinking of the Unconscious, and the Infinite, of Society during Dark Times. *Organisational and Social Dynamics*, 5(1), 57–72.

Layton, L. (2004a). A Fork in the Royal Road: On "Defining" The Unconscious and its Stakes for Social Theory. *Psychoanalysis Culture and Society*, 9, 33–51.

Layton, L. (2004b). Relational No More: Defensive Autonomy in Middle-Class Women. *Annual of Psychoanalysis*, 32, 29–42.

Layton, L. (2005). Notes Toward a Nonconformist Clinical Practice: Response to Philip Cushman's "Between Arrogance and a Dead-End: Psychoanalysis and the Heidegger-Foucault Dilemma". *Contemporary Psychoanalysis* 41, 419–429.

Layton, L. (2006). Racial Identities, Racial Enactments, and Normative Unconscious Processes. *Psychoanalytic Quarterly*, 75(1), 237–269.

Le Bon, G. ([1913, 2014). *A tömegek lélektana* [Psychologie les foules] (Translated by Balla, A.). Belső EGÉSZ-ség kiadó, Budapest. [English source: Le Bon, G. (2009 [1895]). The Psychology of Crowds, ed. by Cuffaro, A. & Kauders, D., Sparkling Books.]

Lőrincz, Zs., Gyomlai, É., Szajcz, Á., Zana, K., & Sinkovics, A. (2019). A bioni mezőelmélet. Egy kortárs interszubjektív megközelítés bemutatása [The Bionian field-theory. Introduction to a contemporary intersubjective approach]. *Lélekelemzés*, 2, 197–231.

Meissner W. W. (2008). Self and Time. *Journal of American Academy of Psychoanalysis*, 36(4), 707–736.

Ogden, H. T. (1985). On Post-Traumatic Space. *International Journal of Psychoanalysis*, 66, 129–141.

Ogden, H. T. (1994). The Analytic Third: Working with Intersubjective Clinical Facts. *International Journal of Psychoanalysis*, 75, 3–19.

Ogden, H. T. (2010). Original Articles on Three Forms of Thinking: Magical Thinking, Dream Thinking, and Transformative Thinking. *Psychoanalytic Quarterly*, 79(2), 317–347.

Peltz, R. (2020). Living Entities that Join and Separate us: A Discussion of "Trump Cards and Klein Bottles: On the Collective of the Individual". *Psychoanalytic Dialogues*, 30, 417–423.

Priel, B. (1997). Time and Self: On the Intersubjective Construction of Time. *Psychoanalytic Dialogues*, 7, 431–450.

Reich, W. (1980). *The Mass Psychology of Fascism* (Translated by Wolfe, P.T.). Orgone Institute Press, New York.

Reiner, A. (2012). *Bion and Being: Passion and the Creative Mind*. Karnac, London.

Søraa, R. A., Manzi, F., Kharas, W. M., Marchetti, A., Massaro, D., Riva, G. & Serranoa, J. A. (2020). Othering and Deprioritizing Older Adults' Lives: Ageist Discourses During the COVID-19 Pandemic. *European Journal of Psychoanalysis*, 16(4), 532–541.

Stolorow, D. R. (2011). *World, Affectivity, Trauma: Heidegger and Post-Cartesian Psychoanalysis*. Routledge, London and New York.

Szondi, L ([1937], 1992, 1996). A tudattalan nyelvei: szimptóma, szimbólum és választás. In: Szondi Lipót életművéből. *Thalassa Alapítvány*, 96(2), 61–82 [Szondi Lipót: Die Sprachen des Unbewussten: Symptom, Symbol und Wahl. Eredetileg megjelent: Szondiana II., (a Schweitzerische Zeitschrift für Psychologie und ihre Anwendungen 26. számának melléklete). Jelen fordítás alapja a Szondiana 1992/2. számában megjelent újraközlés, amely jegyzeteket nem tartalmaz].

Togashi, K. (2014). Sense of "Being Human" and Twinship Experience. *International Journal of Psychoanalytic Self Psychology*, 9(4), 265–281.

Trevarthen, C. (2009). The Functions of Emotion in Infancy: The Regulation and Communication of Rhythm, Sympathy, and Meaning in Human Development. In: Fosha, D., Siegel, D. J. & Solomon, M. F. (ed.) *The Healing Power of Emotion: Affective Neuroscience, Development, and Clinical Practice* (pp. 55–85). Norton, New York.

Trevarthen, C. (2015). Awareness of Infants: What Do They, and We, Seek? *Psychoanalytic Inquiry*, 35(4), 395–416.

Tubert-Oklander, J. (2006). The Individual, the Group and Society: Their Psychoanalytic Inquiry. *International Forum of Psychoanalysis*, 15(3), 146–150.

Tubert-Oklander, J. (2007). The Whole and the Parts: Working in the Analytic Field. *Psychoanalytic Dialogues*, 17(1), 115–132.

Vermote, R. (2019). *Reading Bion* (Series Editor: Birksted-Breen, D). Routledge, London and New York.

Volkan, V. D. (2009). Large-Group Identity, International Relations and Psychoanalysis. *International Forum of Psychoanalysis*, 18, 206–213.

Volkan, V. (2013). Large-Group-Psychology in its Own Right: Large-Group Identity and Peace-Making. *International Journal of Applied Psychoanalytic Studies*, 10(3), 210–246.

Winnicott, D. W. (1953). Transitional Objects and Transitional Phenomena – A Study of the First Not-Me Possession. *International Journal of Psychoanalysis*, 34, 89–97.

Winnicott, D. W. (1956). Mirror Role of Mother and Family in Child Development. In: *Playing and Reality* (pp. 111–118). Tavistock, London.

Winnicott, D. W. (1971). *Playing and Reality* (1–156). Tavistock Publications, London.

Zahavi, D. (2001). *Husserl and Transcendental Intersubjectivity: A Response to the Linguistic-Pragmatic Critique*. Ohio University Press, Athens, OH.

Chapter 3

The Trauma of Reality

In this chapter, we think through the period of COVID from the perspective of reality, interpreting the concept of reality in the theoretical framework of the Atmosphere. We focus particularly on the process by which external events in the *here-and-now* (the real) become inner, subjective realities – in other words, by which they are given meaning. The giving of meaning is a fundamental human need. If the traumatic event is too overwhelming, it outstrips the individual's processing capacity, the giving of meaning will fail, and the *me* remains fixed in a meaningless present (Boulanger, 2002, 62).

In the long term, disintegration of the self is unbearable, so the *me* constantly makes attempts to give meaning. After serious shock, as we saw earlier, the symbolic capacity of the *me* falls; in other words, it temporarily or for a prolonged period loses the ability to give meaning to events in the outside world. At such times, it turns to the *we*, the intersubjective community, and tries to temporarily borrow containing and symbolizing capacity, and meaning from it. In this chapter, we focus on understanding the intersubjective aspect (in the broad sense) of giving meaning. In order to gain more accurate understanding of this aspect, our model distinguishes a third reality between external reality (the real) and the individual's inner, psychic reality: *we* (or collective) reality, the reality of the group, of the intersubjective community in the broad sense. In our approach, the Atmosphere also has a meaning-giving function. In other words, it is able to "dream" an intersubjective reality (the *we* reality) that for many is an integrated reality, and helps individuals to ascribe meaning (see also How the Atmosphere Works). The *we* reality is thus the psychological field created by the we, the result of the function of the Atmosphere; in other words, the Atmosphere's dream. In subsequent chapters, we define the concept of reality, we examine the mutual interplay of the *we* reality and the *me* reality, including how the individual's and the group's perception of reality is changed and distorted by the effect of mass trauma. We consider how the reality of the group, the *we* produced in the constantly changing *here-and-now* can color and shape the *me* reality. We discuss how changes in the *me* reality rebound to the *we* reality, and how past (emotional) reality is woven through the present *me* and *we* realities.

DOI: 10.4324/9781003194064-6

On the Relationship between Outer and Inner Realities

In this book, when we consider reality, we set out from a Bionian and post-Bionian approach; in other words, by reality we mean a psychic construct which is the result of the alpha function, the process of symbolization (Bion, 1962a, 85). In this interpretative framework, reality is the end product of a process of dreaming: using its dreaming, transformative capacity, the mind changes the raw, objective reality of the external world (the real) into an interior psychic reality, which through this process gains a personal meaning, and becomes an integral part of the personality (Ferro & Civitarese, 2013, 647). Another important element of reality in our interpretation is its intersubjective or social aspect. By this we mean that we consider the inner psychic reality to be an intersubjective or a social construct, whose genesis requires not only a receptive other, but also the Social: people jointly give meaning to the external reality they have experienced together (a shared reality) (Bion, 1962b, 309–310; Trevarthen, 2015, 396). Trevarthen writes:

> The function of interpersonal connectedness is, from infancy, more than brains being co-conscious of an external world, and more than emotional regulation of interpersonal states. It is actively aesthetic and moral in the internal purpose and feeling of each moving human body, and the infant is a wise, sensitive, and proud contributor to this sensibility and the meanings it gives to a shared reality.
>
> (Trevarthen, 2015, 396)

In this relational approach, reality comprises both the external and internal realities as they interact with one another (Benjamin, 2005, 451). As Fonagy and Target put it:

> In many ways following in the footsteps of relational theorists (e.g. Bromberg, 1996; Mitchell, 1997, 2000; Renik, 1998), we now recognize that the intrapsychic and interpersonal domains of psychoanalysis come together in the intersubjective, in which reality is defined as a relational matrix that incorporates both the internal and the external world.
>
> (Fonagy & Target, 2007, 919)

When two people meet, the intersubjective reality of the external world (the *we* reality) is always present, weaving through and shaping their unconscious shared reality. "Unconscious structuring is therefore lifelong, organized not only by the impact and influence of early objects on an organismal body but by the repeated and perpetual subjection to group life, made necessary as a human quality of belonging," writes González (2020a, 393). Thus, it is not possible to think in terms of individual psychic processes, to understand them completely, without taking into account the *collective aspect* of the subject, the *we-in-me* (González, 2020a, 389; González, 2020b, 424; Peltz, 2020, 418–421). The inner reality has an important role in ensuring the sense of self-continuity: "It provides a cushion and a container in which the impact of external reality can be absorbed and reworked. Psychic reality is timeless, therefore it provides the personality with the continuity that can be lacking in external reality" (Oliner, 1996, 280). However, external reality also has an important role in maintaining continuity: it provides the *me* with a point of reference, a time (temporality and the eternal). In order to maintain self-coherence, it is important the individual be capable of perceiving and accepting the *here-and-now* reality, and that this experience be allowed to continuously develop his personality. "[T]here is a reciprocal relationship in which external reality is constantly used in the service of fantasy, modifying the self-representation according to these experiences" (Oliner, 1996, 289). A condition for psychic equilibrium is that the inner and outer realities be distinguishable, and also that they be in a mutual dynamic relationship: in other words, the outer, present reality should affect the inner reality, and the inner reality should be able to affect the external world (in other words, the external world should mirror and validate an inner experience). The reality of serious trauma is impossible for the *me* to integrate, and under the effect of trauma, it loses its ability to give meaning.

> The experience of extreme destruction, for example as a result of the atomic bomb, and of violence, as in the concentration camps, can rob the victim of the basis of his identity; it can result in the loss of identity, of reality perception, and of meaning, as well as in the blocking of secondary processes such as, for example, the working through of grief.
>
> (Affeld-Niemeyer & Marlow, 1995, 26)

Inner reality becomes distant from outer reality, and from personal meaning. Unconscious fantasies gather strength. Partly as a defense against complete disintegration and meaninglessness, the self becomes rigid, and reacts no longer to the present reality, but to an external, unchanged, frozen, timeless reality (Bakó & Zana, 2022, in press).

We Reality

Just as the field co-created in therapy, the third, dreams for the patient a new integrated reality (Ferro & Civitarese, 2016; Ferro, 2009, 219; Ferro, 2015, 522; Lőrincz et al., 2019, 217; Vermote, 2019, 82–85), we assume that the *we*, or more accurately the intersubjective field that it creates, "dreams" a new reality, the dream of the social (Lawrence, 2000, 84–88; Bermudez, 2018, 543–547). Using Bion's model of the mind, intersubjective theories and the Transgenerational Atmosphere as an interpretative framework, we consider reality to be a field created by the *we*, the dream of the Atmosphere (see also Me and We, and Their Mutual Interaction in the Atmosphere and The Healthy Functioning of the Atmosphere) (Bion, 1962b; Ferro, 2006; Ogden, 2010; Ferro & Civitarese, 2013; Civitarese, 2019; Vermote, 2019; Bakó & Zana, 2018, 2020a). As we use the term, *we* reality is an intersubjective construct: it is the result of a process of ascribing meaning, in which the intersubjective community (the *we*) "dreams" a reality that is not yet at the individual level, but which has been transformed (and in this sense is internal). We conceive the development and relationship of the *we* reality and the *me* reality to be similar to the dialectic development and relationship of the subject (*me*) and intersubject (*we*) (Civitarese, 2021). In parallel with the birth of the *we* reality, each *me*, each subject also tries to tame, to "dream" the external reality into something that can be received. In our approach, *me* and *we* realities are not hierarchical but are mutually interactive constructs in a dialectic relationship with one another. The constantly changing *me* realities continually transform the *we* reality, and the changing *we* reality also constantly affects the individual's perception of reality. The *we* reality surrounds and permeates the subject without and within from birth, shaping the internal reality. A healthy *me* is able to create (to dream) and to retain an internal reality that is self-consistent. However, in the case of trauma, the effect of the *we* reality may grow, and due to a loosening of the boundaries of the self, the subject temporarily becomes more receptive to the function of the intersubjective environment around him. At such times, the *we* reality of the collective may penetrate his own subjective reality.

Social processes may burden, or even overburden the *me* and thus become traumatic, when a conflict arises between the realities (the multiple smaller group realities and the *we* reality in the broad sense), and this may result in a fragmentation of reality as a construct (Bakó & Zana, 2022, in press).

Healthy We Reality

If the Atmosphere's symbolizing, dreaming capacity is maintained, then it is able to "dream" an intersubjective (*we*) reality (one that is symbolized at the group level, though not yet for the individual) which for the vast majority of individuals is an integratable psychic reality; in other words, it gives space for many kinds of individual realities. "In a healthy group – internal or external – multiplicity is in creative tension with coherence. A group is at its most generative when it contains the greatest diversity among its members while sharing the most unity of purpose" (González, 2020a, 393). Thus, it is a great variety of feelings and opinions that give the reality of the present. It is flexible and constantly changes according to changes in the external reality, the real, and individual realities. If it is functioning properly, the field dreamed by the *we* forms a bridge between the external and psychic realities and enables the individual to share his/her internal world with the other.

Another key condition for the dreaming of a *here-and-now* reality is remembering, because this is what creates the relationship, continuity with the experiences of the past, and enables us to make use of earlier experiences. In healthy cases, the Atmosphere reacts not only to the current situation, the present external reality, but it also contains and transmits the earlier memories of the *we*, the human community, including the pre-symbolic and even the unsymbolized domains (see Temporality and Continuity in the Atmosphere). In the best case, when the Atmosphere's transforming function is maintained, it is able to contain even these unsymbolized contents, so they do not overwhelm.

Anna (32 years old, an interior designer) is bringing up her daughter alone. She loses her ability to orientate herself in interpreting events in the outside world (see Diary, September/October 2020 – Decisions and The Healthy Functioning of the Atmosphere) and follows the current *we* reality like the needle of a compass. This is what she clings to when she has to decide whether or not she should fear. This can be a good coping strategy if the *we* is functioning properly. When the *me* is weaker, it is unable to interpret events in the outside world, and it can turn to the *we* for support, which if it is working well enough can dream a reality which for many can be integrated Bakó & Zana, 2022, in press).

Perversion of the We Reality: The Trauma of Reality

The trauma of reality sets in if the containing function of the *we* is also damaged. The individual, or small group, with their loosened boundaries of the self, is engulfed by overwhelming feelings. Archaic, primitive functions gather strength, and the dreaming of reality as a group-level psychological function is damaged. Reality is no longer a dream, but the unchanged replaying of traumatic events, a post-traumatic nightmare: "such 'dreams' are dreams that are not dreams in that they leave the dreamer psychically unchanged" (Ogden, 2010, 330). Particularly overwhelming is the effect of a trauma perpetrated by humans against humans, a collective societal trauma. At such times, the container capacity of society, of the *we*, suffers serious, prolonged damage, and so is unable to contain and tame individual experiences (Boulanger, 2002, 68; Bakó & Zana, 2020a, 10–11; Bakó & Zana, 2021a, 29–31) (see also Society's Containing Capacity and How It Can be Damaged).

The effect of other large-group traumas, such as natural disasters and the current pandemic, depends on many factors: if the containing capacity of the Whole suffers no damage, or only minor or temporary damage, then the *we* can be nourishing and supportive (with general assistance, empathy, and solidarity dominating), helping the traumatized groups and individuals to regain their security. But other tendencies may also gather strength: the traumatized *we* may lose the container capacity, its capacity to change. In this case, it no longer mirrors the genuine *here-and-now* events, but becomes rigid and permeable to the reality of the past. The Transgenerational Atmosphere conveying the events of the past has an increasingly marked effect on the reality of the present (Bakó & Zana, 2018; Bakó & Zana, 2020a, 30–40; Bakó & Zana, 2021a, 51–63).

Gabriella (41 years old, a secondary school teacher) is normally very wary of infection and cautious, and she didn't even leave home. Just before the latest lockdown, she went to a large shopping mall to buy a much bigger refrigerator than the one she already had (see Diary, March/April 2020 – Scapegoating). In her case, the anxiety of the *here-and-now* (fear of becoming infected) was nuanced, and in fact overridden by the strong *we* experience: the "group-as-a-whole" dream, or nightmare (Bermudez, 2018, 538, 553–555), the *here-and-now* reality became a general sense of threat. The threat in reality is recast even at the group level as a reality of the past – that in wartime there is not enough food. Gabriella, who as a result of the trauma is overwhelmed by her own anxiety due to loosening boundaries of the self, turns to the *we* in vain. For her, the traumatized intersubjective field mirrors not the *here-and-now* reality, but a traumatized reality detached from the real world, one which reinforces her inner fantasies and fears. This is the trauma of reality (Bakó & Zana, 2022, in press).

My own personal experience related to *A Fairytale for Everyone* (*The Therapists' Own Experiences: Where Is the Wolf?* Also see *Diary November/December 2020 – Numbers on the Rise*) captures a similar experience: the individual is easily swayed when a shocking experience affects many people, and when the transforming capacity of the environment is also damaged. The world of the past, the Transgenerational Atmosphere, deeply permeates the world of the present, hampering orientation. Nancy Goodman (2012) tells of a similar experience, the collapse of the space-time construct. She and her colleagues recorded their therapy experiences following the 9/11 attacks, including their own experiences: "Was I like the many upper middle class European Jews who stood by in disbelief as Nazi Germany conducted the Final Solution, while a few others responded by leaving their comfortable professional lives, and saving themselves from death[?]" (Goodman & Meyers, 2012, manuscript). The current threat (the pandemic situation, the horror of terrorism) projected a threat from the past, the Holocaust, onto the present, making it difficult to judge what exactly we fear, what we should fear, in the present day.

The Fragmentation of Reality

The uncontained realities of smaller groups and *me* split off the damaged *we* reality (which is now able to contain the experiences of individuals and groups to a limited extent), and reality is fragmented (see also Trauma and Splitting). Multiple individual and group realities form, and these no longer communicate with one another; they form alongside one another, but do not affect each other.

The case of Mariann, a veterinary in her 30s, well illustrates how she increasingly loses her ability to orientate herself in the events of the outer and inner worlds (see Diary, The Period before Christmas – Extremes). Feelings that are adequately linked to the outer reality (she is overburdened with all the work, and the feelings of the pet owners overwhelm her) are almost imperceptibly woven through with experiences from other people's (the clients' and the external world's) realities, which are more chaotic, less differentiated, and more fragmented. This existential anxiety reflecting the outer reality and the quasi-psychotic fantasies overwhelming her (for instance, they fear that they will implant something in me, or that they will listen to my thoughts, or see into me) become inseparable for Mariann. The microchip and the "listening in" on the phone are particularly good metaphors for what Mariann is experiencing as an inner reality: indeed, as a result of the blurring of the boundaries of the self typical in mass trauma situations, and the growth in self-destructive tendencies (Bohleber, 2010, 174), contents which are alien to the self may move in, overwhelming and taking control over the working of the self, or the opposite: contents from the self may move out. Mariann is overwhelmed not only by her own undigested contents, but also by collective transgenerational fantasies conveyed by a *we*, an intersubjective field, that is ever less able to contain (Bohleber, 2010, 161–170). Although fear of the Russian vaccine is related to the *here-and-now* (at the time the Russian vaccine did not have a European license), at the same time it shows another phenomenon: that the collective experience of the past (for many decades, Hungary was subject to a communist regime and occupied by Russia) weaves through the present reality. The Russian occupation and the eastern vaccine are subsumed in one psychological reality. A weakened, traumatized *me* gives in to temptation (or pressurization) and dissolves into a greater whole (see also the sections Society's Containing Capacity and How It Can Be Damaged, *Me* and *We*, and Their Interaction in the Atmosphere, and The Intersubjective Background to Sharing Experiences). However, since the larger whole is now fragmented, and does not function properly, the *me* does not receive confirmation, but is overwhelmed by collective fantasies, which can be ones of paranoia, anxiety, or even extreme aggression (Bohleber, 2010, 171–177).

These fragments of reality are not flexible, and less able to react flexibly to the *here-and-now*, or mirror or integrate other realities. The external world reflected to the individual is no longer one that has been digested by the Other (the intersubject as a whole); it is rather the inner reality of one or another smaller groups, frozen in the past. A poorly functioning intersubjective field is no longer capable of freely sharing experiences. When reality is traumatized, individual experiences cannot be freely shared, and sharing them may even become dangerous. The *we* is unable to dream a shared, coherent reality. Reality becomes fragmented and multiple psychic realities, or reality fragments, exist in parallel, encapsulated, unable to communicate with others or with events in the outside world. Smaller groups are unable, or able only to a limited extent, to accept the different reality of the Other, and to reflect dynamically on the outer world. For the individual who is part of the group, it is not the events in the outside world which are translated into acceptable contents; rather, the traumatic world, often based on events in the past, is projected onto the present (Bakó & Zana, 2022, in press).

Summary

During the pandemic, we and our patients all experienced the sudden changes in the collective mood, and noticed how these changes deeply affect the experiences of the individual, ourselves included. Setting out from the basic assumption that the individual and the social (the Intersubjective) cannot be conceived of independent of one another, in this book we have sought to answer the question of what happens at the level of individual psychology: How does the subject (the *me*) become receptive to the reality represented by the intersubjective community, the *we*, and what triggers this? How are the multiple *me*-experiences, themselves in continual flux, able to shape the intersubjective reality? How are the *me*-experience and the *we*-experience able to affect each other so rapidly, and so deeply? What does the individual make of the external world as it changes extremely rapidly in mass traumatization? To what extent is it adaptive or dysfunctional when the relationship of the *me* to the external world changes, or fails to change, as a result of the reality represented in the group?

We proposed the concept of Atmosphere, as a development of the notion of Transgenerational Atmosphere. The Atmosphere describes far more generally the relationship between the self and the other, the subject (*me*) and the intersubjective community (*we*), the non-verbal (non-symbolic, or pre-symbolic) transmission of emotions. We envisage the genesis of the Atmosphere as a psychological space to be similar to that of the Transgenerational Atmosphere, inasmuch as it is based on a loosening of the boundaries of the self. This thinning of the boundary between the *self* and the *other* is what enables a shared intersubjective psychological field, the Atmosphere, to come into being. However, one essential difference with the Transgenerational Atmosphere is that we see the Atmosphere as a damaged psychological field arising not only as the result of trauma. Indeed, we posit that the Atmosphere is a constantly present psychological vehicle, both surrounding and simultaneously penetrating the *self*, an intersubjective "container" full of emotions and thought contents. In this sense, the Atmosphere is an intersubjective psychological field of the *we*, which is born of the constantly changing interaction of the *me* and the *we* in the *here-and-now*. In this reading, the Atmosphere has healthy vital functions for the individual: it helps to translate the reality of the external world for the *me*, by dreaming a mass experience, the *we* reality, or it may help to temporarily contain and transform traumatic experiences that exceed the individual's capacity for symbolization and overwhelm him or her.

In our approach, the Atmosphere is not merely a *here-and-now* construct, but it also serves a remembrance function: it is the carrier of collective knowledge, values, the history of previous generations – including pre-symbolic, or even unsymbolized experiences. In this approach, the Atmosphere helps us to understand remembrance and transmission: the Atmosphere is the intersubjective field that creates the opportunities for collective unconscious (or rather pre-symbolic) memories to be preserved and passed on to heirs. The *me* receives and accepts the knowledge, the relationship to the world, offered by the intersubjective community, the *we*, and simultaneously it lets in the collective fantasies and basic assumptions generated by the current *here-and-now*. It constantly adjusts and tunes its own *me*-experience in the light of changes in the "collective mood" transmitted by the *we*, the Atmosphere. As to when and to what extent in this process the *me* is able to retain or regain its own boundaries, this depends on many factors which we have discussed in detail in this book.

In the closing chapters, we focused on understanding the intersubjective aspect (in the broad sense) of giving meaning. In order to gain more accurate understanding of this aspect, our model distinguishes a third reality between external reality (the real) and the individual's inner, psychic reality: *we* reality. The *we* reality is the symbolized experience of the group, its dream of the external world. In this approach, reality is the result of the function of the intersubjective field created by the group, a symbolic process at work at the group level, the crystallization of a group-level experience of the outside world in the *here-and-now*. The trauma of reality is the perversion of the symbolic function of the field created by the *we*, the intersubject. The experience of the group or the effect of the past is always present; they transform and color the individual's experience. This is a natural process; indeed, it is adaptive: when there is no time to think things over, or when logical thinking processes break down as a result of a crisis, or when the individual has no memories from his or her own experience to rely on, then a wealth of procedural memories where the knowledge of many generations is condensed, can be life-saving. In addition, it can be life-saving for the weakened *me* to allow in the experience of the group, to lower the boundaries of his/her own self: when the *me* freezes, the group may be sufficiently capable of reacting. In the case of societal traumas, the processing capacity of the individual is often insufficient. The intersubjective community, the *we*, becomes more prevalent than usual, because even a stable *me* is weakened under threat, relying more on the *we* with its promise of security, and being more inclined to dissolve. In these special periods, the *me* may briefly lose itself partially or completely: this may lead to self-sacrifice or to unaccustomed manifestations of aggression which in retrospect are difficult to interpret. If the containing capacity of society and the group is maintained, it may be able to provisionally support the individual, the *me*, for whom the reality of the outer world is temporarily too much, and overwhelming. A well-functioning *we* can be of great help at such times: it can mirror back to the individual that s/he is not alone, there is a helping other; that what seems unbearable for the individual is digestible for the *we*. It is able to take what for the individual is "too much" and modulate it, dream it, in such a way that it can be integrated.

However, in the case of group-level trauma affecting the vast majority of people, the field created by the *we*, the Atmosphere, may also be damaged. A traumatized Atmosphere is no longer able to dream a psychic reality that can be integrated by many, and destructive tendencies may gather strength. The weak *me*, because of the loosened boundaries of the self, is especially sensitive to the intersubjective reality of the external world, and thus also to destructive, regressive processes: if in the *we*, archaic anxiety gathers strength, along with paranoid and aggressive tendencies and projective mechanisms, then these may, due to the loosened boundaries, affect the individuals in undigested form. In the shared psychic space, these feelings are shared quickly without any control, overwhelming masses of people, and in extreme cases prompting them to action. As a result of overwhelming trauma, the ability of society as a whole to tolerate frustration is lowered, and what was previously acceptable (for instance, any kind of otherness) becomes unacceptable and irritating.

When writing this book we attempted to understand the social effects of mass trauma as related to the COVID pandemic, little suspecting that following the pandemic, not unconnected to its social and psychological effects, we would be witnesses to an even "less containable" destructive event: Russia's war in Ukraine. We attempt to fight against the "incomprehensible" and undigestible with what we have: our psychoanalytical thinking. We hope and trust that reflecting on these issues together helps to repair the fragmented, perverted containing capacity of the Intersubjective as a whole, society (Bakó & Zana, 2022, in press).

References

Affeld-Niemeyer, P. & Marlow, V., Translated by: Barbara Wharton, B. (1995). Trauma and Symbol: Instinct and Reality Perception in Therapeutic Work with Victims of Incest. *Journal of Analytical Psychology*, 40(1), 23–39.

Bakó, T. & Zana, K. (2018). The Vehicle of Transgenerational Trauma: The Transgenerational Atmosphere. *American Imago*, 75(2), 273–287.

Bakó T. & Zana K. (2020a). *Transgenerational Trauma and Therapy. The Transgenerational Atmosphere*. Routledge, London and New York.

Bakó, T. & Zana, K. (2021a). *A transzgenerációs trauma és terápiája. A transzgenerációs atmoszféra*. Medicina kiadó, Budapest.

Bakó, T. & Zana, K. (2022). A trauma realitása – A realitás traumája. *Lélekelemzés*, 2, 13–37.

Bakó, T. & Zana, K. (in press). The Reality of Trauma; The Trauma of Reality (Translated by Robinson, R.). *Psychoanalytic Dialogues.*

Benjamin, J. (2005). Creating an Intersubjective Reality: Commentary on Paper by Arnold Rothstein. *Psychoanalytic Dialogues*, 15(3), 447–457.

Bermudez, G. (2018). The Social Dreaming Matrix as a Container for the Processing of Implicit Racial Bias and Collective Racial Trauma. *International Journal of Group Psychotherapy*, 68(4), 538–560.

Bion, W. R. (1962a). *Learning from Experience* (pp. 1–116). Tavistock, London.

Bion, W. R. (1962b). The Psycho-Analytic Study of Thinking. *International Journal of Psychoanalysis*, 43, 306–310.

Bohleber, W. (2010). *Destructiveness, Intersubjectivity and Trauma. The Identity Crisis of Modern Psychoanalysis.* Routledge, London and New York.

Boulanger, G. (2002). Wounded by Reality: The Collapse of the Self in Adult Onset Trauma. *Contemporary Psychoanalysis*, 38(1), 45–76.

Bromberg, P. M. (1996). Standing in the Spaces: The Multiplicity of Self and the Psychoanalytic Relationship. *Contemporary Psychoanalysis*, 32, 509–535.

Civitarese, G. (2019). The Concept of Time in Bion's "A Theory of Thinking". *International Journal of Psychoanalysis*, 100(2), 182–205.

Civitarese, G. (2021). Intersubjectivity and Analytic Field Theory. *Journal of the American Psychoanalytic Association*, 69, 853–893.

Ferro, A. (2006). Trauma, Reverie, and The Field. *Psychoanalytic Quarterly*, 75(4), 1045–1056.

Ferro, A. (2009). Transformations in Dreaming and Characters in the Psychoanalytic Field. *International Journal of Psychoanalysis*, 90, 209–230.

Ferro, A. (2015). A Response That Raises Many Questions. *Psychoanalytic Inquiry*, 35(5), 512–525.

Ferro, A. & Civitarese, G. (2013). Analysts in Search of an Author: Voltaire or Artemisia Gentileschi? Commentary on "Field Theory in Psychoanalysis, Part 2: Bionian Field Theory and Contemporary Interpersonal/Relational Psychoanalysis" by Donnel B. Stern. *Psychoanalytic Dialogues*, 23(6), 646–653.

Ferro, A. & Civitarese, G. (2016). Psychoanalysis and the Analytic Field. In: Elliott, A. & Prager, G. (eds.) *The Routledge Handbook of Psychoanalysis in the Social Sciences and Humanities* (pp. 132–148). Routledge, London.

Fonagy, P. & Target, M. (2007). Playing with Reality: IV. A Theory of External Reality Rooted in Intersubjectivity. *International Journal of Psychoanalysis*, 88(4), 917–937.

González, F. J. (2020a). Trump Cards and Klein Bottles: On the Collective of the Individual. *Psychoanalytic Dialogues*, 30(4), 383–398.

González, F. J. (2020b). With Fellow Travelers to Nodal Places: Reply to Dajani, Doñas, and Peltz. *Psychoanalytic Dialogues*, 30, 424–431.

Goodman, N. R. & Meyers, M. B. (2012). *The Power of Witnessing: Reflections, Reverberations, and Traces of the Holocaust – Trauma, Psychoanalysis, and the Living Mind* (Chapter 24, pp. 301–318). Routledge Press, London.

Lawrence, W. (2000). Social Dreaming Illuminating Social Change. *Organisational and Social Dynamics*, 1(1), 78–9.

Lőrincz, Zs., Gyomlai, É., Szajcz, Á., Zana, K., Sinkovics, A. (2019). A bioni mezőelmélet. Egy kortárs interszubjektív megközelítés bemutatása. [The Bionian field-theory. Introduction to a contemporary intersubjective approach] *Lélekelemzés*, Budapest, (2):197–231.

Mitchell, S. A. (1997). *Influence and Autonomy in Psychoanalysis*. Analytic, Hillsdale, NJ.

Ogden, H. T. (2010). Original Articles on Three Forms of Thinking: Magical Thinking, Dream Thinking, and Transformative Thinking. *Psychoanalytic Quarterly*, 79(2), 317–347.

Oliner, M. M. (1996). External Reality: The Elusive Dimension of Psychoanalysis. *Psychoanalytic Quarterly*, 65, 267–300.

Peltz, R. (2020). Living Entities that Join and Separate us: A Discussion of "Trump Cards and Klein Bottles: On the Collective of the Individual". *Psychoanalytic Dialogues*, 30, 417–423.

Renik, O. (1998). Getting Real in Analysis. *Psychoanalytic Quarterly*, 67, 566–593.

Trevarthen, C. (2015). Awareness of Infants: What Do They, and We, Seek? *Psychoanalytic Inquiry*, 35(4), 395–416.

Vermote, R. (2019). *Reading Bion* (Series Editor: Birksted-Breen, D). Routledge, London and New York.

Index

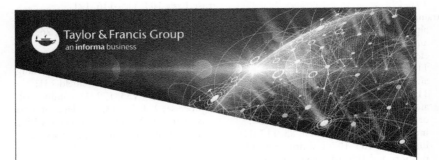

For Product Safety Concerns and Information please contact our EU representative GPSR@taylorandfrancis.com Taylor & Francis Verlag GmbH, Kaufingerstraße 24, 80331 München, Germany

Printed and bound by CPI Group (UK) Ltd, Croydon, CR0 4YY
08/06/2025
01896986-0007